Freud

D0223065

In this fully revised and updated second edition, Jonathan Lear clearly introduces and assesses all of Freud's thought, focusing on those areas of philosophy on which Freud is acknowledged to have had a lasting impact. These include the philosophy of mind, free will and determinism, rationality, the nature of the self and subjectivity, and ethics and religion. He also considers some of the deeper issues and problems Freud engaged with, brilliantly illustrating their philosophical significance: human sexuality, the unconscious, dreams, and the theory of transference.

In this new edition Lear emphasizes the philosophical significance of Freud's *fundamental rule* – to say whatever comes to mind without censorship or inhibition. This binds psychoanalysis to the philosophical exploration of self-consciousness and truthfulness, as well as opening new paths of inquiry for moral psychology and ethics.

One of the most important introductions and contributions to understanding this great thinker to have been published for many years, *Freud, second edition* will be essential reading for anyone in the humanities, social sciences and beyond with an interest in Freud or philosophy.

Jonathan Lear is the Roman Family Director of the Neubauer Collegium for Culture and Society at the University of Chicago, USA. He is also the John U. Nef Distinguished Service Professor in the Committee on Social Thought and the Department of Philosophy. He is a trained psychoanalyst, and the author of several acclaimed books on philosophy and psychoanalysis, including *Aristotle: The Desire to Understand; Love and Its Place in Nature; Open Minded; Happiness, Death and the Remainder of Life and Radical Hope: Ethics in the Face of Cultural Devastation*. His most recent book is *A Case for Irony* (2011). He is a recipient of the Andrew W. Mellon Foundation Distinguished Achievement Award.

Routledge Philosophers

Edited by Brian Leiter

University of Chicago

Routledge Philosophers is a major series of introductions to the great Western philosophers. Each book places a major philosopher or thinker in historical context, explains and assesses their key arguments, and considers their legacy. Additional features include a chronology of major dates and events, chapter summaries, annotated suggestions for further reading and a glossary of technical terms.

An ideal starting point for those new to philosophy, they are also essential reading for those interested in the subject at any level.

Available:

Hobbes
A P Martinich

Leibniz
Nicholas Jolley

Locke
E J Lowe

Hegel
Frederick Beiser

Rousseau
Nicholas Dent

Schopenhauer
Julian Young

Freud
Jonathan Lear

Darwin
Tim Lewens

Rawls
Samuel Freeman

Spinoza
Michael Della Rocca

Merleau-Ponty
Taylor Carman

Russell
Gregory Landini

Wittgenstein
William Child

Heidegger
John Richardson

Adorno
Brian O'Connor

Husserl, second edition
David Woodruff Smith

Aristotle, second edition
Christopher Shields

Kant, second edition
Paul Guyer

Hume
Don Garrett

Dewey
Steven Fesmire

Forthcoming:

Habermas
Kenneth Baynes

Peirce
Albert Atkin

Mill
Daniel Jacobson

Plato
Constance Meinwald

Nietzsche
Maudemarie Clark

Einstein
Thomas Ryckman and Arthur Fine

Plotinus
Eyjólfur Emilsson

Berkeley
Lisa Downing and David Hilbert

Levinas
Michael Morgan

Cassirer
Samantha Matherne

Kierkegaard
Paul Muench

Jonathan Lear

Freud

Second edition

Routledge
Taylor & Francis Group

LONDON AND NEW YORK

First published 2005
This edition published 2015 by Routledge
2 Park Square, Milton Park, Abingdon, Oxon OX14 4RN

and by Routledge
711 Third Avenue, New York, NY 10017

Routledge is an imprint of the Taylor & Francis Group, an informa business

© 2005, 2015 Jonathan Lear

British Library Cataloguing in Publication Data
A catalogue record for this book is available from the British Library

Library of Congress Cataloging-in-Publication Data
Lear, Jonathan.
Freud / by Jonathan Lear. – Second edition.
pages cm – (Routledge philosophers)
Includes bibliographical references and index.
1. Freud, Sigmund, 1856-1939. 2. Psychoanalysis and
philosophy. 3. Psychoanalysts–Austria–Biography. I. Title.
BF109.F74L43 2015
150.19'52092–dc23
2014030452

ISBN: 978-0-415-83179-6 (hbk)
ISBN: 978-0-415-83180-2 (pbk)
ISBN: 978-1-315-77191-5 (ebk)

Typeset in Joanna MT and Din
by Cenveo Publisher Services

In memory of Sam Ritvo

Contents

Acknowledgements

I would like to thank my students at the University of Chicago and my colleagues in the Committee on Social Thought and the Department of Philosophy: they sustain a marvelous environment of questioning and research. I have had longstanding conversations on psychoanalysis and philosophy with Matthew Boyle, Michael Brearley, John Coetzee, David Finkelstein, Irad Kimhi, Gabriel Lear, Lawrence Levenson, Hans Loewald, Anselm Mueller, Edna O'Shaughnessy, Sebastian Rödl, Eric Santner, William Sledge, Martin Stone, Candace Vogler, Bernard Williams and Richard Wollheim; and I am grateful to them all. Sections of this book were read by Tony Bruce, Benjamin Fong, Sebastian Gardner, Brian Leiter, Nir Ben Moshe, Jerome Neu, Skomantas Pocius and Richard Strier and they all gave helpful comments. I want to express special thanks to Isabela Ferreira who served as an invaluable research assistant on this second edition; and to Jennifer Lockhart who played an equally valuable role on the first edition. In addition to my research and teaching, I have over the past decades been seeing analysands in psychoanalysis. It is in that work that I have developed a capacity to interpret Freud, as well as the judgment to decide where I agree and where I disagree. I am deeply grateful to the Andrew W. Mellon Foundation for its Distinguished Achievement Award, which freed up time for the research and writing of this second edition. Finally, my loving thanks to my family Gabriel, Sophia and Samuel Lear.

Preface to the second edition

This book presents an overall view of Freud's work, one that emphasizes its enduring philosophical significance. I am glad to have been invited to write a second edition because, while I continue to agree with the interpretation of the first edition, my sense of why it matters philosophically has developed. In the first edition I wanted to give a straightforward account of how psychoanalysis works. I wanted to eliminate the aura of mystery that sometimes taints presentations of psychoanalysis, while nevertheless preserving the wonder of human being that it reveals. I have long thought that the familiar criticisms of psychoanalysis flow from misunderstandings of what it is. Therefore a resolutely non-mysterious introduction might be the best response.

Still, since writing the first edition I have become ever more impressed with the elegance and significance of what Freud called the fundamental rule of psychoanalysis. It is a simple rule to state: an analysand is asked to say whatever it is that comes into his or her mind, without censorship or inhibition. In an important sense, this is the only rule of Freudian psychoanalysis. For the other rules – for example, coming to sessions a certain number of times a week or lying on a couch – are in place to facilitate an environment in which an analysand can speak his or her mind freely. These subordinate rules should be maintained or altered depending on whether they genuinely support the fundamental rule. Although the fundamental rule is simple to state, it is not at all simple to follow. Indeed, it is basically impossible for anyone to follow the fundamental rule. Psychoanalysis as we know it emerges from the cracks:

from the pauses, intrusive thoughts, changes of subject, bodily complaints, feelings of inhibition – all of which disrupt the free flow of self-conscious thought.

From the perspective of the philosophical tradition, self-consciousness is not simply a special capacity that we humans happen to possess, it constitutes us as the creatures we are. It either makes possible or itself manifests that capacity of the psyche philosophers have called human reason. In this sense, psychoanalysis is located at the core of our humanity, for it really only enjoins one activity: to allow self-consciousness to unfold spontaneously of its own accord. What psychoanalysis discovered is that there is something internal to the free flow self-consciousness that opposes it. This too is constitutive of our humanity.

Freudian psychoanalysis gives us unparalleled access to this internal conflict within self-consciousness to its own unfolding. Since psychoanalysis only asks a person to speak his or her mind, both analyst and analysand can come to see in the minutest detail when and how that process gets interrupted. There is no appeal to authority here; nothing needs to be accepted on faith. There is no behind-the-curtains mystery; indeed, there are no curtains.

Once one comes to see psychoanalysis in this light, two further consequences of philosophical importance quickly emerge. (I shall discuss them both in the Introduction.) First, psychoanalysis is in a position to take up the promise of ancient Greek ethics: namely, the development of a robust moral psychology. Plato and Aristotle are explicit that the virtuous person must have an integrated, harmoniously functioning psyche. But they cannot say in any detail what such harmony consists in. They use suggestive phrases – for example, that the rational and non-rational parts of soul must act 'in concord' or 'speak with the same voice' – but at the time they wrote, such phrases could only serve as placeholders. If moral psychology is to avoid the charge of cheerleading for an illusory image of virtue, it must provide a convincing account of what the required psychic unity amounts to. Psychoanalysis is especially well-placed to respond to this challenge – and thus to take up the legacy of ancient Greek ethical thought.

Second, in the living present of a psychoanalytic session, analysands can become self-consciously aware – immediately and transparently − of the efficacy of their thinking. Since Freudian psychoanalysis works through the unfolding self-conscious awareness of the analysand, as analysands become increasingly aware of the flow of their self-conscious minds, they become increasingly able to change their minds directly through their own self-conscious activity. They are aware of the efficacy of their thinking because this awareness itself helps to constitute the efficacy. Freud himself was not clear about this, but it is an immediate consequence of the principle he laid down.

In this second edition, the Introduction and Conclusion are new. The text has been revised throughout, but there are major revisions in Chapter 6 on psychological structure and object relations and in Chapter 7 on Freud's critique of religion and morality. Although the overall position in those chapters remains the same, the presentation is, I think, significantly improved. My hope is that this book will help others to see − perhaps against the grain of the times − how Freudian psychoanalysis continues to matter, both for human life and for the philosophical traditions that have tried to comprehend it.

1856,
6 May   Sigismund Schlomo Freud born in Freiberg, Moravia (now Pribor in Czech Republic).

1859–60   The Freud family moves first to Leipzig, then to Vienna, motivated in part by financial hardship.

1873   Freud writes to a friend that he has decided not to go into law, but to become a natural scientist. He graduates with distinction from the *Gymnasium*.

1875–80   Freud studies at University of Vienna: zoology with Carl Claus (a follower of Darwin); physiology with Ernst Brücke; and Aristotelian philosophy with Franz Brentano.

1881   Freud becomes a doctor of medicine. Moves to Berggasse 19.

1882   Freud is engaged to Martha Bernays. Joins the General Hospital in Vienna: Theodor Meynert's psychiatric clinic.

1884–85   Studies anesthetic properties of cocaine. Travels to Paris to study with Charcot at the Salpêtrière Clinic and becomes interested in hypnotism.

1886   Marries Martha Bernays. Resigns from General Hospital and goes into private practice as a doctor for nervous diseases.

1887   Begins friendship with Wilhelm Fliess, an ear, nose and throat doctor in Berlin.

1893–94   Works with Josef Breuer on the Studies on hysteria.

Tries to stop smoking cigars; abandons the attempt after seven weeks and writes to Fliess, 'From the first cigars on, I was able to work and was the master of my mood; prior to that, life was unbearable.'

1896   Freud's father Jacob dies. Freud begins to analyze his own dreams. Coins the term 'psychoanalysis.'

1899/1900   Publishes The interpretation of dreams.

1901   Freud begins treating Dora. Publishes The psychopathology of everyday life.

1903   Freud's friendship with Fliess ends.

1905   The Dora case study is published. Freud also publishes Three essays on the theory of sexuality and Jokes and their relation to the unconscious.

1906   Freud begins friendship with Carl G. Jung.

1907   Freud publishes 'Obsessive actions and religious practices' and 'Creative writers and daydreaming.'

1908   First psychoanalytic congress meets in Salzburg. Freud publishes 'On the sexual theories of children.'

1909   Freud goes to America – with Jung and Sandor Ferenczi – to lecture at Clark University. He publishes the Little Hans case study, Analysis of a phobia in a five-year-old boy, and the case study of the Rat Man, Notes on a case of obsessional neurosis.

1910   International Psychoanalytical Association founded. Freud is treating the Wolf Man.

1911   Publishes his analysis of Dr. Schreber, 'Psychoanalytic notes on an autobiographical account of a case of paranoia.' Alfred Adler leaves the Vienna Psychoanalytic Society.

1913   Publishes Totem and taboo. Breaks with Jung. Internationale Zeitschrift für Psychoanalyse is founded.

1914   Freud publishes 'On narcissism: an introduction.' Writes 'Observations on transference-love.' World War I begins.

1915   Publishes 'The unconscious,' 'Repression' and 'Instincts and their vicissitudes.'

1916   Publishes 'On transience' and the first part of Introductory lectures on psychoanalysis.

1917   Publishes 'Mourning and melancholia' and second part of *Introductory lectures*.

1918   Resumption of meetings of international congress of psychoanalysts. Publishes the Wolf Man case study, *From the history of an infantile neurosis*.

1919   Freud writes to Ernest Jones: 'We have grown hungry beggars all of us here. But you shall hear no complaints. I am still upright and hold myself not responsible for any part of the world's nonsense.' He publishes '"A child is being beaten": a contribution to the study of the origin of the sexual perversions.'

1920   Publishes *Beyond the pleasure principle*.

1921   Publishes *Group psychology and the analysis of the ego*.

1923   Freud publishes *The ego and the id*. He smokes too many cigars. His doctor detects the first signs of oral cancer that will plague Freud the rest of his life. Freud almost dies from first attempt to operate on his cancer. He also publishes a serious revision to his theory of dreams, 'Some additional notes on dream interpretation as a whole.'

1924   Publishes 'The economic problem of masochism,' 'The loss of reality in neurosis and psychosis' and 'The dissolution of the Oedipus complex.' Freud declines offer of $25,000 from the publisher of the *Chicago Tribune* to come to the USA to psychoanalyze the two accused killers Nathan Leopold and Richard Loeb.

1925   Freud turns down an offer of $100,000 from Hollywood producer Samuel Goldwyn to write or advise on a screenplay about love. He publishes 'A note upon the "mystic writing pad."'

1926   Publishes *Inhibitions, symptoms and anxiety*, a serious revision of his earlier theory of anxiety; and *The question of lay analysis*, which argued that non-physicians should be allowed to train as psychoanalysts.

1927   Freud publishes *The future of an illusion*. He tells a visiting French psychoanalyst, 'This is my worst book!' *New York Times* publishes article under the headline, 'Religion Doomed/ Freud Asserts/ Says It is at a Point

Where It Must Give Way Before Science/ His Followers Chagrined.'

1928   Freud declares his dissatisfaction with the current state of knowledge of female development and female sexuality. He confesses to a Hungarian analyst that he does not like working with psychotic patients, 'I am angry at them to feel them so far from me and all that is human.'

1929   A week after the stock-market crash, Freud sends *Civilization and its discontents* to the printer.

1930   Freud writes to Lou Andreas-Salomé, 'I have completely given up smoking, after it had served me for precisely fifty years as protection and weapon in the combat with life. So, I am better than before, but not happier.' Awarded the Goethe Prize. His mother dies at age 95.

1933   Freud publishes *New introductory lectures on psychoanalysis*; and 'Why war?' a correspondence with Albert Einstein.

1934   Freud begins his work on Moses and monotheism.

1936   Freud turns 80 and Thomas Mann gives a private reading of 'Freud and the future' at Berggasse 19. He publishes 'A disturbance of memory on the Acropolis.'

1937   Freud publishes 'Analysis terminable and interminable.' He writes to Ernest Jones that the Austrian people are 'thoroughly at one with their brothers in the Reich in the worship of anti-Semitism. Our throat is being choked ever more tightly even though we are not being strangled.'

1938   Hitler takes over Austria. Spontaneous violence against Jews immediately erupts in Vienna. Freud's daughter Anna is ordered to report to the Gestapo for questioning. Freud and family emigrate from Austria to England.

1939   Freud's cancer again becomes active. *Moses and monotheism* is published in English. Freud decides that his cancer-ridden life has become 'nothing but torture and makes no sense.' At his request, his doctor administers three injections of morphine over two days and Freud dies on 23 September.

Introduction
The peculiar conversation

I am still unable, as the Delphic inscription orders, to know myself; and it really seems to me ridiculous to look into other things before I have understood that. ... Am I a beast more complicated and savage than Typhon, or am I a tamer, simpler animal with a share in a divine and gentle nature?

Socrates in Plato's *Phaedrus*[1]

Having already treated of the celestial world, as far as our conjectures could reach, we proceed to treat of animals, without omitting, to the best of our ability, any member of the kingdom, however ignoble. For if some have no graces to charm the sense, yet nature, which fashioned them, gives amazing pleasure in their study to all who can trace links of causation and are inclined to philosophy ... *We therefore must not recoil with childish aversion from the examination of the humbler creatures. Every realm of nature is marvelous:* and as Heraclitus, when the strangers who came to visit him found him warming himself at the furnace in the kitchen *and hesitated to go* in, is reported to have bidden them not to be afraid to enter, as *even in that kitchen divinities were present,* so we should venture on the study of every kind of creature without distaste; for each and all will reveal to us something natural and something beautiful.

Aristotle, *Parts of animals*[2]

While Antiphon was still occupying himself with poetry he invented a method for curing mental distress, no different in its way from being treated for a physical ailment by a doctor; he built himself premises near the agora in Corinth and posted an advertisement to the effect that he had found a talking cure for distress. And by delving into the reasons for their distress he used to bring his patients relief. But he considered this profession beneath his dignity and turned to oratory instead.

pseudo-Plutarch, *Lives of the Ten Orators*[3]

1 Freud's fundamental rule

In the beginning, one person asks another person for help. The other person, after listening for a while and asking some questions, agrees that he can be of help, and explains the rule that will structure their time together: try to say whatever comes into your mind without inhibition or censorship. Freud called this the fundamental rule of psychoanalysis. By 1913, he explained his technique this way:

> What the material is with which one starts treatment is on the whole a matter of indifference – whether it is the patient's life history or the history of his illness or his recollections of childhood. But in any case the patient must be left to do the talking and must be free to choose at what point he shall begin ... The only exception to this is in regard to the fundamental rule of psycho-analytic technique which the patient has to observe. This must be imparted to him at the very beginning: 'One more thing before you start. What you tell me must differ in one respect from an ordinary conversation. Ordinarily you rightly try to keep a connecting thread running through your remarks and you exclude any intrusive ideas that may occur to you and any side-issues, so as not to wander too far from the point. But in this case you must proceed differently. You will notice that as you relate things various thoughts will occur to you which you would like to put aside on the ground of certain criticisms and objections. You will be tempted to say to yourself that this or that is irrelevant here, or is quite unimportant, or nonsensical, so that there is no need to say it. You must never give in to these criticisms, but say it in spite of them – indeed, you must do so precisely because you feel an aversion to doing so. Later on you will find out and learn to understand the reason for this injunction, which is really the only one you have to follow. So say whatever goes through your mind. Act as though, for instance, you were a traveler sitting next to the window of a railway carriage and describing to someone inside the carriage the changing view which you see outside. Finally, never forget that you have promised to be absolutely honest, and never leave anything out because, for some reason or other, it is unpleasant to tell it.'[4]

There may be other rules — coming to sessions on time, paying one's bill, lying on a couch — but from this Freudian perspective they are derivative. They are in place in order to create and maintain an environment in which the analysand can speak her mind. As Freud puts it here, the fundamental rule 'is really the only one you have to follow.'

In calling this rule *fundamental* Freud signals that it is part of the constitutive structure of psychoanalysis. Of course, Freud did not hit upon this rule from the beginning; he came to it over time. But, as Aristotle taught us, the order of discovery is not the same as the order of reality.[5] That is, sometimes we hit upon something almost by chance, but slowly we come to see that this chance discovery is the key to our inquiry. For a brief time at the beginning of his career, Freud tried hypnosis as a therapeutic technique. His account of why he abandoned it is hilarious:

> as soon as I tried to practice this art on my own patients, I discovered that my powers at least were subject to severe limits. ... I soon began to tire of issuing assurances and commands such as 'You are going to sleep! ... sleep!' and of hearing the patient, as so often happened when the degree of hypnosis was light, remonstrate with me, 'But, doctor, I'm not asleep', and of then having to make highly ticklish distinctions: 'I don't mean ordinary sleep; I mean hypnosis. As you see, you are hypnotized, you can't open your eyes', etc., 'and in any case there's no need for you to go to sleep', and so on. I feel sure that many other physicians who practice psychotherapy can get out of such difficulties with more skill than I can. If so, they may adopt some procedure other than mine. It seems to me, however, that if one can reckon with such frequency on finding oneself in an embarrassing situation through the use of a particular word, one will be wise to avoid both the word and the embarrassment.[6]

Freud tells us that there were good clinical reasons to abandon hypnosis as a therapeutic technique: it did not provide long-lasting cure, and it depended on the doctor's suggestion.[7] However, Freud also abandoned hypnosis because he wasn't very good at it.

From the beginning Freud encouraged his patients to speak their minds, but it was an empirical discovery of some magnitude that they had difficulty in doing so. As he said in a footnote to the passage just quoted, 'there comes a time in every analysis when the patient disregards it.'[8] That is why Freud formulated the fundamental rule *as a rule*. We would have no need for a rule if we effortlessly lived by it. It is part of Freud's genius that he is able to convert a problem into a solution. If people have difficulty speaking their minds, let us focus on that very difficulty. By 1914, he conceptualized the culmination of the development of psychoanalytic technique this way:

> Finally, there was evolved the consistent technique used today, in which the analyst gives up the attempt to bring a particular moment or problem into focus. He contents himself with studying whatever is present for the time being on the surface of the patient's mind, and he employs the art of interpretation mainly for the purpose of recognizing the resistances which appear there, and making them conscious to the patient. From this there results a new sort of division of labor: the doctor uncovers the resistances which are unknown to the patient; when these have been got the better of, the patient often relates the forgotten situations and connections without any difficulty. The aim of these different techniques has, of course, remained the same. Descriptively speaking it is to fill in the gaps in memory; dynamically speaking, it is to overcome resistances due to repression.[9]

When Freud talks about the 'surface' of the patient's mind, he means whatever comes to conscious awareness in the moment. The analyst's role in this new 'division of labor' is basically as a facilitator. He notices blocks and inhibitions in the analysand's speech — Freud calls them 'resistances' — and he brings them to the attention of the analysand with the aim of understanding and thereby overcoming them.

The fundamental rule enjoins the free flow of self-conscious speech. Of course, as one tries to speak one's passing thoughts and feelings, one may well do more than just report them. By trying to articulate them in speech, one may develop them. And analysands regularly report that simply by trying to speak their thoughts they become aware of many thoughts of which they were previously unaware. And, as we have seen, one does not do this all on one's own, but in the presence of and with the help of another. Still, if we follow Freud's lead, and insist on the centrality of the fundamental rule, we arrive at a suggestive idea about what psychoanalysis is: it is the activity of *facilitating the development of self-conscious thought* in the analysand. We may not know yet in any detail what this phrase means, but simply by taking psychoanalysis to be organized by Freud's fundamental rule, we can see that it aims at this end.

So, before we know any empirical results – how well psychoanalysis treats this or that disease – we can see simply by looking at its structure, that psychoanalysis is a 'cure' for inhibition and constriction of self-consciousness. That is how it is organized. As such, psychoanalysis commands philosophical attention. For a claim running through the philosophical tradition – from Socrates to the present – is that self-conscious thinking is not simply a special capacity we possess, but a core expression of who we are. Our freedom, as well as our capacity for truthfulness, depends on our ability to think freely, and to act on the basis of freely flowing self-conscious thought. There is this thought too: that our capacity to think freely is something we can develop over time. We can *get better* at the very activity that makes us distinctively human.[10]

In effect, Freud discovered that there is an uncanny force, internal to the spontaneous unfolding of self-conscious thought, that interrupts it, disturbs it, *opposes* it. He called this the unconscious. How we should understand the unconscious will be a topic of this book, but right away we should avoid a misunderstanding that diminishes the philosophical significance of psychoanalysis. At the beginning of his career, Freud conceptualized the unconscious as a hidden and repressed realm of wishes pressing for gratification. But he quickly came to see that such a characterization on its own was inadequate. We need to understand the unconscious as a peculiar *form of thinking*. Ideas and images are associated loosely – sometimes ideas are linked because the words that express them have a similar shape, or, when spoken, they have a similar sound. Sometimes a link is created simply by the mind placing one thought next to another. An image can also be highly condensed in meaning, with one image having layer upon layer of meaning. Freud called this activity of mind *primary process*, and we shall learn about its nature and importance (see Chapters 1, 2 and 3). But that is not all. There are other hallmarks of unconscious mental activity that can have a profound influence on how we live our lives. Freud gives this list:

> To sum up: *exemption from mutual contradiction, primary process* (mobility of cathexes), *timelessness*, and *replacement of external by psychical reality* — these are the characteristics which we may expect to find in processes belonging to the system Ucs.[11]

We will come to understand better what these qualities are as we work through Freud's texts. But even now we can see that these features of unconscious thinking reinforce each other, and together lend stability to the psyche. If an unconscious fantasy is exempt from contradiction, countervailing thoughts need not get in its way. And if the fantasy is timeless, it can cast an aura over an entire life. Suppose, to take a highly simplified case, a child has an unconscious fantasy, 'I am the unloved one.' Precisely because this fantasy is exempt from contradiction and is presented in a timeless mode, the person will tend to interpret life's passing events through a frame of feeling unloved. The person will focus on real-life slights; but even kind gestures will tend to be treated with suspicion, as though there must be some underlying motive ('He was nice to me only because he wants something from me'). The world will come to seem an unloving place, thus reinforcing the fantasy. The person can come to feel that she is somehow *fated* to be unloved. One of Freud's great insights is that the unconscious is always already at work, shaping the events of the day to fit hidden meanings. And he was a master in detecting private gratifications in human suffering. So, it is painful to feel unloved; but there is pleasure in feeling in control. No one can disappoint you (so the fantasy goes) because you got there first and disappointed yourself. One thereby avoids feelings of uncertainty and vulnerability. In this way, 'psychical reality' can come to overrun external reality (see Chapter 5).

That the unconscious is not simply a realm of hidden wishes, but a peculiar mode of thinking is of philosophical significance.

Philosophers tend to think that rationality is the principle of unity in a human life. In Plato's *Republic*, Socrates says that the appetitive part of the soul is multiform, with desires pulling and pushing in all sorts of directions.[12] On this picture, appetitive desires, taken on their own, are chaos. It takes the activity of reason to rule certain desires in, as those one will act upon, and rule other desires out. Again, on this picture, there is plausibility to the thought that it is by these acts of will that we constitute ourselves – for they unify our psyche.[13] If the unconscious were merely a forbidden realm of wayward desires, this picture would be complicated but not particularly challenged. The task would simply be to figure out how to extend self-conscious awareness to these wishes, so that we could either rule them in or rule them out. In effect, Freud discovered that this philosophical picture is based on an inadequate anthropology.[14] In the psychoanalytic treatment of adults we regularly find unconscious core fantasies – such as, *I am the unloved one* – whose rudiments were formed in childhood, but have been imaginatively elaborated ever since. These fantasies are effective in organizing and unifying the psyche, in ways that often bypass – and sometimes distort – rational, self-conscious thought. These fantasies have a way of infiltrating our self-conscious thinking – *inclining* our judgment – so as to make it appear rational that we are 'the unloved one.' We are tempted to think of reason as a capacity to *distance ourselves* from our desires and *judge them* in reflective, self-conscious thought.[15] But, from a Freudian perspective, this very experience of 'reflectively distancing' oneself from one's desire can be an illusion. Desire may already be present in the experience of 'reflective distance' tilting one toward the 'mature' judgment that one is, in fact, unloved. How are we to deal with the fact that fantasy can distort our experience of rational self-reflection? If our task is not simply to deal with desires that press upon us, but also with an alternative mode of thinking, then perhaps the conception of rationality as reflective distance becomes inappropriate.

We want to take seriously the philosophical intuition that human life is valuable in part because it can be shaped and informed by self-conscious thought. We thus need to find an adequate way to take account of this alternative mode of thinking that Freud called the unconscious. Freudian psychoanalysis is that very way. Organized by the fundamental rule, psychoanalysis provides an interface in every-day life where self-consciousness and the unconscious meet. The analysand tries to speak his mind, and he is everywhere *confronted* with interruptions of hitherto unconscious thinking. The abstract question – 'how are we to deal with the unconscious?' – becomes immediate, concrete and pressing. And, even at the beginning of our inquiry, we can see how these moments might have a fractal quality. If in the here-and-now, the analysand's associations are interrupted by the thought, say, that the analyst is bored and would rather be doing something else, we might have right here the key to the shape of a life – I *am the unloved one.*

Let us consider a case study of Freud's, one that has come to be known as the Rat Man.[16] To give him the respect he deserves, I shall call him Mr. R. We shall consider details of the case in the next chapter, but looking at it from a broad perspective, Mr. R's problem is that he inhabits a guilty world. He tends to interpret passing events as though they are bad or, at the very least, ominous – and that they are somehow his fault. Obviously, much needs to be said about how a person gets into such a position and what holds him there. But for now, the point is that self-conscious reflection is part and parcel of this world. Mr. R's problem is not just that he feels guilty but that when he reflects on his feeling, it seems to him like the right response. He looks to the world and sees ever more reasons for feeling like he does. Indeed, his self-conscious reflection is implicated in finding reasons why he should feel guilty. For Mr. R, self-conscious reflection on his desires and impulses is a manifestation of his unfreedom: as he reflects on his reasons for feeling guilty, he digs himself ever deeper into a crabbed and constraining world. Self-conscious reflection is deployed as a defense, one that helps sustain the guilty world. Although Mr. R is an extreme case, in my psycho-analytic experience this general situation is the rule rather than an exception. And it shows that the process of 'stepping back' from one's psychological experience can be an illusion.

Here is a vignette from the case: Mr. R had convinced himself that he was somehow responsible for a torture that would be carried out on his loved ones not only in this life, 'but also to eternity – to the next world.' Freud points out to Mr. R that, although as a child he was religious, he had become an atheist. How could he still believe in otherworldly punishments? Freud is inviting Mr. R to reflect on his impulse to feel guilty. He is asking him to reflect on how his inclination to believe he is responsible fits with his other beliefs. Freud reports that Mr. R,

> reconciled the contradiction between his beliefs and his obsessions by saying to himself: 'What do you know about the next world? Nothing can be known about it. You're not risking anything – so do it.' This form of argument seemed unobjectionable to a man who was in other respects particularly clearheaded, and in this way he exploited the uncertainty of reason in the face of these questions to the benefit of the religious attitude which he had outgrown.[17]

This is an illusion of reflective distance. Mr. R can say to himself that he is subjecting reason to a critique, pointing out its limits. He explicitly takes himself to have shown that he does have legitimate space for his belief. What he cannot see is that his 'philosophical' reflection is a manifestation of his unfreedom.

Freud says that Mr. R, like many obsessional neurotics, had a need for uncertainty and doubt.

> The creation of uncertainty is one of the methods employed by the neurosis for drawing the patient away from reality and isolating him from the world – which is among the objects of every psychoneurotic disorder. ... The predilection felt by obsessional neurotics for uncertainty and doubt leads them to turn their thoughts by preference to those subjects upon which all mankind are uncertain and upon which our knowledge and judgments must necessarily remain open to doubt.[18]

In short, philosophical reflection can be used as a defense, blocking the self-understanding it purports to deliver. Officially, Mr. R reflects on life after death because he wants to know whether he has reason to feel guilty. The fact that our knowledge about the afterlife is uncertain is supposedly the outcome of the inquiry. Unofficially the situation is the reverse: because Mr. R is motivated to keep on feeling guilty, he chooses a realm – the next world – about which knowledge is necessarily uncertain. Philosophical reflection is his disease.

Freud makes an extraordinary claim about self-conscious reflection when it occurs in an obsessional neurotic like Mr. R: 'The thought-process itself becomes sexualized, for the sexual pleasure which is normally attached to the content of thought becomes shifted on to the activity of thinking itself.'[19] Freud's conception of sexuality is very different from the popular conception – as we shall see in Chapter 2. But, for now, we can see Freud's point: in an obsessional like Mr. R, the activity of thinking takes on its own peculiar pleasure, and it takes on a life of its own. In this way, it subverts the thinking process. If Mr. R were genuinely to consider his guilt, his thinking would need to stay on target, aim towards some kind of resolution. Instead, the thinking itself becomes so charged that it becomes ever more loosely moored to its content. He is purportedly reflecting on his guilt, but as he goes back and forth – 'Should I feel guilty? But it wasn't my fault! Maybe it was? What a bad person I am!' – genuine reflection becomes ever more tenuous. He tries to keep up the appearance that he is thinking *about* his guilt, but his mental activity becomes ever more the trading of guilty thoughts in an endless back-and-forth. The 'thinking' goes on without end because that has become its aim. (We shall consider the case of Mr. R in Chapter 1.)

2 An adequate moral psychology

Plato and Aristotle believed that ethical life – a life lived well among family, friends and fellow citizens in political society – would also be a happy, rich and meaningful life. Doing well in the company of others would coincide with faring well as a human being. Such a conception of ethical life often strikes contemporary readers as too rosy. And the idea that one might ground ethics in a conception of human flourishing, or happiness – what the Greeks called *eudaimonia* – strikes many as an impossible task. Why should the demands of ethical life be conditions of personal happiness?

The plausibility of this approach to ethics rises or falls with a substantive claim about human psychology. Namely, that ethical life, when properly lived, can be the expression of a genuinely unified, integrated, harmonious psyche. That gives content to the thought that the virtuous person's actions are truly flowing from him. And it suggests that ethical life is the condition of a *wholehearted* life. The idea that a life lived wholeheartedly is a happy one is appealing; but Plato and Aristotle do not value psychic harmony simply for harmony's sake. They think that psychic integration is the condition in which human reason – that is, thoughtful self-consciousness – can permeate the human psyche. For Plato and Aristotle, psychic integration is the condition of a life lived according to reason, untroubled by countervailing factors. That is why they thought that psychic integration mattered: it provided the opportunity for a distinctively human way to flourish. But is this claim about human psychology true? And how would we find out?

We need to be wary either of accepting or rejecting this claim too quickly. The danger of accepting the claim too quickly is obvious: we need to avoid wishful illusion. The philosopher Bernard Williams warned us of an ever-present tendency in moral psychology to collapse into what he called *moralizing*: one that unwittingly assumes the very categories one needs to vindicate, and ends up preaching to the choir.[20] But the danger of rejecting the claim too quickly is equally real: that of falling into the contemporary cultural cliché that the story is the true one. It seems to me we need an honest and detailed account of the scope and limits of this ancient Greek philosophical project.

This is something that the ancient Greek philosophers cannot give us. Although Plato and Aristotle valorize harmonious relations between parts of the psyche, they are sketchy at best about what it consists in. I will give one example from Aristotle, but I think it shows a limitation that runs through ancient approaches to moral psychology. Aristotle says that the non-rational part of the psyche needs to 'listen well to,' obey and 'speak with the same voice' as reason.[21] But he has virtually nothing to say about what this means. His statements about training our non-rational natures are mainly at the level of public policy. He emphasizes the importance of early habituation into the virtues, and notes that fine people will emerge from this process with their non-rational souls well trained. This is the basis of ethical virtue.[22] But he does little to explain how this comes about. Perhaps more serious: Aristotle's moral psychology seems to assume the categories it seeks to vindicate. This would make him vulnerable to Williams' charge of moralizing. So, when Aristotle says that the non-rational soul of the virtuous person is *obedient* to reason, he uses a concept he wants to valorize without giving us an account of what the right kind of obedience consists in.[23] Why, after all, should *obedience* be the best conception of what healthy intrapsychic communication consists in? With the benefit of hindsight, this does not look like a good choice. But even if one does settle on obedience, the *manner* of the obedience ought to matter. In terms of understanding the integrated unity of a virtuous person's psyche, there is all the difference in the world between servile compliance or obsessional obedience, on the one hand, and the genuine harmony of a non-rational part of the soul that 'listens well to' and 'speaks with the same voice as' reason on the other. And yet Aristotle does not give us a satisfying account of how one might distinguish one from the other.

Bernard Williams suggested that a robust moral psychology 'uses the categories of meaning, reason and value, but leaves it open, or even problematical, in what way moral reasons and ethical values fit with other motives and desires, how far they express those other motives and how far they are in conflict with them.' Williams thought that the ancient Greek philosophers could not live up to this standard; and he looked elsewhere for a genuine moral psychology. 'Thucydides and (I believe) the tragedians, among the ancient writers, had such a psychology, *and so in the modern world did Freud.*'[24] Williams took himself to be leaving ancient Greek ethics behind, but I think we can take up his suggestion and move in a different direction. Instead of thinking of ancient ethics as inevitably moralizing, think of it as unfinished. It bequeaths us a project that it itself could not complete. The Freudian approach to the human psyche gives us a new way of inheriting the ancient philosophical legacy.[25]

3 The 'immorality' of psychoanalysis

We have not been able to see the possibility of this approach, I suspect, because some of our most influential thinkers have argued that it is impossible. Jacques Lacan, to take a prominent example, argued that psychoanalysis comes both too soon and too late to fit into a broadly Aristotelian approach to ethics.[26] It comes too soon in the sense that it is ostensibly not concerned at all with promoting the familiar virtues, such as justice or temperance. Aristotle tells us that there is no right way to commit adultery.[27] But if an analysand starts talking about his adulterous desires or his adulterous behavior, the analyst's job is not to talk him out of it, but to help him understand what it means for him. This feature of psychoanalysis strikes many critics as amoral or immoral. And, for Lacan, psychoanalysis also comes too late in the sense that Freud stands on the other side of a historical divide – between modernity or post-modernity and the ancient world – such that on this side we can no longer assume that ethics and politics are in place to make humans happy. The 'virtues' of any civilization, so the objection goes, are just manifestations of power relations by which one social class dominates others. And what philosophers of any given period call 'reason' is a hodge-podge of valorizing self-justifications for the dominating ideology of the time. For Aristotle, the good polis should function to promote the happiness of its citizens, and vice versa. For Freud, by contrast, it is an illusion to think that civilization is in place to make humans happy: rather, it secures a basic order, indifferent to the human costs, and is the source of neurotic discontent.[28]

This outlook has its power, but it is a mistake to think we have no choice of inheritance.[29] As for the charge that psychoanalysis comes 'too late': there is more than one way to read Freud's critique of civilization and the individual's discontent. Instead of reading it as a timeless account of an inevitable, tragic conflict between individual and society, read it as pointing out a fault-line – a place where the needs of the individual and the aims to which society tends come into conflict. One can then read Freud as providing the material for a political critique of the conditions of bourgeois modernity. That is, one can read him as making the historical claim that in the social conditions in which he encountered his patients, the discrepancy between the conditions needed for humans to flourish and the demands imposed by society had become too great. On this reading, the aim need not be stoic fortitude in the face of the inevitably tragic human condition – and we should be suspicious of such 'fated' accounts – but rather political commitment to change social conditions so as to support human flourishing (see Chapter 7).

Aristotle is emphatic that ethics must be understood in the context of an adequate politics.[30] And he insists that political society must support and be supported by the flourishing lives of its citizens. One can insist on this ideal while rejecting the aristocratic values Aristotle held. And one can further insist that we lack a substantial understanding of what such an ideal consists in so long as we remain ignorant of the detail that psychoanalysis reveals about what it is for us to flourish.

As for the charge that psychoanalysis comes 'too soon': It is true that psychoanalysis is not directly concerned with promoting the classical ethical virtues – justice, temperance, courage. But one need not think of this as amorality (or immorality), but rather as a *teleological suspension of the ethical*.[31] That is, we put familiar ethical values into abeyance for the sake of developing the virtue of truthfulness. As we shall see, truthfulness is not simply one virtue among others, but is fundamental: a condition for the possibility of ethical virtues. So, in this sense, psychoanalysis ironically enjoins a teleological suspension of the ethical for the sake of the ethical.

4 Truthfulness

The psychoanalytic notion of truthfulness is rich and unusual, and I can here only provide an introduction. Some of what I will say goes beyond Freud's explicit pronouncements, but it is in a Freudian spirit. The first entry for 'truth' in the *Oxford English Dictionary* is 'the quality of *being true*', and it explicates this as 'the character of being or disposition to be true to a person, principle, cause, etc.; faithfulness, fidelity, loyalty, constancy, steadfast allegiance.' The question is: how could coming to psychoanalysis multiple times a week and trying to speak one's mind according to the fundamental rule – how could this become a manifestation of 'faithfulness, fidelity, loyalty, constancy, steadfast allegiance' *to oneself*?

The answer, in a nutshell, is that the activity of speaking one's mind in this way can, at one and the same time, be efficacious in integrating the psyche. As the analysand tries to speak her mind, she in effect establishes a membrane across which hitherto unconscious thoughts can pass into self-conscious awareness. There will be disruptions of thought, momentary intrusions of daydreams and passing thoughts, uncanny connections, suddenly remembering a dream, and so on. These are conscious experiences of the analysand; they are not merely inferences to some hidden realm. The immediacy of this experience is enhanced as the analysand's unconscious fantasy weaves the analyst into its web. (This is the phenomenon known as transference, and I shall discuss its meaning and significance in Chapter 4.) Because in these circumstances the unconscious is not completely hidden – because it emerges in the microcosm, in the here-and-now of self-conscious attention – it becomes possible for the self-conscious mind to exert efficacious control, precisely through its self-conscious understanding.

With some luck, much practice and some help from the analyst, the analysand can come to recognize the unconscious *as it speaks* across this membrane. This is a *practical* recognition, not just a theoretical appreciation of hitherto hidden truths. That is, the analysand develops a capacity to appropriate the emerging unconscious thinking into her self-conscious thinking – and she does so precisely through the direct and immediate exercise of her self-conscious thinking. Such direct causal efficacy is not everywhere present in psychoanalytic discourse, but when it occurs, it is compelling in that an analysand can experience her efficacy immediately and self-consciously. To use our simplified example, after much analytic work, there can be a moment when the analysand's utterance – 'I have lived my life as an unloved child' – can be the very act that breaks open the false world of possibilities that have hitherto constrained her life. Before the analysis, all of her possibilities were ones in which she felt unloved – although she was not aware of how active she was in constructing such a world. It is via the direct activity of her self-conscious mind that she is able to open up genuinely new possibilities for living. I believe that critics of psychoanalysis have not paid sufficient attention to this aspect of psychoanalytic practice.[32] When it is well done, and at critical moments in the therapy, the efficacy of the mind is immediately and transparently available to the self-conscious awareness of the analysand. By way of analogy: Imagine yourself breaking up with a partner in an important, longstanding, but ultimately unhealthy relationship. After much indecision, many back-and-forths, a slow working towards the conclusion, you finally say, 'This relationship is *over.*' Obviously, you might be mistaken: you might be back with your partner after a few emotionally fraught hours. But consider the case where you are right about yourself: you have done the preparatory emotional work and are finally ready to end the relationship. In saying the words, 'This relation is *over*' you end the relationship. The utterance is not reporting on a distinct event, it is the very activity of ending the relationship. And the efficacy of your act is immediately available to your self-conscious awareness. This is because the breaking up and the awareness of breaking up are '*one reality*.'[33] The analogy needs qualifications, but, roughly, I want to claim that when analysis is successful, the analysand learns how to break up with an unhappy form of living. And through the fundamental rule, Freud gave us the self-consciously transparent method for bringing this about.

This self-conscious efficacy of mind is, at one and the same time, an activity of integrating the psyche. After much preparatory work, and on occasion when the unconscious is actually speaking through the membrane, the very utterance of the analysand can bring together the emotional and unconscious and self-conscious parts of her psyche. To use Aristotle's terms, the rational and the non-rational parts of the soul come to *speak with the same voice*. Analysands who take themselves to have had successful analyses regularly report that one of the benefits of analysis is that they feel more alive. They may have been successful in their jobs all along, but now they feel *enlivened* by a sense of creativity and possibility. This enhanced sense of vibrancy is, I think, a manifestation of psychic integration, and it makes plausible the thought that such integration is a constituent of human flourishing.

Obviously, much more needs to be said about this unusual efficacy of self-conscious mind, but already one can see how it opens up a realm of truthfulness. Psychoanalytically understood, truthfulness is not merely a matter of facing up to hidden wishes and fantasies; it is a matter of facing up to them *in such a way as to break open falsely constraining worlds of possibility* (see Chapter 4 on transference). At the same time this is the activity of integrating the psyche. And psychic integration, insofar as it is achieved immediately and directly through the activity of self-conscious understanding, is a form of fidelity to oneself. By way of analogy, think of a true friend. A true friend is a genuine friend, a loyal friend, one who maintains steadfast fidelity to the friendship. He is, one wants to say, a friend *through and through*.[34] By actively integrating one's

psyche via self-conscious appropriation of one's hitherto unconscious thinking, one maintains a loyalty to oneself by becoming
oneself *through and through*. Aristotle thinks that the virtuous person
needs to have a unified psyche. One needs, as it were, to become
oneself through and through, if one's acts are to be a full-blooded
expression of oneself.

That is why truthfulness, psychoanalytically understood, is a foun-
dational virtue for ethics. Psychoanalysis offers at least the promise of
a robust account of what this unity consists in (see Chapter 6). In
this way, psychoanalysis can be seen as an attempt to resume the
ancient project of an ethics and politics grounded in and explained
by a robust conception of human flourishing. This is the project the
ancient Greek philosophers could not themselves complete.

It is easy to misunderstand this claim about psychic unity – in
part because we are not yet in a position fully to understand it. We
should be wary of thinking we already understand what psychic
integration consists in.[35] At most, it seems to me, we have a preliminary understanding. As we have seen, Freud discovered that the
unconscious is not merely a hidden realm of unconscious wishes,
but an alternative manner of thinking. We are still at an early stage
of reflection of what that means. What would it be to thoughtfully
and self-consciously take this mode of thinking into account?
If reason is, among other things, a capacity for thoughtful, self-
conscious appropriation of the non-rational soul, then it seems fair
to say that we do not yet fully understand what human reason is.
In particular, Aristotle's conception of reason as that to which the
non-rational soul should listen well and be obedient to seems
off the mark. For the unconscious, Freud discovered, is in its own
non-rational way thinking about fundamental problems of human
existence. To return to the simplified example: it is not unusual for
an analysand to be working out in unconscious fantasy basic questions about the nature of love, as well as the extent to which one is
capable of loving and being loved. In a funny way, the unconscious
acts like a philosopher who happens to lack the capacity for rational
thought. Since unconscious mental activity is such a fundamental,
pervasive and insistent aspect of human life, it seems misguided to
think of reason as *telling* it what to do. Rather, reason needs to learn
how to *listen* to the unconscious, engage in thoughtful conversation

with it, perhaps become playfully thoughtful in response. It seems to me that psychoanalysis offers a unique opportunity for philosophy. We will come to understand in robust detail what we mean by *psychic unity*, *integration* and the *exercise of reason* as we come better to understand what is involved in the thoughtful, self-conscious appropriation of unconscious mental activity.

Freud said that 'anyone who has succeeded in educating himself to truth about himself is permanently defended against the danger of immorality, even though his standard of morality may differ in some respect from that which is customary in society.'[36] It is impossible to know with confidence precisely what he meant, but it is inviting to read Freud through the lens of virtue ethics. 'Educating oneself to the truth about oneself' is not merely a matter of learning new facts about oneself, but is rather the activity of self-consciously appropriating these wishes, efficaciously taking responsibility for them as one's own. It is a matter of actively integrating unfamiliar ways of thinking into self-conscious thinking. This developing 'self-knowledge' is in and of itself the active, self-conscious unifying of the psyche.[37] Why should such 'education' protect one against 'the danger of immorality'? From a Platonic-Aristotelian perspective, an ethically virtuous life requires psychic integration: the temptations of immorality issue from psychic fragmentation. The non-rational part of the psyche is tempted by acts that actually interfere with one's happiness; but it remains isolated from (and thus out of communication with) the rational part of the psyche. Acting unethically, for Plato as for Aristotle, was always acting in a psychically fragmented way – with the different parts of the soul speaking with different voices. Psychoanalysis is not directly a training in familiar ethical virtues, but it is a training in the truthfulness that such virtues require. In that sense, psychoanalysis may be prior, but it does not come 'too soon': it can help open the possibility of an ethically virtuous life.

5 The egalitarian impulse

'We must not recoil with childish aversion from the study of humbler creatures,' Aristotle tells us, 'for *every realm of nature is marvelous*.' The Greek word that is here translated as *marvelous* is basically the same as the word Aristotle uses when he, following Socrates and

Plato, says that philosophy begins in *wonder*.[38] His point is not simply that even humble creatures can arouse our curiosity. It is that, as we come to understand their workings, even humble creatures can *stun* us, fill us with awe and thereby provoke us to philosophy. Of course, in talking about humbler creatures, he was talking about the wild boar that will castrate itself in order to relieve an itch, or how birds have voice while scallops (in spite of their whizzing sounds) do not.[39] He is not talking about the humble human being. When it came to human ethical life, Aristotle is concerned with excellence, and with those who are capable of achieving it. By contrast, we are inheritors of millennia of Judeo-Christian traditions, and centuries of Enlightenment traditions, and we thus have a concern for individual human beings, however well or poorly they happen to be doing. Ironically, it may be just this widened concern for individuals – however we encounter them – that enables us to break out of the confines of moralizing, and open up the possibility of a robust and honest moral psychology.

Aristotle cites Heraclitus with approval:

> as Heraclitus, when the strangers who came to visit him found him warming himself at the furnace in the kitchen *and hesitated to go in*, is reported to have bidden them not to be afraid to enter, as *even in that kitchen divinities were present*, so we should venture on the study of every kind of creature without distaste; for each and all will reveal to us something natural and something beautiful.[40]

Notice that Heraclitus is encouraging his visitors to overcome their inhibitions; so too does Aristotle encourage his reader. Only thus will revelation of the natural and the beautiful become possible. Two-and-a-half millennia later, Sigmund Freud invited us, not into the kitchen, but into his consulting room. It was a similarly humble place. Freud was willing to listen to ordinary people who came into his office – and these were, by and large, bourgeois women and men of late nineteenth- and early twentieth-century Vienna.[41] He listened to them and, on the basis of what he heard, he transformed our conception of the human. He not only discovered systematic aspects of how the mind works unconsciously, he came to see that each of us unwittingly participates in dramatic struggles – the stuff that had hitherto been reserved for heroes of myth and literature.

Surely one of Freud's most admirable working principles, implicit in his practice, is this: nothing is beneath our notice. Psychoanalysis is constituted by a refusal to say ahead of time that anything we do is insignificant, unworthy of contemplation.

Equally important is that, when Freud is at his best, theory emerges naturally from clinical details. Much of the criticism of psychoanalysis as extravagant occurs because theoretical terms are invoked in isolation, cut off from clinical reality. It is worth reminding ourselves that the central concepts of psychoanalysis emerge as a response to human suffering. Freud listened to people who came to him in pain, and his ideas emerged from what he heard. Some of his ideas are speculative excesses that deserve to be discarded, but the central concepts of psychoanalysis are closely tied to clinical reality. One aim of this book is to bring the reader back to clinical moments and show how theoretical ideas develop out of them.

When Heraclitus invited the strangers in, they were not only strangers to Heraclitus, they were strangers to the kitchen. This was an odd place to search for truth. Until quite recently in the history of civilization, the kitchen was a place for women and servants. It was a place where private gossip was exchanged as meals were prepared – a warm, sheltered locus of human intimacy. When Heraclitus says that *even here* divinities are present, he is usually interpreted as meaning that divinities are present in the kitchen as everywhere else. But suppose the divinities present were special to the kitchen. Maybe they don't get along with the other divinities. Might they like to cause a ruckus? In which case, certain insights might emerge only in the kitchen.

As Freud invites us into the consulting room, we are the strangers. And we are being invited into a strange space. Yet it does bear an uncanny resemblance to Heraclitus' kitchen. A preponderance of Freud's patients were women, and if one considers some of the classic case studies – Anna O, Elizabeth von R, Dora – one can see that they used Freud's 'kitchen' as a place to share intimacies, gossip, explain their situations ... and complain. Of course, they took themselves to be going to a medical doctor, and in the first instance they complained of particular ailments – a pain in the

thigh, difficulty walking, fainting spells, facial tics, vaginal discharge, recurrent disturbing thoughts. But as one listens to all the
specific complaints one begins to hear an underlying master-
complaint: 'in my own attempt to figure out how to live, *something
important is going wrong.*'

Freud was not well placed to hear this master-complaint. He took
himself to be a medical doctor engaged in scientific research, and
he had particular conception of what that consisted in. Just as a
doctor probes for the hidden causes of physical diseases, so Freud
took himself to be probing the unconscious for specific hidden
meanings that were making the patient ill. On occasion he could be
insensitive to the large-scale structures in which those meanings
operated. He could become impatient with his patients when they
did not accept his specific diagnoses. At times his impatience seems
painfully insensitive (see, for instance, Freud's case study of Dora,
discussed in Chapter 4). It also blinds him to the philosophical
and ethical significance of his discoveries. Another aim of this book
is to bring this significance to light.[42]

6 The journey of a human life

By way of example, let me raise a question about a core value of
Western philosophical, ethical and religious traditions: are we to
remain creatures who consider our humanity partially to consist
in the journey – often slow, sometimes painful – of self-conscious
self-discovery? Are we to continue to be creatures who constitute
ourselves via the celebration, the mourning and memorialization
of the suffering we have already gone through? There are powerful
cultural currents that run counter to this value – and we need to
admit that, on occasion, the psychoanalytic profession contributes
to them. Although Freud speaks in a wonderful polyphony, in his
more medical moments, he too is implicated. If all we need is a
cure for a discrete medical condition – say, lifting depression or
calming anxiety – then perhaps a pill can do that better, and do so
more cost-effectively than psychoanalysis. If we have a discrete
behavioral problem – drinking too much, difficulty writing papers
for a deadline – perhaps there are effective behavioral modifications available.

Psychoanalysis commends itself not simply because of the final outcomes it achieves, but by the process of self-conscious self-discovery that it is. This is what it is to deepen our humanity, at least according to this core value. Indeed, it seems to me that one of the 'final outcomes' of psychoanalysis is the capacity to *keep on* with the activity of self-discovery after one's official treatment is over. This is at least one way of interpreting Freud's claim that psycho-analysis is both terminable and interminable. 'Educating oneself to the truth about oneself' is not meant to be an activity that comes to an end, at least while one is alive and well. It is a way of life. In that sense, the aim of psychoanalysis (understood as a treatment) is to prepare one to engage in a life of more psychoanalysis! No other form of treatment can match psychoanalysis for that outcome.

7 A philosophical introduction to a non-philosopher

This book is unusual in that it means to be a philosophical intro-duction to a non-philosopher.

Born in 1856, Freud spent his early twenties working in research labs at the University of Vienna; first in anatomy, then in neurophy-siology. Working in the lab of the renowned physiologist Ernst Brücke, Freud wrote, 'I found rest and full satisfaction at last.'[43] But by the age of 26, he was engaged to Martha Bernays – and concerned about earning a living. The anti-Semitism of the time made the prospect of promotion to a top academic post unlikely, and he began training for private practice. The university awarded him a travel grant in 1885, and he went to Paris to study brain-physiology and psychology with Jean Charcot at the Salpêtrière clinic. He spent some time doing microscopic studies of children's brains, but Charcot fascinated him with his use of hypnosis in the treatment of hysterics. Apparently, Charcot could induce hysterical symptoms and cure them via hypnotic suggestion. Anyone who has ever seen a hypnotist perform will know how uncanny it is to watch other people being hypnotized. And it is tempting to speculate that this experience put the thought in Freud's mind that physical effects might have a psychological cause. He, of course, believed the psychological cause had an organic substrate of some sort, but in terms of understanding the process, it was the hypnotic suggestion that was important. For although Charcot's words started the air vibrating, and made a physical impact on the neurological systems of his patients, it was the suggested idea of paralysis that seemed to immobilize his hypnotized patients. Perhaps equally important, Charcot rescued hypnotism from the carnival, the nightclub and the quack; he insisted on its significance for medical research and treatment. He certainly provided a striking example of someone who believed that mysteries were in our midst, there for the solving.

Freud returned to Vienna in the spring of 1886, he resigned his low-level position at the General Hospital and began seeing patients in private practice for nervous disorders. If he had remained in the research lab, he would not have been able to show us the same things. For the extended conversation in the privacy of the doctor's office opened up avenues of intimacy that could never be replicated in ordinary empirical research. And it was in this context that Freud was able to grasp the workings of unconscious mental activity that we might not otherwise be able to see.

Of course, as a well-educated European of the late nineteenth century, Freud received a classical education. He studied Aristotle with Franz Brentano, but he was more interested in ancient literature and history than he was in philosophy. Throughout his career he remarks with admiration on the works of the great philosophers such as Plato, Anaxagoras, Empedocles. Indeed, he invokes Plato to justify his own work in psychoanalysis:

> anyone who looks down with contempt upon psychoanalysis from a superior vantage-point should remember how closely the enlarged sexuality of psychoanalysis coincides with the Eros of the divine Plato.[44]

> what psychoanalysis calls sexuality was by no means identical with the impulsion towards a union of the two sexes or towards producing a pleasurable sensation in the genitals; it had far more resemblance to the all-inclusive and all-embracing Eros of Plato's *Symposium*.[45]

> In its origin, function and relation to sexual love, the 'Eros' of the philosopher Plato coincides exactly with the love-force, the libido of psychoanalysis.[46]

But he did not pursue Plato's thought with any rigor. The same holds for his contemporaries, Schopenhauer and Nietzsche whom he cited with admiration. By contrast, he held the academic world of philosophy professors in low esteem. He was impatient with their facile 'proofs' that the unconscious could not possibly exist because 'unconscious mental' was a contradiction in terms. He also thought that philosophy was too concerned with building overarching systems and that it overvalued logic.[47] Some of his criticisms are fair, some are irritated grumbling: to my mind, none of it matters much. What does matter is that if we want to take our concerns with happiness, freedom, truthfulness and value seriously, we should not ignore Freud.

It is time to get clear on what I mean by a *philosophical* introduction. There are already many books that will introduce you to Freud the man, introduce you to the central ideas of psychoanalysis, locate Freud in the history of ideas or offer trenchant criticisms of his views. A philosophical introduction is different. A biographer will want to know what Freud's life was like and, perhaps, how his ideas arose out of that life. An historian of ideas will want to know the historical context in which these ideas arose, and what influence they had on subsequent thought. A psychoanalytic introduction will aim to explain what the central concepts are, and how they work within psychoanalytic theory and practice. A philosophical introduction, by contrast, will want to show why these ideas matter for addressing philosophical problems that still concern us. Given this aim, there are bound to be aspects of such a book that, from any other perspective, appear strange. The book will pay scant attention to the details of Sigmund Freud's life. Obviously, one has to be historically sensitive simply to read a book from another time and culture. But the emphasis will always be on why Freud's ideas continue to have significance, not on how they arose. And Freud may not be the best arbiter of this. Nor is he the final arbiter of what counts as psychoanalysis. There may then be interpretations in this book to which Freud, the man, would have objected. His views are always significant, but psychoanalysis stays alive via a vibrant engagement with them.

That being said, I shall everywhere try to make the best possible case for Freud's ideas and arguments. This is not because I have a desire to defend Freud, but because if we are going to see how these ideas might continue to matter, we need to see them in their best possible form. Obviously, there are important criticisms to be made of Freud and, more generally, of psychoanalysis. But we have to beware of a certain kind of argument from decadence. So, to give a notorious example, psychoanalysts are sometimes criticized for pulling rank on their patients. If their patients disagree with their interpretation, so the objection goes, then they are 'resisting.' No doubt this happens and, humanly speaking, it is awful when it does. But, philosophically speaking, the question is not whether some analysts are bullies. Rather, the question is, 'When psychoanalysis is practiced well, is there even so a tendency towards bullying?' Similarly with Freud: there is no doubt that he did not treat the patient he called Dora as well as he should have. Still, one fitting tribute to Dora is to learn from her case as much as we can about the possibilities for human freedom. The aim, then, is not to achieve a balanced historical view of who did what to whom, or who thought what when. Nor is it to make all the criticisms that might legitimately be made. It is to show why these ideas continue to matter insofar as a philosophical understanding of the human soul still matters. And so, when I do offer a criticism, it is because I think that the best possible construal of Freud's position is still open to criticism and that this criticism is of philosophical significance.

Finally, this is a philosophical introduction. I do not pretend to be able to uncover the hidden philosophical meaning of psychoanalysis; I do mean to engage in a conversation with Freud. My hope is that the book will stimulate others to pursue these thoughts, for I am convinced they are crucial to our self-understanding.

Notes

1 Plato, *Phaedrus* 229e–230a (Alexander Nehamas and Paul Woodruf trans., in *Plato: Complete Works*, ed. John M. Cooper, Indianapolis, 1997).
2 Aristotle, *Parts of animals* I.5, 644b21–645a23; revised Oxford translation; my emphases.
3 Pseudo-Plutarch, *Lives of the Ten Orators* 833c–d. In *Pseudo-Plutarch, Photius and the Suda: The Lives of the Attic Orators* (trans. R. Waterfield with commentary by Joseph Roisman and Ian Worthington. Oxford: Oxford University Press, 2015).
4 Freud, 'On beginning the treatment,' SE XII: 134–35; my emphases.

5 Aristotle, *Posterior Analytics* 71b19–72a5.

6 Freud, *Studies on hysteria*, SE II: 108–9.

7 See Freud 'Two encyclopedia articles,' SE VIII: 237, 250–51; and 'On psychoanalysis,' SE XII: 208. 'Suggestion' works in psychoanalytic theory similarly to the position 'sophistry' has in philosophy. It is a contrast term, that which psychoanalysis defines itself against. Freud was also concerned that the apparent 'cure' depended too much on an unexamined relationship with the hypnotist – and if that relationship was disturbed, so too was the 'cure.'

8 Freud, 'On beginning the treatment,' SE XII: 135n1.

9 Freud, 'Remembering, repeating and working-through,' SE XII: 147–48.

10 See Lear, *A case for irony*, Chapter 1: 'To become human does not come that easily' (Cambridge, MA: Harvard University Press, 2011), pp. 3–41.

11 Freud, 'The Unconscious,' SE XIV: 187.

12 Plato, *Republic* IX.580d11. (The Greek for 'multiform' is *polueidia*.)

13 See Christine Korsgaard, *Self-constitution: agency, identity and integrity* (Oxford: Oxford University Press, 2009).

14 It seems to me that Aristotle too was aware that his Platonic anthropology was inadequate – and was moving in a similar direction to Freud. At the beginning of *Nicomachean ethics*, he says that there seems to be *another nature (physis) of the soul* that, while non-rational, *in a way participates in reason* (*Nicomachean ethics*, I.13, 1102b13–14). The Oxford and Loeb translations suppress the fact that Aristotle is talking about a nature, perhaps because the English sounds a bit awkward. Instead they have Aristotle saying that there is another non-rational *element* of the soul. But, for Aristotle, nature is an inner principle of change and rest. So, Aristotle seems to be saying that there is a non-rational part of the soul with its own inner principle of change. This makes intuitive sense. If we think about our emotional lives, we can see the workings of an inner principle of change, not altogether rational. Sometimes we get angry, and even when we tell ourselves we have no reason to be angry, we continue to brood. Sometimes our erotic life seems to take on a life of its own, and seems impervious to our own attempts to calm ourselves down. Freud's discoveries from this perspective, are: first, that this 'other nature' of the soul is not confined to our conscious emotional life, but permeates unconscious mental life; second, that there are very peculiar hallmarks of this other form of mental life.

15 See C. Korsgaard, *The sources of normativity* (Cambridge: Cambridge University Press, 1996), pp. 92–93.

16 Freud, *Notes on a case of obsessional neurosis*, SE X: 151–257.

17 Ibid, SE X: 169–70.

18 Ibid, SE X: 232–33.

19 Ibid, SE X: 245.

20 See B. Williams, 'Naturalism and morality,' in J.E.J. Altham and R. Harrison (eds.), *World, mind and ethics: essays on the ethical philosophy of Bernard Williams* (Cambridge: Cambridge University Press, 1995), pp. 202–5.

21 Aristotle, *Nicomachean ethics* I.13, see especially 1102b25–1103a31; Aristotle makes a distinction within the non-rational soul between that vegetative and

nutritive part that, he thought, does not participate in reason, and another part concerned with emotions and desires that in its way does participate. We are here concerned with this part.

22 Aristotle, *Nicomachean ethics* I.13, 1103a3–10; cp. VI.2, 1138b35–1139a6.

23 Ibid, I.13, 1102b31–32. Aristotle does offer an intriguing model. The non-rational soul, he says, participates in reason as though it were listening and obedient to a father (Ibid, I.13, 1102b31–32, 1103a3). This is a patriarchal image, and that raises problems of its own, but there is something thought-provoking in Aristotle's idea that the non-rational soul is essentially childish. It is as though it is permanently en route to maturity; but its excellence does not consist in actually reaching adulthood. Rather, the excellent non-rational soul is an excellent instance of a childish soul. Its excellence consists not in 'what it will be when it grows up', but in a distinctively non-rational ability to listen to and communicate with reason. The external, social model of intra-psychic speaking-with-the-same-voice would thus be excellent parent–child communication. The excellent child is excellent at attending to his parent's communication; the excellent parent is excellent not only in knowing what to say, but in how to communicate it to a child. Still, Aristotle's psychology leaves us without the resources to understand what such a communicative relationship consists in.

24 Williams, 'Naturalism and morality,' p. 202, my emphasis. See also, Williams, *Ethics and the limits of philosophy* (Cambridge, MA: Harvard University Press, 1985), pp. 30–53.

25 I begin to explore this option in Lear, 'Integrating the non-rational soul,' *Proceedings of the Aristotelian Society* 114 (April 2014), pp. 75–101.

26 Jacques Lacan, *The ethics of psychoanalysis, 1959–1960, The seminar of Jacques Lacan, Book VII* (London and New York: Routledge, 1992).

27 Aristotle, *Nicomachean ethics* II.6, 1107a14–17.

28 Freud, *Civilization and its discontents*, SE XXI: 64–145. Moreover, there is Freud's postulation of the so-called death drive: purportedly, a principle within us that works against our flourishing. (See Freud, *Beyond the pleasure principle*, SE XVIII: 7–64). This is a paradigm of a non-Aristotelian principle. I discuss this in Chapter 5.

29 I take this lovely phrase from David Bromwich, *A choice of inheritance: self and community from Edmund Burke to Robert Frost* (Cambridge, MA: Harvard University Press, 1989).

30 Aristotle, *Nicomachean ethics* I.2, 1094a18–b11; I.3 1095a1–12; I.13, 1102a7–25; *Politics* I.1, 1252a1–7; I.2.1252b29–30; III.6, 1278b17–24; III.9, 1280b39; VII.2, 1325a7–10.

31 This term is due to Kierkegaard, see *Fear and trembling* by Johannes de Silentio, ed. and trans. H.V. Hong and E.H. Hong (Princeton: Princeton University Press, 1983), pp. 54–67.

32 See, e.g., Adolf Grünbaum, *The foundations of psychoanalysis: a philosophical critique* (Berkeley: University of California Press, 1984).

33 This lovely way of putting it is due to Sebastian Rödl, *Self-consciousness* (Cambridge, MA: Harvard University Press, 2007), e.g., p. 62.

34 Think too of true blue, true north or the true Cross.
35 A thought running through the Aristotelian tradition (and developed by Aquinas) is that reason is not an extra capacity that is, as it were, added on to our animal capacities for desire, perception and locomotion. Rather, it is transformative of the human psyche: it influences desire, shapes perception and directs movement. Human being is thus not animality plus rationality, but rational animality. This is what is meant by the claim that rationality is the form of the human psyche: it is, from an Aristotelian perspective, the principle of unity in a human life. The best contemporary explication of this thought is in Matthew Boyle, 'Essentially rational animals,' in G. Abel and J. Conant (eds.), Rethinking epistemology, vol. 2 (Berlin: Walter de Gruyter, 2012), pp. 395–427; and 'Additive theories of rationality: a critique,' forthcoming in European Journal of Philosophy, and online: http://dash.harvard.edu/handle/1/8641840.
36 Freud, Introductory Lectures on Psychoanalysis, SE XVI: 434.
37 I discuss this at more length in Lear, 'Wisdom won from illness: the psychoanalytic grasp of human being,' International Journal of Psychoanalysis (2014).
38 Aristotle, Metaphysics I.2, 982b12–13. (to thauamdzein; thaumastos for the Parts of animals passage)
39 Aristotle, History of animals VI.28, 578a4–6; IV.9 535b13–32; VIII.3, 593a3–14.
40 Aristotle, Parts of animals I.5; my emphasis, my translation.
41 See L. Appignanesi and J. Forrester, Freud's women (New York: Basic Books, 1992); N. Chodorow, 'Freud on women,' in J. Neu (ed.), The Cambridge companion to Freud (Cambridge: Cambridge University Press, 1991), pp. 224–48; H. Decker, Freud, Dora and Vienna 1900 (New York: Free Press, 1991).
42 For other attempts to probe the ethical or philosophical significance for Freud see J. Cottingham, Philosophy and the good life (Cambridge: Cambridge University Press, 1998); P. Rieff, Freud; the mind of the moralist (Chicago: University of Chicago Press, 1979); S. Scheffler, Human morality (Oxford and New York: Oxford University Press, 1992).
43 P. Gay, Freud: a life for our time (New York: W.W. Norton, 1988), p. 32.
44 Freud, Three essays on the theory of sexuality, SE VII: 134.
45 Freud, 'Resistances to psychoanalysis,' SE XIX: 218. See also Beyond the pleasure principle: 'the libido of our sexual instincts would coincide with the Eros of the poets and philosophers which holds all living things together' (SE XVIII: 50).
46 Freud, Group psychology and the analysis of the ego, SE XVIII: 91.
47 Freud, 'Resistances to psychoanalysis,' SE XIX: 216–17; An outline of psychoanalysis, SE XXIII:158–59; New introductory lectures on psychoanalysis, SE XXII:160–61.

One
Interpreting the unconscious

When I set myself the task of bringing to light what human beings keep hidden within them … I thought the task was a harder one than it really is. He that has eyes to see and ears to hear may convince himself that no mortal can keep a secret. If his lips are silent, he chatters with his finger-tips; betrayal oozes out of him at every pore.[1]

1 Analysis of the psyche

Although we may on occasion mystify ourselves, and although others may mystify us in ways that incline us to invoke unconscious motivation, there is no reason why the unconscious itself needs to remain mysterious. Freud was not a magician; nor did he have supernatural powers. He looked carefully at strange phenomena of everyday life, and he thought hard about how to make sense of them. 'How are we to arrive at a knowledge of the unconscious?,' Freud asks. 'It is of course only *as something conscious that we know it*, after it has undergone transformation or translation into something conscious. Psychoanalytic work shows us every day that translation of this kind is possible.'[2] What is the unconscious and how does it work? The following chapters are devoted to answering this question.

Freud begins with easily observable phenomena and works his way backwards in systematic ways. The word 'analysis' comes directly from ancient Greek and it was used to describe a special geometrical practice. The geometry we learn in school, deriving from Euclid's *Elements*, was called *synthesis*. One begins with elementary items and operations – points in space, the ability to draw a line between any two points, and so on – and then, in a step-by-step way, one constructs ever more complex figures. But what if one cannot figure out how to construct a particular complex figure? One strategy is to start with the complex figure itself and work in the reverse direction, breaking it down step-by-step into its component parts. This is analysis. If one succeeds in analyzing the figure all the way, one can just reverse the process for a synthesis, or what we would now call a proof.

This is the model Freud is drawing on when he offers us an analysis of the psyche. He begins with behavior that is puzzling, and treats it as a complex psychological construction. That is, myriad motivations are responsible for the behavior, and we shall come to understand the behavior when we can see it as the outcome of these disparate forces. So, to take a moment from the life of Mr. R:

[margin handwritten note: Obsessive compulsive neurosis]

> He is walking along a road on which he knows his lady-friend will later be traveling in a carriage. He removes a stone from the road so that the carriage will not be damaged. A bit later he feels compelled to go back to replace the stone in the road.[3]

[margin handwritten note: obsessive compulsive neurosis operating from the unconscious]

There are two aspects of this moment which command our attention. First, Mr. R cannot himself say what he is doing in the latter part of his act. Obviously, he knows he is replacing a stone – he can track his behavior – but he doesn't know why. Thus his own behavior has become puzzling to him. Second, the latter half of the act looks like what Freud calls a 'critical repudiation' of the first half. Mr. R knows that he originally removed the stone out of love and concern for his lady-friend, but he has no idea why he replaced it.

[handwritten note: Freud would argue this is due to the inner hatred that is suppressed by love]

2 A second mind?

It is tempting to think another mind is at work. I am going to argue that this is the wrong way to conceive of the unconscious, at least in its deepest forms, but it is important to see what leads us – and led Freud – in this direction. The reasoning is plausible enough. The second part of Mr. R's act looks like a reversal of the first part, but the first part flowed from love and concern for his lady-friend of which Mr. R was aware. Might the second part, then, flow from anger towards her of which he is unaware? But then there must be reasons for his anger of which he is also unaware. It makes no sense for anger to exist as an isolated atom – having nothing to do with the rest of mental life. Is he angry at her because she doesn't return his affection?; or because she once insulted him?; or because he hates her taste in clothes?; or because she has bad breath? At this point, who knows? The reasons might not be good ones, but they must somehow hang together and give the anger at least superficial plausibility. There would be no reason to think that replacing the stone was an expression of anger if one could not also uncover some basis for the anger – however loopy. Thus we arrive at the idea that the unconscious is itself an articulated, rationalizing structure: a second mind.

Freud says we should apply this reasoning to ourselves as well: 'all the acts and manifestations which I notice in myself and do not know how to link up with the rest of my mental life must be judged as if they belonged to someone else: they are to be explained by a mental life ascribed to this other person.'[4] The point of assigning these acts to another *person* is that we assume that they hang together in some more or less coherent way. Mr. R is definitely engaging in stone-removing behavior; but we take this behavior to be an action of his. But in order to view this first part of Mr. R's performance as an action, we must attribute certain beliefs to him, for example, that there is a stone in front of him, that it might be an obstacle or danger, etc. – and a desire to remove it. As the philosopher Donald Davidson says, 'Such explanations explain by rationalizing: they enable us to see the events or attitudes as reasonable from a point of view of the agent. An aura of rationality, of fitting into a rational pattern, is thus inseparable from these phenomena, at least as long as they are described in psychological terms.'[5] And the beliefs and desires radiate out indefinitely. For Mr. R to believe that there's a stone in front of him, he must have certain minimal beliefs about stones: say, that they are hard and durable, that they come from the earth, that they won't just pop like a balloon, and so on. And we should expect his desire to remove the stone to fit with other desires, such as a desire to protect his lady-friend, be of help, and so on. This is an example of what Davidson calls the *holistic* character of the mental.[6]

A problem thus arises when we consider Mr. R's removing-and-replacing the stone as a whole. For there doesn't seem to be any perspective from which this behavior looks reasonable. We seem to have, rather, a particular form of irrationality: 'the failure, within a single person, of coherence or consistency in the pattern of beliefs, attitudes, emotions, intentions and actions.'[7] A sign of irrationality is that Mr. R suffers a reflexive breakdown: he himself cannot give an account of what he is doing in replacing the stone.[8]

Davidson argues that to make Mr. R's act intelligible, we must partition his mind into quasi-independent structures – a conscious mind and an unconscious mind – each part having a certain rationality of its own. The act of removing the stone reflects the conscious part of his mind: he is aware of his love for his lady-friend, aware that the stone poses some kind of danger for her, and so on. Here his beliefs, desires and acts all hang together in a coherent whole. But then there is this other part of his mind, the unconscious part, in which he is angry at her, resents her for not caring about him and seeks revenge. Of all of this he is unaware, but, again, all this hangs together more or less coherently. And it is these seething emotions that explain his putting the stone back in its original place. Thus within each part of the mind there is a holistic coherence; the incoherence arises when motivations from these disparate parts clash.

Freud says that 'a battle between love and hate' was raging in Mr. R's breast.[9] On this picture, the loving part of the mind is rational enough and the hating part of the mind is rational enough; the irrationality is in the battle between these parts – a battle that is all but unintelligible to Mr. R himself. This is a fascinating and plausible picture – but ultimately it does not do justice to the peculiar nature of the unconscious Freud discovers. In particular, it makes the unconscious look more rational than it often is.

Of course, there are occasions when unconscious motivations do have this rational structure. Consider an unhappy couple where each partner has, over the years, built up many reasons to be angry at the other. But, somehow, in order to stay together, each has devised a strategy of keeping the reasons for anger out of conscious awareness. Officially and sincerely, each is not angry with the other. But every now and then a vengeful act slips out – although the partner who acts is not really aware of what he or she is doing.

Here each partner has an articulated set of reasons for being angry – all that's missing is awareness that they're angry. This describes a structure Freud called the preconscious.[10] It has the same

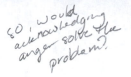

So, would acknowledging anger solve the problem?

basic structure as the conscious mind, although it is either not presently conscious or is actively kept out of consciousness. What's in a name? This couple is able to endure as a couple *and* hold onto their fury precisely because they each lack the name 'anger' to apply to their articulated structure of reasons. It's a certain kind of hell, but there are couples who live it.

But this does not seem to be the situation with Mr. R. Let me simply state my intuition, which I shall explain and defend in the rest of this chapter.

1 Mr. R is angry *at* his lady-friend *because* she does not return his love. And in replacing the stone, he expresses his angry feelings. However,

2 Mr. R does not understand what he is doing in replacing the stone, *not* because he has an articulated structure of angry reasons in his unconscious mind which he cannot (yet) name; rather, he doesn't understand what he is doing because he doesn't yet have angry reasons.

Although Mr. R is angry at his lady-friend because she does not return his love, he is not angry *that* she doesn't love him. That is, Mr. R's mental state does not express what philosophers call a pro-positional attitude.[11] Nevertheless,

3 Mr. R's replacing-the-stone does count as an action.

In acting, he knows what he is doing in the minimal sense that he is replacing the stone, and he sees something to be said in favor of it. He cannot say much about it – 'I shouldn't have removed it in the first place' – but he does see himself as acting to correct a previous error; and that's enough to make it an action.

If this picture of Mr. R is correct, we do not need an unconscious as a 'second mind' with its own rational structure to explain his behavior. But then, how are we to understand it? Before we answer that question, there is one crucial caveat: our aim is not to get to the truth of what was *really* going on with Mr. R. Rather, it is to get to the truth of what *might* have been going on with him. As a philosophical introduction, our aim is to work out the possibilities of human mentality, the possibilities of interpretation. For what we are concerned with here is the scope of human meaning. Mr. R is dead, he is not our patient and our evidence about him is limited. A biographer would want to know what was actually going on with him; an historian of psychoanalysis would want to know if Freud was right in his diagnosis; but a philosopher only needs to work out what might have been going on with him. For the philosopher's aim is to open up interpretive possibilities. Obviously, I do have a hunch about what Mr. R was like; and for the sake of simplicity I shall talk about what he *was* like, rather than what he *might* have been like. But what really matters here is possibility. If this picture of Mr. R is a real possibility, then we have to work out a conception of the unconscious that makes sense of it.

To get the interpretive problem into sharper focus, let us consider a similar moment from another of Freud's patients, whom I shall call Mr. S. Mr. S was walking through a park when he kicked his foot against a branch lying on the ground. He picked it up and threw it in the hedge.

Fear of action
doing more harm
than inaction.
On the way home he was suddenly seized with uneasiness that the branch in its new position might perhaps be projecting a little from the hedge and might cause an injury to someone passing by the same place after him. He was obliged to jump off his tram, hurry back to the park, find the place again, and put the branch back in its former position – although anyone else but the patient would have seen that, on the contrary, it was bound to be more dangerous to passers-by in the original position than where he had put it in the hedge.

Freud says, 'The second and hostile act, which he carried out under compulsion, had clothed itself to his conscious view with the motives that really belonged to the first and philanthropic one.'[12]

Now if one thinks of the unconscious as a second mind, with a rationality of its own, one will be tempted to think that each of these component-acts makes sense in itself, the only problem is how they fit together: for each of these acts flows from a part of the mind which is in itself more or less rational. This is just what Davidson thinks:

Here everything the agent does (except stumble on the branch) is done for a reason, a reason in the light of which the corresponding action was reasonable. Given that the man believed the stick was a danger if left on the path, and had a desire to eliminate the danger, it was reasonable to remove the stick. Given that, on second thought, he believed the stick was a danger in the hedge, it was reasonable to extract the stick from the hedge and replace it on the path. Given that the man wanted to take the stick from the hedge, it was reasonable to dismount from the tram and return to the park. In each case the reasons for the action tell us what the agent saw in the action, they give the intention with which he acted, and thereby give an explanation of the action. Such an explanation, as I have said, must exist if something a person does is to count as an action at all.[13]

This does not seem the right description of Mr. S. If Mr. S had decided the stick in the hedge was a danger, he would have had a reason to go back and remove it. But what reason could there be to *replace it on the path*? There seems to be a compulsion, not merely to remove the danger of the stick poking out of the hedge, but to restore it to its original position. Where is the reason in that? Freud describes Mr. S as 'suddenly seized with uneasiness,' 'obliged' to jump off the tram, acting 'under a compulsion,' and unable to see 'what anyone else would have seen.' One gets the sense that Davidson is forced to see the act of replacing the stick as more rational than it is precisely because he conceives of the unconscious as a second mind.[14] He sees the irrationality one level up – in how the two component-acts fit together – but in fact the second act seems nutty all on its own. How, then, might we otherwise conceive of the unconscious?

3 Fear and trembling and the couch

To answer this question, let us look to the analytic situation and consider a crucial moment in Freud's treatment of Mr. R:

> Things soon reached a point at which, in his dreams, his waking fantasies and his associations, he began heaping the

grossest abuse upon me and my family, though in his deliberate action he never treated me with anything but the greatest respect. His demeanor as he repeated these insults to me was that of a man in despair. 'How can a gentleman like you, sir,' he used to ask, 'let yourself be abused in this way by a low, good-for-nothing fellow like me? You ought to turn me out; that's all I deserve.' While he talked like this, he would get up from the sofa and roam about the room, a habit which he explained at first as being due to delicacy of feeling: he could not bring himself, he said, to utter such horrible things while he was lying there so comfortably. But soon he himself found a more cogent explanation, namely, that he was avoiding my proximity for fear of my giving him a beating. If he stayed on the sofa he behaved like someone in desperate terror trying to save himself from castigation of terrific violence; he would bury his head in his hands, cover his face with his arm, jump up and suddenly rush away, his features distorted with pain. He recalled that his father had had a passionate temper, and sometimes in his violence he had not known where to stop.[15]

What is Mr. R doing? In the moment, he is not sure himself. He flails about for a self-interpretation and finally hits on one that Freud says is 'more cogent': Mr. R is afraid that Freud is going to give him a beating. But how are we to understand this claim? It is implausible to assume that Mr. R is consciously afraid that good Dr. Freud is going to beat him. In the first instance he himself had no idea what he was doing. And he couldn't really believe, at least consciously, that a bourgeois, Viennese doctor was about to thrash him in the consulting room. Does that mean that Mr. R is unconsciously afraid that Freud is going to beat him? That is the line of reasoning taken by Mr. R and accepted by Freud.

But it seems that they are not making a discovery about the unconscious so much as following out the logic of the concept of fear. For the concept of fear makes a claim to its own rationality. If we fear something we believe it to be a danger – and we take that danger to be a legitimate cause of our fear.[16] And thus if one assumes Mr. R is afraid, and there is no conscious belief that Freud is a threat, then there is conceptual pressure to conclude there must be an unconscious belief. In short, Mr. R and Freud seem to think the following interpretive inference is legitimate: from

1 Mr R is acting fearfully;

and

2 there is no conscious belief that Freud is a threat;

it is valid to infer that

3 there must be an unconscious belief.

They are already en route to conceptualizing the unconscious as a rational structure with a 'mind of its own.' For, as we have seen, it makes no sense that there should be only one unconscious belief on its own. Perhaps Mr. R also believes that Freud is like his father, who did beat him ... , and so on. It is in this way that the unconscious starts to look like a second mind.

And this conceptualization does have therapeutic consequences. Freud's treatment of Mr. R should be importantly different depending on whether or not he has an unconscious belief. For if Mr. R is acting for inappropriate reasons – and he is unconscious that those are his reasons – then the proper therapeutic technique would be to bring these reasons to light. Mr. R would then be able to see that his hitherto unconscious reasons were bad reasons. When good reasons can interact with bad reasons, one should expect Mr. R's fear to diminish and eventually to evaporate. But if all this is a rationalizing defense, if Mr. R does not have an unconscious belief that Freud is going to beat him, then what at first sight looks like a therapeutic technique – 'making the unconscious conscious' – on further reflection looks like the construction of a false self. Mr. R starts to think of himself as having this unconscious belief, when no such thing is true about him. He can then go down the rabbit-hole of wondering what all his other hidden beliefs are. In this case, the interpretation of Mr. R as unconsciously afraid that Freud was going to beat him would facilitate Mr. R's self-misunderstanding.

For the sake of the argument, let us simply assume that our skeptical worries are justified, and that it is a mistake to interpret Mr. R as unconsciously afraid that Freud is going to beat him. We then have a situation in which

1 Mr. R is not consciously afraid that Freud is going to beat him;

and

2 He is not unconsciously afraid that Freud is going to beat him.

And yet it also seems true that

3 Mr. R is afraid of Freud.

But how could 1, 2 and 3 all be true? Don't they form an inconsistent triad? I don't think so. And seeing how they all can be true together, we shall gain some insight into the expression of unconscious mental life.

Here is what I suspect was happening with Mr. R. As the analysis is progressing, Mr. R is feeling ever more anxiety – anxiety that is inextricably bound up with his relation to Freud. Mr. R never developed the capacity to tolerate anxiety, thus he does not have the capacity to let the anxiety develop into more fully formed emotions. At some point the anxiety becomes too much to handle; and Mr. R jumps from the couch and cringes in an about-to-be-attacked kind of way. The immediate effect of this jump is to break the flow of the analysis. He cannot continue to talk about his thoughts and feelings if he's jumping-and-cringing. Thus he disrupts what would otherwise have been a more continuous development of his emotional life – one in which his emotions acquired texture and complexity by continuing to talk about them.

Let us grant that this is an emotional outburst. If we are going to understand the emotion, we need to see how it is functioning *as an outburst*. Emotions such as fear or anger are present in infancy, and they recur throughout life. But in a healthy life, a recurrence of fear is not a mere recurrence. An emotion such as fear has a developmental history: the fearful reaction of an infant has important similarities but also important dissimilarities to the expression of fear in an emotionally mature adult. The infant is overcome with terrifying bodily sensations: racing pulse, heavy breathing, cramping stomach. Bodily reactions never go away completely, and in extreme situations they come back with a vengeance, but in healthy adult life and relatively normal circumstances they become tempered by thought. This tempering is possible because, as we have seen, fear makes an implicit claim that it is an appropriate response to the situation.[17] Not only does a mature adult not feel fear at the same things a child does – for she can see they are not a danger – when she does start to feel afraid, she can use her own thought to calm herself. If she can persuasively say to herself that this looming challenge is not actually as threatening as she is taking it to be, she can thereby calm down. In a mature adult and in a relatively normal range of circumstances – excluding torture, horrific accidents and so on – fear is responsive to thought.

The mature capacity to experience fear is the outcome of a complex developmental process. And, like any developmental process, it can be interrupted, inhibited or distorted. In a mature and healthy expression of fear, a person takes up various fearful somatic responses – many of them automatic – and embeds them with reasons. On the one hand, fear reaches down into our gut; on the other hand, it reaches out to the world and makes a claim that fear is the right response. How might this emotional maturation fail to come about?

In the case of Mr. R, Freud gives us a clue. As a little boy he had done something naughty and his father had given him a beating.

> The little boy had flown into a terrible rage and had hurled abuse at his father even while he was under the blows. But as he knew no bad language, he had called him all the names of common objects he could think of, and had screamed: 'You lamp! You towel! You plate!', and so on. His father, shaken by such an outburst of elemental fury, had stopped beating him, and had declared: 'The child will be either a great man or a great criminal.' The patient believed that the scene made a permanent impression upon himself as well as upon his father. His father, he said, never beat him again; and he also attributed to this experience a change which overcame his own character.

> From that time forward he was a coward – out of fear of violence of his own rage. His whole life long, moreover, he was terribly afraid of blows, and used to creep away and hide, filled with terror and indignation, when one of his brothers or sisters was beaten.[18]

Freud is describing a childhood scene in which Boy R is surprised and terrified by his own rage. He becomes a coward – as Freud calls him – but what really scares him are aspects of himself. We can also see that in this moment he develops a certain emotional tic: when he gets anxious, he cringes and creeps away. Why, after all, does he cringe when a sibling is getting thrashed? One possibility, of course, is that Boy R is afraid that he's next. In which case he has a reason to cringe and creep away. But suppose that this was not Boy R's situation. Rather, the cringe-and-creep, which he acquired in that horrific moment with his father, is taken over as a more or less automatic response to feelings of anxiety. It's just what he does when he starts to feel fearfully anxious.

We are now in a position to appreciate a poignant emotional irony: Mr. R's cringe simultaneously expresses fear and inhibits the development of his capacity to experience fear. The infant's scream or Boy R's cringe is, of course, an expression of fear. As English speakers, we count every fearful expression along the developmental route from infancy to adulthood an expression of fear. A house that is being built does not count as a house until it is sufficiently constructed to shelter people; but even elemental and infantile expression of fear counts as fear. Thus Mr. R's cringe – whether it occurred in childhood or in the consulting room with Freud – is an expression of his fear. The danger we interpreters must avoid is to witness an immature emotional outburst and feel obliged to find all the features of the mature emotion. Just because the emotion is being displayed in a biologically mature adult, does not mean that the emotion itself is mature. I suspect this is the trap Freud and Mr. R fall into when they conclude that Mr. R must be afraid that Freud is going to beat him. Mr. R is afraid; he may even be afraid of Freud; but he isn't afraid that anything. His fear isn't sufficiently developed to have propositional structure. Thus he has no belief, conscious or unconscious, that Freud is about to beat him.

bodily response to traumatic triggers

The poignancy is that Mr. R uses his cringe to disrupt the development of his own emotional life. He is, after all, in a therapeutic setting, talking about his emotions with Freud. If he could have tolerated the situation, it would have been an occasion in which he imbued his feelings with more self-conscious thought. He could, for instance, have talked about his anxiety and his fearful feelings. The analytic situation could then have been part of a process of emotional development. This is just what his jump-and-cringe disrupts. Thus his expression of fear disrupts the process by which he might acquire a more mature capacity to express fear. In good-enough circumstances, a fearful experience is also an occasion to learn how to be afraid. That is, it is an occasion to mature with respect to fear – to think about one's reasons, to think about the danger, to think about how one has reacted in the light of the danger. And in healthy development, this kind of reasoning will come to permeate one's capacity to experience fear. However, if there is something about the fearful experience that is too much, then one can learn nothing from it.[19] Perhaps the danger is overwhelming; or perhaps one has little capacity to tolerate fear and is quickly flooded with anxiety. In such cases, the experience of fear *inhibits* the development of the capacity to experience fear.

Now Mr. R's problem is that, unbeknown to himself, he has taken over this inhibiting process and made it his own. From childhood on he has felt threatened by the intensity of his own angry emotions. So, when he starts to feel threatened, he reacts with that behavioral and emotional pattern he learned from childhood: he jumps-and-cringes-and-flees. This response disrupts what would otherwise have been the unfolding of his emotional life; and thus he inadvertently locks himself into an infantile emotional life. He is deploying his own emotions to disrupt his own emotional development.

It may at first seem counterintuitive that a genuine expression of fear can itself disrupt the development of the capacity to express fear. Normally we are inclined to think that the expressions of emotional life are themselves part of a developmental process in which the emotions gain in complexity and structure. But there are two aspects of this fear-filled outburst that are worth noting. First, although it is itself an emotional experience it has the effect of disrupting Mr. R's emotional life. Second, although Mr. R genuinely experiences fear – and fear is a reaction to an experienced threat – it is also true that he actively deploys this fearful reaction. That is, the fearful jump-and-cringe has strategic value for him – it disrupts the unfolding of other threatening emotions – and that is why it is happening. Although there is no conscious decision, and no intention to cringe, conscious or unconscious, he has taken over this cringe and is deploying it to disrupt his emotional life.

[margin handwritten note: almost like a protective measure]

It is difficult to capture this activity accurately. Freud discovered that anxiety is not simply an emotional state that overcomes us; it is a state we can learn to induce in ourselves. This learning is not a conscious process, and producing the anxiety is not an action. Although it is a mental activity, it is not the outcome of beliefs and desires. Rather, inducing anxiety – however painful – has some strategic value; and that is why it has been selected. The philosopher Mark Johnston has called this a mental tropism.[20] Mr. R 'learns' to trigger anxiety in himself, but he has no conscious awareness that he is doing this. And this activity is occurring at a more primitive level than that of belief, desire and intention.

Thus we can say that Mr. R actively induces anxiety to disrupt himself and the analysis – this is purposeful mental activity – and yet he is not acting on the basis of any beliefs, desires or intentions. He does not believe that he can disrupt the analysis in this way; he does not desire that the analysis be so disrupted; and yet disrupting the analysis is the aim of his activity. This is what Freud called a defense mechanism.[21] Following him, I am going to call this the anxiety defense.

We do not yet fully understand how this mechanism works. We need to learn how a primitive emotional activity such as self-induced anxiety can take on a specific form – like a jump-and-cringe; and we need to learn how these meaning-laden activities are preserved and used over and over, both to express and disrupt emotional life.

For that we need a better understanding of the Freudian conceptions of sexuality, wish and fantasy – and we shall get to them in the next chapters. But we are already in a position to see how

Mr. R's jump from the couch can be a meaningful activity, even though it does not express a fear *that* Freud is going to beat him (conscious or unconscious). Again, Mr. R's mental state does not express a propositional attitude. For although the jump is an expression of his fear – it is even an expression of his fear of Freud – he does not have reasons for it, conscious or unconscious. The emotional outburst is motivated, it does flow from an emotional orientation towards Freud, but that orientation does not have sufficient structure to count as a reason. And thus there is no easy or clear language with which to describe that orientation. It is the stuff from which a reason might develop – if only emotional outbursts like this one were not themselves preventing the development of reasons.

If this account is correct, then simply to interpret Mr. R's act as fear that Freud is going to beat him is to go off in the wrong direction. For we will then be inclined to search for reasons for Mr. R's fear; and if Mr. R is not consciously aware of his reasons we will be inclined to interpret him as having unconscious reasons. And, as Davidson has shown us, we shall then be conceptually obliged to interpret the unconscious mind as a whole network of mutually supporting beliefs and attitudes. But Mr. R's problem is not that he has unconscious reasons – nor that he has an unconscious second mind that is set against his conscious projects. Rather, his problem is that he suffered so much anxiety he never got around to formulating reasons. Indeed, it makes more sense to say he is afraid of the development of his own emotional life. To put it paradoxically, he is too afraid to be afraid. Less paradoxically, Mr. R suffers so much anxiety that he disrupts the development of his own emotional life. And because he is constantly disrupting his own development, he never gets to the point where he can experience fear maturely. Mr. R looks like an adult, biologically speaking he is an adult, and yet his expressions of fear are those of a child. It should no longer be a mystery how this is possible. His childhood emotional reactions were so powerful that they disrupted the normal development of his emotional life, and in this way they are preserved. He grows older biologically speaking, but his angry and fearful emotions remain more or less the same.

4 The non-mysterious unconscious

Let us return one last time to Mr. R's stone-removing-and-replacing behavior. According to Freud, there was a 'battle between love and hate' raging in Mr. R's breast. Like fear and anger, love and hate are emotions that are there in elemental forms in infancy, but that develop complexity, structure and depth throughout life. We are now in a position to see that in all his stone-placing activity, Mr. R is not only expressing his love and his hate, he also is inhibiting the development of those very emotions. As we read the case history, we see that Mr. R keeps himself so busy expressing obsessional acts, so busy expressing this emotion, warding off that fear, that he has no time or space to develop the very emotions that he is expressing in immature forms. Mr. R feels anxiety quickly and he tolerates it badly. As soon as he feels it, he rushes off in one direction or other.

The hectic rushing from one task to the next expresses his anxiety – but it also keeps it at bay. It gives him something to do. The overall outcome of this rushing around is to inhibit the maturation of emotional life.

And so, it is an interpretive mistake to think that what we need to account for are two actions – removing the stone and replacing it – for each of which he has reasons. Obviously, in a minimal sense Mr. R has performed two acts – he knows he is removing the stone, he knows he is replacing it – and he can give some minimal account of something to be said in favor of doing so. But this level of explanation is not capturing what is really motivating Mr. R. Rather than see him as performing two acts, each of which is rational in itself – and wondering how they could possibly fit together – it seems more accurate to see him as performing an emotional dance: it's the love-and-hate two-step. The dance is a surrogate for emotional integration. Mr. R cannot bring his loving and angry feelings together, and thus he cannot modulate his feelings towards his lady-friend. Thus he can love with idealized fervor. But as soon as he acts on those loving-idealizing feelings, angry feelings are also triggered (although these are feelings he does not well-understand or recognize as such). Now the question is not how the two acts could ever fit together, but how either of them could ever exist apart.

Is it possible he is only more anxious that something worse will happen if he doesn't put the stone back?

Given that Mr. R has performed the loving segment of the dance, he feels compelled to get to the hating part. Without it the dance remains incomplete. If this is Mr. R's situation, then of course he is going to suffer reflexive breakdown. For he does not see himself as dancing, he takes himself to be acting and he assumes a certain rationality in his behavior. But as he tries to interpret himself he has to come to grief. For taken as discrete actions, these acts do not fit together. To search for unconscious reasons is only to increase the confusion. It is to treat the unconscious as though it were a repository for already formed reasons, the only problem being to discover what they are. But among Mr. R's problems is that he doesn't have the reasons he takes himself to have.

We are now in a position to see one non-mysterious way in which 'the unconscious' can appear in adult life. Imagine Mr. R as a pre-linguistic infant. Baby R doesn't yet have the capacity to formulate complicated thoughts, for he hasn't yet acquired the language in which he might think them and feel them. Still, he has a powerful emotional life: he experiences elemental forms of love and hate, anger and fear. And he has a (small) repertoire of behaviors to express those feelings: he angrily throws his bottle away, anxiously pulls it back; when startled, he cringes and cries.[22] A pattern of emotional reactions is laid down and in various ways preserved alongside his developing personality. The adult Mr. R is no longer pushing away and retrieving bottles, the cultural vehicles with which he expresses these emotions has shifted. He is now pushing away and retrieving stones, but it is in the context of a city park, a complex social scene, he is expecting the carriage of his lady-friend, and so on. The infantile behavior is unrecognizable as such because it is embedded in adult social life. Yet because it is a remnant of infantile life it appears strange, incomprehensible. And as self-interpreters we grope for an explanation. But if we find too many reasons for our behavior, we thereby hide from ourselves its infantile roots. The behavior is motivated, meaningful, expressive of emotional life, and flowing from sources of which we are unaware. But if we take it to be flowing from an unconscious mind, a quasi-independent structure of propositional thoughts, we are attributing more thought – and thus more rationality – to the act than is there.

5 How the unconscious escapes our notice

Freud says 'betrayal oozes out of every pore' – and yet all we see is perspiration! We need to train our eyes to see things that are right there before them. Here is one significant way we fail to see the unconscious at work: we tend to assume that if we are in a relatively sophisticated situation – say, an adult conversation – that the elements of that situation will be sophisticated. One would think that the use of language to assert beliefs, express desires, fears and hopes would be a bastion of propositional thought. For unlike pushing and pulling on sticks and stones, unlike jumping-away-and-cringing, we use language to express our thoughts. But consider Freud's description of Mr. R's attempt to say a prayer:

> At the time of the revival of his piety he made up prayers for himself which took up more and more time and eventually lasted for an hour and a half. The reason for this was that he found, like an inverted Balaam, that something always inserted itself into his pious phrases and turned them into their opposite. E.g., if he said 'May God protect him' an evil spirit would hurriedly insinuate a 'not.' On one such occasion the idea occurred to him of cursing instead, for in that case, he thought, the contrary words would be sure to creep in. His original intention, which had been repressed by his praying was forcing its way through in this last idea of his. In the end, he found his way out of his embarrassment by giving up the prayers and replacing them by a short formula connected out of the initial letters or syllables of various prayers. He then recited this formula so quickly that nothing could slip into it.[23]

Mr. R has an obsessional fear that a particularly cruel torture is going to be inflicted on his father and he is trying to utter a prayer that God should protect him. (As readers of the case history will know, Mr. R's father is already dead, and the prayer is meant to protect him in 'the next world.' The torture is one he had heard about from a cruel Captain: rats burrowing into the anus of the prisoner.)

It is tempting to see Mr. R as bursting forth with a contradictory prayer from the one he intended to utter. If so, then Mr. R has an unconscious desire to harm his father. And how could there be an unconscious desire other than as part of a rationalizing network of beliefs and desires of an unconscious mind? This unconscious desire makes sense if it is located in an unconscious mind in which Mr. R also hates his father, fears his revenge, desires his own revenge, and so on. And this may be what is going on. This would be the case if Mr. R had a fairly well-elaborated hatred of his father and all he lacked was awareness of these complex feelings. But such complexity of thought is not required to make sense of this event, and it need not have been what was going on with Mr. R.

Here is another interpretive possibility. We are witnessing a mental activity too primitive to be understood as the outcome of belief and desire. Mr. R is not uttering a contradictory prayer, although it sounds like he is − and thus there is no need to posit a desire or intention to utter such a prayer anywhere in the mind. He is not asserting a prayer contradictory to the one he consciously intended; he is, rather, primitively attacking his prayer-making activity by forcibly inserting a 'not.' This is a quasi-physical activity. Note that the thought could have been disrupted by coughing or repeated sneezing or gagging or a massive anxiety attack. Every attempt to utter the prayer might have been disrupted by vomiting, dry heaves or stomach cramps. He might have had to run to the bathroom every time he tried to pray. There are lots of physical and emotional acts that could have defeated the attempt to pray. Here it is the quasi-physical intrusion of the utterance 'not.' Note that it is the rat-torture he fears, but what he is doing is shoving a little 'not' up into the middle of his sentence. He thereby disrupts his own thought.[24]

In some ways this example is amusing, but it is not far removed from something terrifying. Suppose every time you tried to formulate a thought a voice broke in yelling 'Not! Not! Not! Not!' Here the situation would not be that you were somehow forming the negations of the thoughts you were trying to think. Rather, you could never get to have a single thought − and thus would never have a single thought to negate − because before you formulated the thought, there came the voice of 'Not! Not! Not!' In short, thinking would become impossible. This would not be a case in which mental life was taken up with a lot of negative thoughts; it would be a case of mental life disintegrating.[25]

It is not an accident that Mr. R settled on a vehicle of meaning –
the word 'not' – to engage in his negating activity. Children can
learn to say 'no!' to utter their protests before they learn how to
negate propositions. Indeed, children can scream 'no!' as a way of
disrupting their parents' attempts to tell them what to do. The parents may not be able to finish their sentence – or the child's screams
will drown it out.[26] The children are not thereby forming the contradictory judgment to that of their parents. In some cases, they are
attacking their parents' attempts to make the judgment at all.[27]

[handwritten margin note: Is that Mr R, what Mr R is do mgo]

6 The unconscious is timeless

Freud said that one of the hallmarks of the unconscious is that it
is timeless.[28] What does this mean? We have already begun to
see how fairly sophisticated thought-activity can at the same time be
expressing a primitive struggle. It is important to see that there is
no limit to the sophistication and complexity of living situations
that can simultaneously embed struggles that go back to earliest
childhood. So, to continue with Mr. R: while he is on active military
duty, he orders a pair of eyeglasses – a pince-nez – by mail. One
evening the cruel Captain hands him a packet and says, 'Lieutenant
A has paid the charges for you. You must pay him back.'

[handwritten margin note: OCD?]

> At that instant, however, a 'sanction' had taken shape in his
> mind, namely that he was not to pay back the money or it
> would happen – (that is, the phantasy about the rats would
> come true as regards his father and the lady). And immedi-
> ately, in accordance with a type of procedure with which he
> was familiar, to combat this sanction there had arisen a com-
> mand in the shape of a vow: 'You must pay back the 3.80
> kronen to Lieutenant A.' He had said these words to himself
> almost half aloud.[29]

One needs to read the case history to see the contortions Mr. R goes
through to pay back *and* not pay back Lieutenant A. He makes
enormously complex plans to make a train trip to a town near
where A was staying, only not to get on the train, then to get on it
because a conductor happens to say to him 'Ten o'clock train, sir?'

then to get off at a station along the way, only to get back on. And so on. He gets himself into a confused tizzy, and finally decides to get himself to Vienna where he can lay out the whole problem to his friend. *Let him decide!* He meets his friend in the middle of the night and tells him his story. 'His friend had held up his hands in amazement to think that he could still be in doubt whether he was suffering from an obsession, and had calmed him down for the night, so that he slept excellently.'[30] *Did he only need that confirmation?*

Readers who are familiar with psychoanalysis or psychotherapy will know that there is an enormous amount we might learn about Mr. R by listening to him speak about what the Captain means to him; what his associations are to train travel; to eyeglasses; to the torture, and so on. As we shall see in the next chapters, the unconscious makes connections among ideas that from the perspective of conscious judgment look very loose. If we let the analysand just say whatever comes into his mind without inhibition, some of these connections will come to light. So, for example, it turns out that Mr. R thought of his father *as a debtor.* Indeed, he was a 'Spielratte' – a 'play-rat,' one who lost at cards.[31] Thus the very idea *This* that Mr. R must pay back Lieutenant A links him (in his own mind) *feels like* not only to his father, but also to rats. If he is a debtor like his *a stretch..* father, then maybe, like his father, he is also a rat. *once there*

Now these associations do reveal how Mr. R's imagination *any more* works – and the associations themselves may work through the *examples* meanings of the ideas. The Captain suggests to him that he is a *of this?* debtor, the idea of a debtor is linked to his father, but his father is a particular kind of debtor, a *Spielratte*, and so on. But complex and revealing as these associations may be, they should not blind us to a more primordial structure that is getting expressed at the same time. For whatever interesting associations Mr. R may have to trains, whoever Lieutenant A reminds him of, whatever eyeglasses mean for him, it is *also* true that in getting on and off the train, in trying to pay back and not pay back Lieutenant A, in trying to return and retrieve eyeglasses, Mr. R is re-enacting the same basic structure as he did in removing and replacing the stone. The cultural vehicles have become more sophisticated – and one should expect that the meaning of, say, trains for Mr. R will radiate out in all sorts of fascinating ways – but the primordial struggle of removal and retrieval endures. We have already speculated that this struggle began in infancy. It began with a bottle, moved onto a stone, and then to trains, eyeglasses and paying back debts. No doubt there were countless stages in-between. And with each new item there will be all sorts of associations that are linked to the meaning of that particular item. Still, the primordial struggle endures – as if nothing had changed.

We begin to glimpse what Freud means by repetition. On the surface, it looks as though a baby's bottle, a stone in the road, some eyeglasses and a train ticket to Vienna have nothing in common. And, indeed, they mean many different things even to Mr. R. But as he uses them he finds ways to enact the same struggle over and over again. Indeed, we begin to wonder whether the phrase 'over and over again' is giving us the deepest characterization of what is happening. Certainly, from the perspective of conscious judgment there is a passage of time in which Infant R does X, Boy R does Y, Mr. R does Z – and it is a real psychoanalytic breakthrough to see that X, Y and Z have something in common. Thus there is genuine insight to see that <X,Y,Z> form a structure of repetition.

But from the perspective of the unconscious – if we may speak loosely – it is less like 'the same thing happens again' and more like 'the same primordial struggle endures.' There is no passage of time; there is just the primordial struggle of removal and retrieval. This is the Typhonic monster with a hundred heads: it may feed off of the tidbits of the moment – bottles, stones, eyeglasses, train tickets – but it is never full. The only time is the present and the monster is always hungry. This point is hard to grasp because we are so used to thinking in temporal terms. As a heuristic device, imagine the same mythic tale told from two perspectives, ours and the monster's. Our best poet tells us this myth: 'Once upon a time there was a monster who lived in a cave and first he ate bottles, and then he ate stones, and then he ate eyeglasses and then he ate train tickets, and then ... '

The monster living in the cave, however, has no sense of the passage of time and he has only one message: 'ME WANT COOKIE!'[32] That is all he has ever expressed, all he has ever done, and all he has ever experienced. This is what Freud meant by calling the unconscious timeless.

By now, I hope that there is no longer any temptation to think that the unconscious must be a second mind with a rationality of its own. But it is worth noting that such a conception cannot do justice to the timeless, repetitive nature of the unconscious. Does Mr. R want to pay back Lieutenant A? Why? He knew all along that he didn't actually owe him any money. The debt was owed to the official at the post office; the Captain had made a mistake.[33] The picture of Mr. R having two minds, each with its own network of beliefs and desires, cannot make good sense of this vignette. Consider Mr. R's conscious mind: Having heard the Captain's order, Mr. R is able to suppress from conscious awareness that he doesn't in fact owe money to Lieutenant A. He has heard the Captain's order; and let us suppose he has a belief that he ought to obey. But suppose we were able to intervene at just this moment and ask Mr. R: why? He might be able to say a few things, such as 'One ought to obey orders' or 'Because the Captain told me to,' but in fact he cannot give any articulated set of reasons why he ought to pay back the Lieutenant because he doesn't have any and there aren't any. So, when it comes to Mr. R's conscious mind, there is no articulated structure of beliefs and desires that support his attempts to pay back Lieutenant A. Is that what pressures us into thinking that this rationalizing structure must be hidden in a 'second mind'? But what could that hidden structure be? Perhaps he unconsciously believes that he really does owe Lieutenant A the money? But then what else must he unconsciously believe for it to be rational to believe that? We'd have to construct a whole other universe of experience – for which there is basically no evidence. We would be extravagantly attributing all sorts of other unconscious beliefs to him only because we wanted to rationalize a single belief. Or perhaps he unconsciously believes that if he doesn't pay back Lieutenant A, the torture will occur to his loved ones. But how could any part of the mind rationalize that superstition? No doubt Mr. R does have superstitious fears. And we might loosely express the content of his fears by saying 'He fears that if he doesn't pay the money back, the torture will occur.' But there is no part of the mind – conscious or unconscious – that can rationalize that fear. The hallmark of Mr. R's situation is that *his thought runs out*. There is no rationalizing structure – conscious or unconscious – for these beliefs.

[Handwritten margin note, bottom left:] It doesn't have to if anxiety is high enough

[Handwritten margin note, bottom center:] Why would you take the risk that this torture would happen? It is, in a way, irrational then to pick the path that does not lead to torture.

Here is a better way of interpreting the situation. The phrase 'You must pay back Lieutenant A' is inserted almost mechanically into Mr. R's mind by the Captain's utterance. The Captain is a man of importance to Mr. R, and he utters an injunction directed specifically to Mr. R, but it is also crucially important that this utterance comes next. It is the utterance that confronts Mr. R. And precisely because it is largely cut off from Mr. R's beliefs and desires – after all, why should he have had any thoughts about Lieutenant A given that he didn't owe him any money? – the power of the words is experienced as uncanny. It is like an oracle: Mr. R experiences the words as addressed to him, he experiences them as fateful, but he doesn't really understand why. The experience is similar to an infant's experience of hearing parental utterances before it can fully understand what they mean.[34] And it may well have been experienced by Mr. R as a repetition of such. Once the utterance is in place, it is easy enough to attack it with a 'not' – 'you must not pay back the money' – and to associate this newly formed prohibition with the rat-torture. In a funny way, Mr. R is right to make this association. For the rat-torture is a recurrent, intrusive fantasy that is threatening to take over his mind. And when the fantasy occurs, the rat-torture is occurring (at least, in Mr. R's mind). It has, for him, the reality of a vivid dreamlike experience. The only way to keep this fantasy at bay – and thus (in Mr. R's mind) the only way to prevent the torture from occurring – is to keep the mind occupied with other things. The Captain is associated in Mr. R's mind with the torture, so it makes a crazy kind of sense that by prohibiting his command, one would thereby prevent the torture.

Note that there is nothing inherent in the meaning of 'You must [not] pay back Lieutenant A' that has anything to do with a torture occurring or not occurring. The meaning becomes fateful for Mr. R because it is uttered by the Captain and because this now happens to be the thought intruded into Mr. R's mind. Mr. R is now going to respond to a sophisticated meaning, and he is going to respond in sophisticated, if confused, ways. But it is nevertheless the outcome of rather elemental mental operations and physical transpositions. Looking on as interpreters, it is easy enough for us to assume that Mr. R wants to pay back Lieutenant

A, and that he doesn't want to pay him back; that he wants to follow the Captain's orders, and that he doesn't want to. It may look as though he believes that if he pays back Lieutenant A the rat torture will occur and that if he doesn't pay back Lieutenant A the rat torture will occur (after all, he will have disobeyed the cruel Captain). (Again, in a funny way he is right: either way, the fantasy of the rat torture will eventually recur.) But if we try to locate any of these individual desires and beliefs in a larger, rationalizing network, we cannot succeed. *Fear of the captain*

7 The unconscious and the fundamental question

Our inquiry has shown us that, in trying to understand the unconscious, it is a mistake to conceive of ourselves as searching for a second mind – one that is split off from the conscious mind, yet having a rationality of its own. And while there may indeed be thoughts and wishes that are unconscious, our first priority should not be to seek thought-contents hidden somewhere in the mind, but rather to discover elemental forms of mental activity that dominate one's life.

In Mr. R's case, there is an archaic structure of removal-and-restoration that infiltrates virtually all aspects of his thinking and being. He is himself aware of many of the instances of this structure. What he lacks is a deep understanding of the structure itself. The word deep here is crucial. It is not enough that Mr. R has a merely cognitive grasp that this elemental form dominates his life. He needs to acquire practical mastery over its fractal nature. That is, precisely because this structure is primordial, it will recur in the macrocosm and microcosms of Mr. R's life. A person like Mr. R, dominated by the structure of removal-and-restoration, will experience it as he opens and closes doors, pays bills, walks in the park, thinks about the meaning of life, goes out on dates ... the variations are endless, and they occur in the large and the small. He may experience individual instances of this structure, but he will, for the most part, not be able to recognize it *as* an instance of this structure; and, for the most part, he will feel helpless to intervene. His inability to recognize it as such is what constitutes it as unconscious. Thus he needs to develop the ability to recognize this structure *as it is unfolding*, and acquire the ability to intervene and change its course. A psychoanalytic therapy would help a person acquire this perceptual-practical skill. This is the process Freud calls *working-through*.[35]

We are beginning to grasp a more nuanced sense of what it is to fulfill the Delphic oracle's injunction to know oneself – at least, with respect to the unconscious. And we can begin to think about what a psychoanalytic interpretation must be like. At the beginning of his career, Freud thought that the therapeutic project was simply to discover a hidden memory or wish in a person's mind – and just tell the patient what it was.[36]

This technique did not help his patients – indeed, in some cases it provoked a therapeutic disaster, as we shall see in Chapter 4. Freud thus had to abandon it as an adequate model of what is involved in 'making the unconscious conscious.' There is, of course, an enormous amount to be said about the nature of psychoanalytic interpretation. But even at this early stage of our inquiry, we can see the inadequacy of this picture of interpretation as discovering the contents of the analysand's mind that are already there. However, this does not mean that with interpretation we just make things up, or that anything goes.

Here is a different model of psychoanalytic interpretation: a phrase that

1 names an experience, emotion, behavior as it is emerging in the here-and-now; and
2 in the naming serves to augment a *practical* skill by which the analysand can monitor their life-experience and intervene in satisfying ways.

The interpretation will typically

3 bring to light aspects of that experience that have hitherto remained unconscious.

What makes psychoanalysis into a master-craft is the challenge to the analyst to help bring 1, 2 and 3 into harmony. It is not enough for an analyst to tell analysands the unconscious contents of their minds. The analyst must work with the analysand in such a way that the analysand can experience the unconscious emerging in the here-and-now and can thus incorporate a practical understanding of it. The analyst's ability to formulate an interpretation is itself a practical skill, one that is developed in a lifetime of training and practice.

Obviously, it is beyond the scope of an introduction to Freud to discuss the technique of interpretation in any detail. But basically psychoanalytic interpretation tries to facilitate a process by which what has hitherto been repressed and unconscious can come to light. (That is, it tries to combine 3 with 1 and 2.) Psychoanalysis itself is the building up of a practical-cognitive skill of recognizing the fractal nature of one's unconscious conflicts as they are unfolding in the here and now – and of intervening in ways that make a satisfying difference. A good interpretation is simply a form of words that accurately grasps those conflicts at the right level for the analysand to make a conscious, efficacious intervention in her own thinking and acting – and that thereby augments this practical skill. Without the skill, the words are all but empty. Freud might tell his patient, 'You want to kill your father and marry your mother' – but even if Freud is right, and even if his patient believes him because Freud is the expert, the words cannot make the right kind of difference.[37] With just this piece of information, it is not an exaggeration to say the patient has no idea what Freud is talking about. Indeed, this phrase can now be used to keep real self-understanding at bay. It can be used as an empty intellectualization that falsely persuades one that one already has self-knowledge.

A proper psychoanalytic interpretation cannot come before the analysand has acquired the skills needed to make good use of it. These are skills of monitoring and experiencing one's thoughts and feelings as they are emerging in the here-and-now, in the details of life. The interpretation gives these emerging thoughts and feelings a name – at just the point where the only thing missing from self-awareness is the name. In this way, a good interpretation both completes the emerging experience and helps analysands develop their own practical skills of self-understanding. Over time, they will develop the capacity to supply their own interpretations of their experience.

Further reading

Readings from Freud

Notes on a case of obsessional neurosis (The Rat Man), SE X: 152–249. It is strongly recommended that one read this case history in conjunction with reading this chapter.

Inhibitions, symptoms and anxiety, SE XX: 87–174. A marvelous account of how anxiety can serve as a signal.

'The Unconscious,' SE XIV: 166–204. Freud's classic statement about the unconscious. This conception is developed in the following two works:

'Repression,' SE XIV: 146–58.

'The psychology of the dream process,' The interpretation of dreams, Chapter 7, SE V: 509–621.

Other readings

W. Bion, 'Attacks on linking,' in E.B. Spillius (ed.), Melanie Klein today: developments in theory and practice, Vol. 1, Mainly theory (London: Routledge, 1988), pp. 87–101. A classic account of the mind's ability to disrupt itself.

M. Cavell, The psychoanalytic mind: from Freud to philosophy (Cambridge, MA: Harvard University Press, 1993).

D. Davidson, 'Paradoxes of irrationality,' in R. Wollheim and J. Hopkins (eds.), Philosophical essays on Freud (Cambridge: Cambridge University Press, 1982). An excellent defense of the unconscious as a second mind – a view that I think should ultimately be rejected.

D. Finkelstein, Expression and the inner (Cambridge, MA: Harvard University Press, 2003). An outstanding account of how we express our inner mental states.

S. Gardner, Irrationality and the philosophy of psychoanalysis (Cambridge: Cambridge University Press, 1993). An excellent critique of the unconscious as a second mind. And a fascinating account of how unconscious motivations – wish and fantasy – are significantly different from preconscious and conscious motivations such as desire and hope.

E. O'Shaughnessy, 'W.R. Bion's theory of thinking and new techniques in child analysis,' in E.B. Spillius (ed.), Melanie Klein today, Vol. 2, Mainly practice (London and New York: Routledge, 1988), pp. 177–90.

Notes

1 Freud, Fragment of an analysis of a case of hysteria, SE VII: 77–78.
2 Freud, 'The unconscious,' SE XIV:166.
3 Freud, Notes on a case of obsessional neurosis, SE X: 191–92.
4 Freud, 'The unconscious,' SE XIV: 169.
5 D. Davidson, 'Paradoxes of irrationality,' in R. Wollheim and J. Hopkins (eds.), Philosophical essays on Freud (Cambridge: Cambridge University Press, 1982), p. 289.

6 Ibid, p. 302. Obviously, a person can get very confused. A person in Mr. R's position could think that, in moving the stone, he was sending a message to Mars. Still, to attribute that belief to him, we'd need to know more about what he believed. Did he also think he was moving a stone? How would that get the message across? And if he didn't think it was a stone, what did he think it was? And so on.

7 Ibid, p. 290.

8 The philosopher Sebastian Gardner thinks it is a hallmark of the peculiar form of irrationality that concerns psychoanalysis: 'Irrational phenomena have the following form: a person exhibits irrationality when he does not, or could not – without altering himself in a way that would tend towards the eradication of the phenomenon in question – think about himself in a way that would both make adequate sense of his own thought and/or action, and at the same time avoid exhibiting incompleteness, incoherence, inconsistency, lapse into unintelligibility, or some other defect of a kind to signify, in a suitably broad sense, *self-contradiction*. An irrational subject is thus one who will in some loosely cognitive sense fail the test of self-confrontation: either he will be unable to provide an explanation-cum-justification of himself, or, in the course of attempting to do so, he will betray a failure of self-knowledge. The definition locates a problem of reflexivity at the heart of irrationality: the same subject who at each instant of wakeful self-consciousness experiences himself ineluctably as rational contradicts his own rationality' (S. Gardner, *Irrationality and the philosophy of psychoanalysis* (Cambridge: Cambridge University Press, 1993), pp. 3–4.) See also S. Gardner, 'The unconscious', in J. Neu (ed.), *The Cambridge companion to Freud* (Cambridge: Cambridge University Press, 1991), pp. 136–60. Anyone interested in the relation of psychoanalysis to irrationality should read this book.

9 Freud, *Notes on a case of obsessional neurosis*, SE X: 191.

10 Freud, 'The unconscious,' SE XIV: 166–67, 192.

11 Propositional attitudes are expressed in sentences with verbs such as 'believes,' 'desires,' 'fears,' 'hopes,' 'wishes' followed by *that P* – where P is a sentence that expresses the state of affairs that is the object of belief, desire, fear or hope.

12 Freud, *Notes on a case of obsessional neurosis*, SE X: 192–93n.

13 Davidson, 'Paradoxes of irrationality,' p. 292.

14 Because Davidson sees the individual acts as necessarily tending towards rationality – otherwise they wouldn't be actions at all – he must locate the irrationality one level up, in the way the acts fail to fit together. He does this by conceptualizing the moment as a case of weakness of will – a case in which a person acts against his considered judgment. It is easy to imagine that the man who returned to the park to restore the branch to its original position in the path realizes that his action is not sensible. He has a motive for moving the stick, namely, that it may endanger a passer-by. But he also has a motive for not returning, which is the time and trouble it costs. In his own judgment, the latter consideration outweighs the former; yet he acts on the former. In short, he goes against his own best judgment. (Davidson, 'Paradoxes of irrationality,' p. 294.) Of course, it is possible for a person's act to fit this structure. But this

doesn't seem to be Mr. S. He does have a motive to remove the stick; he doesn't have a rational reason to place it exactly where it had been. Moreover, imagine if just before jumping off the tram, Mr. S had said to himself: 'All things considered, I have a reason to get off the tram and replace the stick exactly where it was.' This would no longer seem to be a case of weakness of will. But would it in any way reduce our sense that this behavior is odd – and calls for some different form of explanation? And even if Mr. S himself thought his behavior *was* an instance of weakness of will, we'd still have reason to be suspicious. Suppose he reported to his analyst at his next session, 'It's funny; I decided that all things considered it was best to stay on the tram – probably no one would get hurt by the stick in the hedge. But I jumped off the tram anyway and ran to remove the stick. Strange.' At last, this looks like a straightforward case of weakness of will. But I think the analyst would do well to be hermeneutically suspicious of this account. There is reason to suspect that the analysand, Mr. S, is being overly intellectual in his account of what happened. And it is possible that finding reasons for his act – even less good reasons – is covering over the fact that this act did not happen for reasons in this way – and this is not, as is claimed, a case of weakness of will.

15 Freud, 'Notes on a case of obsessional neurosis,' SE X: 209.

16 See Aristotle, Rhetoric II.5.

17 Aristotle, *Rhetoric* II; J. Neu, *Emotion, thought and therapy: a study of Hume and Spinoza and the relationship of philosophical theories of the emotions to psychological theories of therapy* (Berkeley: University of California Press, 1977) pp. 61–62; J. Lear, *Love and its place in nature: a philosophical interpretation of Freudian psychoanalysis* (New Haven: Yale University Press, 1990), pp. 47–51; R.M. Gordon, *The structure of the emotions* (Cambridge: Cambridge University Press, 1987); R. de Sousa, *The rationality of emotion* (Cambridge, MA: MIT Press, 1987); D. Davidson, 'Hume's cognitive theory of pride,' in *Essays on actions and events* (Oxford: Clarendon Press, 1980); R.C. Roberts, 'What an emotion is: a sketch,' *Philosophical review* XLVII (1988), pp. 183–209.

18 Freud, *Notes on a case of obsessional neurosis*, SE X:205–6, my emphasis. We shall see in Chapter 3 that a paternal utterance such as 'He shall either be a great man or a great criminal' can have significant effect on psychological development. Obviously, we do not know enough about Mr. R to know how things actually were with him. But as we look at the obsessive back and forth in his personality, we can see all of it as the expression of a master question: am I a great man or a great criminal?

19 See W. Bion, *Learning from experience* (London: Karnac, 1984).

20 See M. Johnston, 'Self-deception and the nature of mind,' in C. and G. Macdonald (eds.), *Philosophy of psychology: debates on psychological explanation* (Oxford: Blackwell, 1995); and J. Lear, 'Restlessness, phantasy and the concept of mind', in *Open minded: working out the logic of the soul* (Cambridge, MA: Harvard University Press, 1998), pp. 80–122; J. Lear, 'Jumping from the couch,' *International journal of psychoanalysis* 83 (2002), pp. 583–93. Note that there is an analogy with Darwin's model of natural selection. Mr. R's anxiety defense is serving as a censor for his mental and emotional life much as death serves as a 'censor' in

natural selection. The anxiety defense disrupts a thought-in-the-making or an emotion-in-the-making – it dies before it can reproduce itself in the environment of Mr. R's mental life. Here the censor does not have to be particularly thoughtful – a little homunculus with a mind of its own – it just has to be a triggering of anxiety in response to anxiety. In this way, a simple mechanism can have profound outcomes for the person deploying it.

21 Freud, 'The unconscious,' SE XIV: 184; 'Repression,' SE XIV: 187.

22 See Freud's account of a child's playing 'fort/da' with a spool in *Beyond the pleasure principle*, SE XVIII: 14–17. I give an interpretation of this game in *Lear, Happiness, death and the remainder of life* (Cambridge, MA: Harvard University Press, 2000), pp. 90–98.

23 Freud, 'Notes on a case of obsessional neurosis,' SE X: 193.

24 One might wonder: how is Mr. R able to inject that 'not' at just the right place so as to contradict the original prayer? Maybe he didn't. Imagine that in the actual event he said, 'May God NOT!' or 'May God protect him. NOT!' It would be natural for him to later report to Freud that he had said, 'May God not protect him.' He would thereby unintentionally make himself look more thoughtful than he was. It also seems to me plausible to assume that a person who has the capacity to negate sentences and form contradictions can thereby develop an intuitive 'feel' for when to forcibly inject a 'not.'

25 See W. Bion, 'Attacks on linking,' in E.B. Spillius (ed.), *Melanie Klein today: developments in theory and practice*, Vol. 1, *Mainly theory* (London: Routledge, 1988), pp. 87–101. It is overwhelmingly plausible to assume that if in the course of thinking and acting a person utters 'May God not protect him!' then that thought must be occurring in his 'stream of consciousness.' The assumption needs to be qualified. For the 'not' is not a part of the stream of consciousness, it is a disruption of it and an attack upon it.

26 A colleague and friend of mine, whom I'll call X, related this story: When he was newly married and his wife was first pregnant, they decided that if the child was a boy they would name him Y. On a vacation trip to visit his parents, he told them of that decision – at which point the parents became agitated. It turned out that X's original name was Y, that X was in fact adopted and his name was changed to X at the adoption, and that X was unwittingly about to name his child after himself. Since X and his family were Jewish, and in the Jewish tradition one is not supposed to name a child after a living member of the family, X was unwittingly about to commit a forbidden act. And, for X's parents to prevent this forbidden act they had to explain to their grown son that he was adopted. Incredulous, X asked his parents why they never told him he was adopted. They answered: 'We tried to tell you when you were six years old, but you stuck your fingers in your ears and kept screaming.'

27 Consider the so-called Valley Girl use of the word 'not' that was popular a number of years ago: 'That's a pretty dress you're wearing. ... Not!' I suspect the reason this locution caught on as a fashion, and provided some amusement, was that it was systematically ambiguous between being a contradiction and a more primitive attack. It *looks* like the subsequent 'Not' is a form of contradiction – as

though one was saying, 'That's not really so.' But there is also a hidden pleasure in the more primitive disruption of the compliment. The 'Not!' disrupts the compliment in a manner similar to Mr. R's disruption of his prayer.

28 Freud, 'The unconscious,' SE XIV: 187.
29 Freud, 'Notes on a case of obsessional neurosis,' SE X: 168. The *Standard edition* uses the word 'phantasy' to denote the special types of fantasy that concern psychoanalysis – in particular, unconscious fantasy.
30 Freud, *Notes on a case of obsessional neurosis*, SE X: 172.
31 Ibid, X: 210.
32 Obviously, the Cookie Monster is an amusing idealization. Not all infantile wishes are so charming. But adults and children find Cookie Monster amusing, I suspect, because there is some internal recognition of the timeless presence of appetite. The specifically oral nature of infantile desire will be discussed in Chapters 3 and 7.
33 Freud, *Notes on a case of obsessional neurosis*, SE X: 172.
34 Jean Laplanche, 'The unfinished Copernican revolution,' in *Essays on otherness* (London and New York: Routledge, 1999), pp. 52–83.
35 See Freud, *Studies on hysteria*, SE II: 288, 291; 'Remembering, repeating and working-through,' SE XII: 155; 'Inhibitions, symptoms and anxiety,' SE XX: 159.
36 See, e.g., Freud, 'Remembering, repeating and working-through,' SE XII: 147.
37 See D. Finkelstein, *Expression and the inner* (Cambridge, MA: Harvard University Press, 2003).

Two

Sex, Eros and life

1 What's sex got to do with it?

Freud claims that sexuality goes to the heart of human being – that is, of our being. But he also says that what he means by sexuality differs radically from the popular conception.[1] His aim, then, is not merely to show that sexuality is more pervasive in our lives than we have assumed; it is to change what we mean by sexuality. He wants to bring about a paradigm shift, a conceptual revision. Thus if we want to understand Freud and psychoanalysis, we must avoid the confusion of thinking we already know what sex is and assuming that Freud wants to reduce all of our marvelous complexity to that.

This picture is mistaken in two important ways: first, Freud never thought that sexuality was the only important force in our lives; second, what sexuality is remains a fascinating and enigmatic question. Still, a challenge can be put to Freud right away: if his conception of sexuality differs that much from the popular conception, why should we think of it as sexuality? Why not think of it – whatever it is – as something else? This is an important question and, to my mind, it has not yet been answered adequately. It is easy enough to see why Freud began thinking about human sexuality. The first patients of psychoanalysis made sex an unavoidable issue. Even Freud was not up to the task of reporting on it fully and accurately. Anna O, the first patient in the early work *Studies on hysteria*, gave the name 'talking cure' to psychoanalysis.[2] Her doctor was Josef Breuer, Freud's distinguished senior colleague, and his treatment would not today count as psychoanalysis. Ms. O would fall into a self-induced hypnotic state in afternoons and early evenings, and Dr. Breuer's technique consisted of letting her 'talk herself out.'[3]

She would talk about anxieties, angers, fears and memories of which she had no awareness when in her normal conscious state. 'A few moments after she had finished her narrative she would wake up, obviously calmed down.' Breuer reports that she was then 'clear in mind, calm and cheerful.' However, 'if for any reason she was unable to tell me the story during her evening hypnosis she failed to calm down afterwards, and on the following day she had to tell me two stories in order for this to happen.'[4] The details of this case make fascinating reading, but the main point is this: Breuer reports that when Ms. O fully 'talked out' her memories and associations to each of her symptoms, the symptom itself would disappear.

> These findings – that in the case of this patient the hysterical phenomena disappeared as soon as the event which had given rise to them was reproduced in her hypnosis – made it possible to arrive at a therapeutic technical procedure which left nothing to be desired in its logical consistency and systematic application. Each individual symptom in this complicated case was taken separately in hand; all the occasions on which it had appeared were described in the reverse order, starting before the time when the patient became bed-ridden and going back to the event which led to its first appearance. When this had been described the symptom was permanently removed.[5]

Freud and Breuer called this the cathartic method – harking back to ancient Greek medicine, where catharsis was both a purgation and a purification. It is important to realize that they were trying not only to cure their patients; they were trying to solve the problem of hysteria – a problem that preoccupied the medical profession in nineteenth-century Europe.[6] Hysteria was noticed primarily among women. The symptoms could be dramatic, and they often looked like medical ailments. The problems were, first, that the physical infirmities did not coincide with anatomical reality (so, for example, a paralysis would correspond to the patient's *idea* of her arm rather than to what doctors took to be the actual limb); second, doctors could find no cause for the illness.

The aim of the Studies on hysteria was to show that hysteria was indeed a genuine illness, and that it had a real cause. The causal explanation had eluded scientists, Breuer and Freud claimed, because, given ordinary methods of observation, the cause had remained hidden. Under hypnosis it was revealed that there was a memory of a past event that was split off from conscious awareness and was active in causing symptoms. 'We must presume ... that the psychical trauma – or more precisely the memory of the trauma – acts like a foreign body which long after its entry must continue to be regarded as an agent that is still at work.' And this discovery had 'an important practical interest':

> For we found, to our great surprise at first, that each individual hysterical symptom immediately and permanently disappeared when we had succeeded in bringing clearly to light the memory of the event by which it was provoked and in arousing its accompanying affect, and when the patient had described that event in the greatest possible detail and had put the affect into words. Recollection without affect almost invariably produces no result.[7]

Freud and Breuer famously conclude, 'Hysterics suffer mainly from reminiscences.'[8] This claim has been misunderstood. The hidden memory, as Freud understands it, is not part of a long causal chain beginning in childhood that led, step by step, to the creation of a symptom. Rather, because the painful memory had been split off from consciousness, it had thereby been preserved – and it was alive in the present as a 'directly releasing cause.' So the point of the technique was not to work back along a causal route to a moment in the remote past when things started going wrong; rather, it was to find a poisonous memory alive in the present causing the present illness, although split off from conscious awareness.

In retrospect, it is easy to see why Breuer and Freud might think of this method as catharsis. The hidden memory was conceived of as a 'foreign body,' a resident alien of the mind. And speaking it with feeling under hypnosis led to the elimination of its causal power: thus the process could plausibly be conceived as talking it out. No doubt this conceptualization was facilitated by Ms. O's description of the treatment as 'chimney sweeping.'[9] And perhaps Breuer and Freud also unwittingly drew upon fantasies we all share in which emotional processes are experienced in corporeal terms. So, for example, we talk about 'getting something off our chests.'

Could such a metaphor underlie the conceptualization of a medical treatment? If so, then fantasies of cure are working their way into the theory of cure. It is an interesting question whether this should matter – and why.

But there is a more serious problem: this conceptualization is only possible because of a crucial omission from the case study. In 1932, approximately fifty years after Breuer's treatment of Ms. O, Freud wrote a letter to a colleague about 'what really happened to Breuer's patient.' According to this letter, on the evening of the day on which all her symptoms had supposedly been cured, Breuer was called back and found Ms. O distraught, confused and suffering from abdominal cramps. When asked what the matter was, she replied, 'Now comes Dr B's child.'[10] What happened next remains a matter of historical controversy, but it does seem that by July 1882 Breuer had referred Ms. O to a private clinic and abandoned directing her treatment. Freud came to think that Breuer could not handle Ms. O's erotic transference, and he fled the treatment; others think that Freud was unfair in his criticism. Either way, what can we learn from this incident? Ms. O seems to have given the entire treatment a sexualized interpretation. The doctor experienced himself as getting something out of Ms. O; Ms. O experienced the doctor as putting something in. Ms. O's description of the treatment as 'chimney sweeping' captures this bivalence perfectly. The obvious meaning is that one is clearing out the accumulated debris hidden inside the chimney. But a less obvious meaning, which seems to have eluded Dr. Breuer, is that something will come out of the chimney only after a Dr. Breuer has stuck his brush up inside.

It is a mistake to think Ms. O actually believed that her doctor had sexual intercourse with her. (And we'll get into the same mess we saw in the last chapter if we say she had an unconscious belief. For we'd have to attribute to her all sorts of other beliefs – about pregnancy, sexual relations, her relation with her doctor – and the only basis for doing so was that we wanted to rationalize a single belief.) It is difficult to find the right vocabulary to describe this scene, but it is more like a heartfelt dramatization. Ms. O is emotionally engaged in the situation – thus it is too weak to call this play-acting or pretend – but it is an engagement that is reminiscent of our own experience when we are in the midst of an upsetting dream.[11]

Ms. O is giving her own account of what happened in a dreamlike language – and the meaning is overtly sexual. In terms of the 'popular conception' of sexuality nothing happened (there was no procreative intercourse between doctor and patient). And yet it is clear in retrospect that Ms. O did have sex on her mind – and her ideas both interpreted and shaped what did happen. Thus, even in this first case history, Freud is confronted with an *extension* of the sexual as commonly understood. The dramatization is of an overtly sexual nature. But Freud needs to understand not merely how such an idea should arise; he needs to understand the imaginative force by which this idea *spreads itself out*: how the idea provides a dreamlike interpretation of the entire therapeutic situation.

Certainly, Ms. O's dramatization undermines a doctor's comfortable assumption that, in treating an hysterical patient, the doctor can stand outside the hysteria. In retrospect, there is reason to suspect that the supposed cures of symptoms were little gifts that Ms. O bestowed upon her doctor-lover. If her loved one wanted to play doctor, so be it! For all we know, Breuer's 'cure' of Ms. O's symptoms was the greatest hysterical symptom of all. Ms. O was a brilliant and sensitive woman. Perhaps even her description of the treatment as 'chimney sweeping' was designed to confirm Breuer's conception of his method as cathartic. On this reading, Breuer's entire treatment – as well as his 'scientific' conceptualization of the treatment as catharsis – was a part of Ms. O's imaginative world.

Ms. O's dramatization should also make us humble about how much we understand what is going on in a therapeutic conversation. Ostensibly, Dr. Breuer was coming to visit her as a doctor and, under hypnosis, Ms. O would talk her problems out. But pervading this conversation, we can see in retrospect, was a fantasy of pregnancy. In a funny way, the fantasy was an unconscious 'theory' of what was going on between them all along. So, to understand what the conversation meant for Ms. O, one would have had to understand how her imagination works. That eluded Breuer during the treatment, and it seems to have been suppressed from the case study. But in this dramatic moment, there could have been no doubt to Breuer and Freud that Ms. O's bodily imagination was expressing sexual ideas.

Still, there is as yet no reason to treat sex *as fundamental*. Sexual ideas are certainly arising as some kind of symptom, but why think that sexuality is the underlying cause? Another hysterical patient might blame her doctor for putting angry thoughts into her head; or for giving her a craving for chocolate ice cream. Ms. O's hysterical pregnancy is interpreted by Freud as a symptom: perhaps the cause is different. Perhaps sexual ideas are no more than the hysterical flavor of the month.[12] Obviously, Freud and Breuer hit upon some stunning imaginative phenomena. But how to understand them is far from clear.

2 How sex hides as physical pain

In the fall of 1892, Freud saw a woman patient who for two years had suffered pains in her legs, and who had difficulty walking.

> The pain was of an indefinite character; I gathered that it was something in the nature of a painful fatigue. A fairly large, ill-defined area of the anterior surface of the right thigh was indicated as the focus of the pains, from which they most often radiated and where they reached their greatest intensity. In this area the skin and muscles were also particularly sensitive to pressure and pinching.[13]

On the surface, it looks like this symptom has nothing to do with sexuality; it looks like a straightforward medical condition. However, even here there is some room for doubt. Elizabeth von R, as Freud calls her, was referred to him by another doctor. And there is reason to think the first doctor had given up; for neither of the two doctors could find any 'ground for suspecting the presence of any serious organic affection.'[14] Freud did not leave the medical model behind – he gave her a physical examination – but he did experiment with its boundaries. As Socrates looked for contradictions hidden among his interlocutor's beliefs, so Freud looked for contradiction inside the physical symptom.

If one stimulates an area sensitive to pain in someone with an organic illness … the patient's face takes on an expression of discomfort or physical pain. Moreover he flinches and draws back from the examination and resists it. In the case of Fräulein von R., however, if one pressed or pinched the hyperalgesic [sensitive] skin and muscles of her legs, her face assumed a peculiar expression, which was one of pleasure rather than pain. She cried out – and I could not help thinking that it was as though she was having a voluptuous tickling sensation – her face flushed, she threw back her head and shut her eyes and her body bent backwards. None of this was very exaggerated but it was distinctly noticeable. Her expression of face did not fit in with the pain which was ostensibly set up by the pinching of her muscles and skin; it was probably more in harmony with the subject-matter of the thoughts which lay concealed behind the pain and which had been aroused in her by the stimulation of the parts of the body associated with those thoughts.[15]

Freud is treating the bodily symptom not simply as something caused by the mind's hidden contradiction, but as directly expressing it. The mind's body was 'saying' that which Ms. von R was not yet in a position to put in full-fledged linguistic speech.

Freud conceives of himself as a medical doctor, looking for the causes of a symptom, trying to diagnose and cure a disease. But he is also looking to the larger scene, trying to make sense of what is going on. The details of this case make fascinating reading – every reader of this book should read the case history. In outline, Ms. von R suffered conflicts between certain erotic attachments to men and attachments and obligations to her family. On a rare night out of the house, taking a break from tending to her sick father, she had met a young man who interested her. But when she came home she found her father had gotten worse.[16] It is then that the pain in her leg intensified. *association of pain and pleasure*

In another incident, Ms. von R rushed to the sickbed of her sister, only to arrive too late. At her sister's deathbed, Ms. von R found herself having an involuntary thought about her brother-in-law: 'Now he is free again and I can be his wife.'[17] She repressed this thought from her consciousness. *intrusive thought*

It is difficult to find the right vocabulary to describe Freud's engagement with Ms. von R. But in a broad sense, he is offering an ethical critique. That is, he is raising a question of how to live in the company of others.[18] Freud is not critical of any of the particular life-decisions Ms. von R makes: he does not think that she should/ should not have stayed home with her father, should/should not have spent more time with the handsome young man, should/ should not have tried to make her former brother-in-law into her future husband. Freud's criticism is not about *what* she decides to do, but how she goes about living. The failure here is what, in the Introduction, I called a failure in truthfulness. So, when she comes home from her exciting night out and finds her father has gotten worse, she does not confront her conflicting feelings; rather, the pain in her leg gets worse. Freud does not think that Ms. von R consciously chose physical pain over erotic pleasure. And there is no reason to suppose that Ms. von R is aware of any conscious choices, no reason to suppose that, from a conscious perspective, she has made a choice.

And thus it is a mistake to think that Freud is offering a *moral* criticism of Ms. von R.[19] Moral criticism is usually directed towards intentional acts and conscious choices, but falling ill was not something that Ms. von R consciously or intentionally did. Moreover, moral criticism is directed against someone for violating the rule of a moral system or for breaking the moral norms of society. Freud offers no such critique.

But he does hold her *ethically* responsible in this sense: as a result of her own mental activity, she is leading an unhappy, restricted life. And in a strange way, she is responsible for her mental activity. In describing her conflict around her feelings over her brother-in-law, Freud says,

> She succeeded in sparing herself the painful conviction that she loved her sister's husband, by inducing physical pains in herself instead; and it was in the moments when this conviction sought to force itself upon her (on her walk with him, during her morning reverie, in the bath, by her sister's bedside) that her pains had come on, thanks to successful conversion.[20]

This is not a conscious choice, but Freud portrays Ms. von R as active in producing the symptom and as securing a strategic outcome. There is a strategic gain to the physical pain: she is thereby able to avoid a painful thought. Put another way: she thereby disables her capacity for ethical thought on how to live. She cannot think about how to live – with her brother-in-law or alone or with someone else or ... – because the very attempt to formulate a thought is disrupted by physical pain. She thereby disables her capacity for living honestly with herself.

It is striking that such a remarkable (and awful) outcome can be produced by a relatively simple mechanism. Repression is sometimes thought to be a mysterious mechanism – and perhaps someday neuroscientists will show us how sophisticated forms of repression work in the brain. But look at how easily it occurs in this case. As Ms. von R begins to experience a forbidden thought, she becomes anxious – and the experience of anxiety is itself disruptive. And suddenly she is seized with a pain in her leg. Ms. von R's capacity for thinking is disturbed by an outbreak of anxiety and pain. *mental conditioning*

Much needs to be said about how this occurs. But underlying the details is a simple truth: if one is disrupted by anxiety every time one tries to formulate a thought, one never gets around to having that thought. Some forms of repression may be more sophisticated; but it need be no more mysterious than that. It is a selective attack on the capacity to form the salient thought.

It is important to recognize that Ms. von R's symptoms are idiosyncratic and contingent. The fact that she developed pains at a particular area on her thigh was due to the fact that that was where her sick father had rested his leg:

> on a long succession of days one of her painful legs came into contact with her father's swollen leg while his bandages were being changed. The area on her right leg which was marked out by this contact remained thereafter the focus of her pains and the point from which they radiated. It formed an artificial hysterogenic zone whose origin could in the present case be clearly observed.[21]

In calling it an *artificial* hysterogenic zone, Freud implies that there is nothing about Ms. von R's thigh itself that makes it the locus of this heightened sensitivity. It became a sensitive place because it is where her father rested his leg. And in calling it *hysterogenic*, Freud means that the purportedly physical ailment is also a place where the intensity of mental life is getting expressed.

Freud does not yet have a theory of sexuality – Ms. von R comes to him at the beginning of his career. But it seems to him as though she has somehow displaced her sexual life onto her thigh. Officially, she has no sexual life: she has no erotic thoughts (at least, so the official story goes), she is spending her life at home taking care of her sick father; she has no time for dates. It's just that she has this pain in her thigh. Freud is convinced there is an economy here. There is an intensity to life; and as this intensity is expressed in certain ways, it is diminished in others. Speaking of Ms. von R, Freud says,

> We may ask: what is it that turns into physical pain here? A cautious reply would be: something that might have become mental pain. If we venture a little further and try to represent the ideational mechanism in a kind of algebraic picture, we may attribute a certain quota of affect to the ideational complex of these erotic feelings which remained unconscious and say that this quantity (the quota of affect) is what was converted. It would follow directly from this description that the 'unconscious love' would have lost so much of its intensity through a conversion of this kind that it would have been reduced to no more than a weak idea. This reduction of strength would then have been the only thing which made possible the existence of these unconscious feelings as a separate psychical group.[22]

It is fashionable to criticize Freud for having an old-fashioned model of the mind, one based on nineteenth-century models of hydraulics. But what he is pointing out here is an important truth: that there is an intensity to life that can be experienced self-consciously, that is transferable and can show up in myriad ways. A physical pain can take the place of a mental pain; a sensitive area in the thigh can take the place of sensitivities elsewhere.

Once Ms. von R has a pain in her leg, she forms a life around it. This is an insight that can be obscured if one thinks merely of

considering medical knowledge at the time, is Freud's reasoning logical?

the symptoms of a disease. The pains cause difficulty with walking; and this keeps her at home. She is confined to taking care of her sick father; yet even after his death there is little sign of her being able to go out into the world. So while it is easy for Freud to focus his curiosity on the symptom, in fact, the symptom is no more than an eye-catching aspect of an entire way of life that is going wrong.[23] Ms. von R's life is pervaded with irrationality in this sense: on the one hand, she wants very much to be rid of her pain. That is why she has gone to the doctor. On the other hand, she is active in keeping that pain alive. She may not be aware of this but: there is strategic value in having that pain and *that* is why the pain is in place.

- It keeps her at home with her father, without her having to admit that is something she wants; indeed, she gets to spend a significant part of her young adult life in a bedroom with him;
- it gives her a reason not to go out into the social world, and thus keeps her from having to confront the tough ethical and erotic conflicts involved in growing up and growing away;
- if she does feel guilty for her erotic thoughts, this pain might serve as a kind of punishment for her;
- it gives her a vehicle for expressing a fundamental meaning in her life: 'I can't take another step forward.'

As is well known, 'Oedipus' means 'swollen foot': Oedipus has difficulty walking because of a painful binding in infancy. Ms. von R has difficulty walking because of an imaginary binding in her thigh. But in each case, the physical deformity expresses a life-meaning. And insofar as there is pressure to express life's meaning, the pain in Elizabeth's thigh also affords (hidden) gratification.

- It provides substitute gratification for the explicit and overtly erotic life that she has, in effect, renounced.

None of these outcomes has been consciously chosen by Ms. von R. Nor are they consciously understood by her as such. Somehow the symptom gets selected and held in place because it serves and expresses certain functions.

The symptom, thus, is motivated. But her capacity for ethical thought is thereby crippled. Ms. von R is not able to formulate a conception of what is important to her in life, nor is she able to deliberate about how to achieve her life's projects. She cannot consider whether she should stay home with her father or find ways to go out with young men or find ways of combining the two. For whatever conflicts she feels are being experienced as physical pains, not as thoughts that are available for her consideration. She is able to engage in self-conscious reflection, but the reflection is cut off from what matters in her life. And if we try to put her mental activity into the form of a conscious deliberation, it comes out incoherent: 'I feel I ought to stay home and take care of my father; and I do also enjoy staying with him. But I'd also like to get out; I'm attracted to other men, and I'm attracted to my widowed brother-in-law. Therefore, the best thing to do is to fall physically ill and forget all about it.' Although this makes a certain crazy sense, it is a *crazy* sense. These are not the terms in which an agent can consciously deliberate and act. And since this is the shape Ms. von R's mental activity has taken, her capacity for reflective understanding must break down. Indeed, the breaking down is the process by which she 'forgets all about it.' The physical pain makes reflective deliberation all but impossible: not only because it is a substitute for conscious thought, but also because it disrupts and distracts the activity of reflective thought. It is difficult to think about life's projects if one's attention is constantly brought back to a pain in one's thigh. But even in moments when reflective thought becomes possible, it will tend to be about whether she or her father is receiving the best medical treatment, and so on. Ms. von R is living a life in which she will inevitably subvert any serious question of how to live. Consider, for example, her forbidden thought, 'Now he is free again, and I can be his wife.' As we have seen, she attacks and represses this desire and thus cannot take it into account. But the situation is worse than that. This forbidden thought is traumatic in the following sense: there is no way she could simply recover it without dreadfully damaging her self-conception. Her sense of what it is to be a loving sister, a dutiful daughter, her sense of herself as a person with desires, her basic sense that she is a decent human being – all this is challenged by one fleeting thought. That is why

anxiety

[Handwritten note in top margin: There is a trend here of people not understanding that intrusive thoughts are normal]

the thought causes so much anxiety, and that is why she represses it. Her challenge, then, is not simply to incorporate a hitherto forbidden thought into conscious awareness; it is to undergo a transformation of self-understanding such that this incorporation becomes possible. This would be one aim of analytic therapy.

Suppose Ms. von R began to reflect on how she ought to live. She thinks: 'I must act responsibly about this pain. I can't just let it drag on. I must do something about it.' On her own, she is in no position to consider the underlying conflicts for which the pain is a substitute. She goes to a medical doctor, as though what is basically wrong with her is a physical disease. In this way, her reflection on how to live collaborates with her self-misunderstanding. It is only because Freud subverts this subversion that Ms. von R finally gets into a position where she can engage in a genuine deliberation on how to live.

3 Abandoning the seduction theory

In his first few years of practice, a number of women patients told Freud that, in childhood, they had been seduced by their fathers or other older male family members – and Freud initially took what they said at face value. He hypothesized that sexual abuse in child-hood was traumatic, and was the cause of hysteria and neurosis in later life.[24] But as early as 1897 he realized he had to give the theory up: what he was hearing were stories of sexual seduction to which he had given too much credence. In a letter to his colleague Wilhelm Fliess, Freud cites a confluence of reasons: his patients weren't getting better, indeed, they were fleeing the treatment at crucial moments; if all the reports were true, sexual abuse would be widespread beyond belief; indeed, if he were going to give equal credence to all such 'memories,' he would have to accuse his own father of sexual abuse.[25] This last realization was for him a reductio ad absurdum of the theory. He knows that some people mistake fantasies of childhood abuse for the real thing because he himself has done it. He was now impugning his own purported memory. It is important to note that Freud never abandoned the idea that children were abused, and that abuse caused lasting psychological harm.[26] What he abandoned was the idea that the stories of sexual seduction he was hearing from the couch – however sincere – were always and everywhere giving a true account of actual events.[27] Abandoning the seduction theory presented Freud with a significant intellectual opportunity. He was able to expand his understanding of what might count as sexual. For if some of his patients were giving vivid accounts of sexual encounters that, in fact, never occurred, it gave him reason to think that sex was alive in the imagination in ways that needed to be explored and understood. The imagination seemed to be able to endow a person with a sexual life even though the person had no sexual life – at least, as ordinarily understood.

But there was also a significant danger. His patients were regularly telling him that childhood abuse was the cause of their problem. This is the *hysterical theory of hysteria*. That is, fantasies of abuse were being incorporated by the patients into an account of how they came to be this way. But this was not merely an account of the hysteria, the account itself *was* the hysteria – masquerading as a search for truth in the therapeutic situation. And though Freud came to doubt whether the abuse actually occurred, and thus came to recognize the role of fantasy, there is a question of whether he got snookered one level up, at the level of theory. For according to the hysterical theory of hysteria, sex is the root cause. Freud may have doubted the specific events, but he accepts the overall picture that sex is the root cause. But why think this? Obviously, with Freud's early patients, their imaginations, sex lives and symptoms are entangled in fascinating ways. But it is not yet clear how best to conceptualize what is going on, and there is a genuine danger that Freud will unwittingly follow his patients in giving an hysterical theory of hysteria.

4 A theory of sexuality

It is easy enough to see from these early cases how Freud might have been led to think that his patients' symptoms were pathologies of sexual life. But by the time Freud writes *Three essays on the theory of sexuality* (1905), he sees that these pathologies force us to rethink the nature of the sexual. 'Popular opinion,' Freud says,

> has quite definite ideas about the nature and characteristics of the sexual drive. It is generally understood to be absent in

childhood, to set in at the time of puberty in connection with the process of coming to maturity and to be revealed in the manifestations of an irresistible attraction exercised by one sex upon the other; whilst its aim is presumed to be sexual union, or at all events actions leading in that direction. We have every reason to believe, however, that these views give a very false picture of the true situation.[28]

It is worth paying attention to Freud's rhetoric. On the one hand, this is not just a revision of scientific theory, even a significant one. It is an argument for the revision of the 'definite ideas' of popular opinion. These are ideas about what we are like, so in rethinking the nature of sexuality, we have to rethink ourselves. On the other hand, Freud is talking about the definite ideas *of popular opinion*, in much the same way that Aristotle talks of the beliefs of 'the many': it leaves the reader wondering what the wise should think. In short, Freud appeals to our intellectual narcissism to nudge us along in a transformation of our self-conception.

The transformation is much more remarkable than some trivial conclusion such as 'sexuality is more pervasive in our lives than we are aware of' or 'we hide our sexuality from ourselves.' If that's all Freud amounted to then we could safely leave him in nineteenth-century Europe. Rather, Freud's point can be put this way: in our sexuality we imitate nature and mock it. It is part of our nature to imitate nature.

To understand Freud's conception of human sexuality, we need to get clear on what he means by the human sexual drive. One way to do this is by showing how different it is from an animal instinct.[29] But a preliminary word of caution is in order. Freud did not spend much time observing other animals carefully; thus he did not have a sophisticated sense of what animal instincts are really like. No doubt zoologists will continue to teach us about all sorts of feats of which animals are capable. Freud is working with a common *image* of what an animal instinct is. And he is differentiating the human sexual drive from that. This nevertheless serves as a useful heuristic device. For Freud's aim is not to get clearer about what other animals are like, but to get clearer about what we are like. Thus there is value in differentiating the human sexual drive from a common under-standing of animal instinct.

So, to work with this image, birds have a nest-building instinct: it is part of their innate, biological inheritance to be able to build nests when they reach maturity. There may be variations in how birds build nests, birds may have the capacity to draw on the available materials in their environment and build in different kinds of spaces; still, there is a characteristic activity that constitutes nest-building; the capacity for engaging in this activity is innate; and the activity contributes to the overall life of the species. In evolutionary terms, we can easily see how the nest-building instinct was naturally selected for it so clearly contributes to the survival of the species. And when we consider the rest of the animal kingdom, the sexual instinct seems just like that. The instinct for reproduction is innate, naturally selected, issues in a characteristic activity and aims at a certain outcome. Freud's point is that the sexual drive in humans differs from an animal instinct in important ways.

Think of it this way: a bird may happen to build a nest in a lady's shoe. And, in building the nest, the bird may show a heightened concern for the shoe. But the bird cannot thereby make the shoe into a fetish. Why not? Is it lack of imagination on the bird's part? In an important sense the answer to this question is 'yes.'

Freud defines the _sexual object_ as the person or thing towards which we feel sexual attraction, and the _sexual aim_ as the act towards which the drive tends.[30] If the sexual drive in humans were merely an animal instinct – at least, as that is commonly understood – one should expect a fairly rigid and innate pattern. The sexual object would be a person of the other sex, the sexual aim would be reproduction. And, of course, speaking at the level of the species, it is part of our biological nature that innate pressures towards sexual reproduction have been naturally selected. But what is uncanny about human beings is that this innate pressure towards reproduction has itself been selected to run its course through a drive that imitates an instinct. For, if we actually look at sexuality in human beings, we will see that there is wide variation, both in object and in aim. Freud begins with homosexuality and he then considers the human fascination with fetish objects. The reason for this choice is pedagogical: these are phenomena that we can see right away are sexual, but they exhibit variation in object and aim. In the case of homosexuality, one's choice of sexual partner rules out reproduction as the aim of the activity; but there is also no fixed set of activities towards which the drive tends. If Freud were only trying to describe what he took to be pathology, his account would not be particularly interesting. His point, though, is that homosexuality forces us to rethink our conception of the normal:[31]

> we have been in the habit of regarding the connection between sexual drive and the sexual object as more intimate than it in fact is. Experience of the cases that are considered abnormal has shown us that in them the sexual drive and the sexual object are merely soldered together – a fact which we have been in danger of overlooking in consequence of the uniformity of the normal picture, where the object appears to form part and parcel of the drive. We are thus warned to loosen the bond that exists in our thoughts between drive and object.[32]

By way of contrast, we can imagine a disruption in a bird's nest-building activities: perhaps an environmental pollutant altered a bird's genetic makeup and it now engages in frenetic activity that, from the point of view of building a nest, looks bizarre. But from this example we see that *the very identity* of the instinct as a nesting instinct depends on its being tied to characteristic activities and objects. If, impossibly, the instinct were to be cut loose from its characteristic activities and objects, one would lose any grounds for identifying it as a nesting instinct. With human sexuality, on the other hand, the possibility for wide variation in activity and object seems to be built into the nature of the drive itself. Thus the very idea of the pathological in relation to the normal is different in the case of human sexuality than in the case of other animal instincts. With the sexual instinct in other animals, we have a fairly clear idea of what would constitute a breakdown in their functioning precisely because the teleological goal of reproduction is so tightly integrated into the expression of the instinct.

Freud's point is that in the case of human sexuality, the tie between sexual activity and purported aim has been so loosened that we can no longer think of the aim as providing a criterion for the activity. No doubt there are evolutionary constraints: human sexuality has been selected to facilitate reproduction. But what has been selected allows for such variation in activity and object that no particular variation could possibly count as an instance of its breakdown. Human sexuality in its very nature is open to variation. Overall, what is getting selected is an inextricable entanglement of sexuality and imagination. Unlike other animals, human sexuality is essentially imaginative – that is, it is essentially open to imaginative variability. One consequence is that all sorts of activities are going to count as sexual that have no relation to reproduction; another consequence is that when humans finally do get around to reproducing, they are going to reproduce imaginative animals.

As a result, one cannot simply read the forms of sexuality off outward behavior. Even in what society takes to be the normal case of adult, heterosexual intercourse, complex fantasies will be swirling around in the minds of each partner that help to shape what this activity means for them. So, for example, it is possible for two people engaging in heterosexual intercourse to each be fantasizing about same-sex partners. In such a case, it is possible that the homosexual fantasies make heterosexual intercourse possible. From the point of view of outward behavior, it would look as though the genitals have the meaning of heterosexual genitals for those involved in the activity. But if, following Freud's radical proposal, we take imaginative life to help shape the meaning of sexual activity, this need not be true. The meaning of sexual life is being shaped by a vivid and variable human imagination; and we need to know the shape of this imagination if we are to know the meaning of sexual life.

Moreover, whatever moral norms (if any) there should be for our sexual behavior, they are not given to us by the sexual drive itself. Perhaps God did endow human beings with a sexual drive in order that they should reproduce. If so, we should follow God's plan. But the drive God gave us is not itself impelling us in just this direction. Similarly, in evolutionary terms, sexuality was selected to ensure the survival of the species. Still, the Freudian response is: even if sexuality did get selected because of the contribution it makes to survival, what ended up getting selected in human beings – namely, sexuality – does not only contribute to that survival. Whatever reasons there may be for imposing or recognizing sexual norms, Freud's point is that it is a misunderstanding to see those norms as arising from the functioning of the sexual drive itself.

The lesson of this insight is not at all that 'anything goes.' It may well be that precisely because human sexuality is so variable and so entangles the imagination that humans have a need to formulate ethical norms that express our best conception of what constitutes human flourishing and respect for others. The point is only that sexuality will not itself be dictating to us what those norms should be.

Freud regularly causes offense because he is seen as trying to reduce our mental life to our animal nature. But in our sexuality, as Freud understands it, we are unlike the rest of animal nature. And if we think of the ancient philosophical classification of humans as *rational animals*, there is a question of how we could locate sexuality as Freud understands it. It is certainly not a manifestation of our rationality; but it doesn't express our animal nature either. The case of fetishism is of particular interest to Freud because, while it is so obviously sexual in its manifestations, it is equally obviously unsuited to sexuality as biologically understood. 'There are some cases which are quite remarkable – those in which the normal sexual object is replaced by another which bears some relation to it, but is entirely unsuited to serve the normal sexual aim,' Freud tells us.

> What is substituted for the sexual object is some part of the body (such as the foot or hair) which is in general very inappropriate for sexual purposes, or some inanimate object which bears an assignable relation to the person whom it replaces and preferably to that person's sexuality (e.g. a piece of clothing or under-linen). No other variation of the sexual drive can lay so much claim to our interest as this one.[33]

There is, Freud thinks, a tendency towards fetishism in ordinary sexuality. For we naturally tend to 'overvalue' those we are attracted to: we tend to think our lovers are prettier, smarter, wittier than they in fact are.[34] And this overvaluing extends to things associated with them: we may become fascinated with the way they dress, the way they cut their hair, and so on. And we can see how this heightened interest in clothes can contribute to an interest in fashion. So far, one can understand this within the context of sexuality as ordinarily understood. Women may dress for women as well as/instead of for men; men may dress for men as well as/instead of for women. Still, all this striving for admiration on the basis of one's sartorial appearance overall does support selection of sexual partners, and thus reproduction. We can also see how a knight errant might hold onto his lady's handkerchief, how it might take on heightened importance as a memorial to his lady faraway. The handkerchief will help to keep her memory alive and stoke the knight's impulse to behave nobly in battle and eventually to return to his true love. So far, nothing is peculiar. But what are we to make of the knight when he becomes so involved with the handkerchief that he loses interest in the lady?

> The situation only becomes pathological when the longing for the fetish passes beyond the point of being merely a necessary condition attached to the sexual object and actually takes the place of the normal sexual aim, and further, when the fetish becomes detached from a particular individual and becomes the sole sexual object. These are, indeed, the conditions under which mere variations of the sexual drive pass over into pathological aberrations.[35]

With a shoe fetish, for example, a fascination with shoes becomes all-absorbing, cut off from whatever imaginative routes that led to it. This is an example of the variation in sexual object. Such people may get overtly sexually excited around ladies' shoes; but there might also be a shift in erotic activity.[36] So, for example, a person might feel a fascinated excitement just at looking at ladies' shoes – at peeking at them. Or he may just want to rub his foot against them, or put them on. The excitement, the fascination – the tittering – may have no obvious relation to sexual activity as commonly understood. It is even possible for a person to find expression in higher cultural forms: he or she might literally put shoes on pedestals, curate at a fashion museum, write treatises on the history of footwear, and so on. This is a process that Freud called sublimation.[37] There is no reason why this charged activity need bear any resemblance to sexual activity biologically construed.

Freud also thought that different parts of the body can take on exaggerated sexual significance. Obviously, sexual activity as popularly understood expresses itself in all sorts of bodily activities and feelings. Freud is making a different claim: 'Certain regions of the body, such as the mucous membrane of the mouth and anus, which are constantly appearing in these practices, seem, as it were, to be claiming *that they should themselves be regarded and treated as the genitals.*'[38] Freud's point is not merely that the mouth and anus get involved in sexual activity – after all, they are 'constantly appearing in these practices' – it is, rather, that the *way* they get involved suggests the mouth and anus are making a certain claim. What does this mean?

On the most superficial level, the idea is that, given the variability in object and aim, other parts of the body can take over as the focus of what we already recognize as sexual life. Indeed, they can take over imaginative roles usually associated with the genitals. To begin with an obvious case, I know of an analytic patient who would start to gag whenever a man's penis would begin to enter her vagina. It is absurd to say that she *believed* her throat was her vagina; but her throat is reacting as though it were her vagina. Or, to take a less obvious case, consider Freud's patient Ms. von R: her thigh became erotically charged because that is where her father rested his leg. Ms. von R and her father are not actually going to have sexual intercourse – neither of them wants that – but because Ms. von R has certain erotic wishes, the place where they do have physical contact became highly charged. I call this a superficial understanding of Freud's claim because we begin by assuming we already know what sexuality is, and we then see Ms. von R's sexual life as displaced onto her thigh.

But what if we do not assume that we already know what sexuality is? Then it becomes possible to understand Freud's claim at a deeper level. Other parts of the body are 'claiming that they should be regarded as the genitals' not merely in the sense that they should be the locus of familiar sexual activity, but rather in the sense that they are exemplary of *what sexuality means.* This will take time to explain. But it clearly goes beyond the familiar idea that for some people the mouth and oral cavity can become the focus of their sexual life: that their sense of excitement, sensual pleasure and imaginative activity are located there. That may all be true, but in addition there is the idea that what sexuality means itself gets tinged with orality. In this case there is no assumption that the genitals provide any paradigm for sexuality. Thus there is no claim, for instance, that the mouth is functioning as though it were the vagina.

Rather, the mouth and oral cavity are putting themselves forward as a paradigm of what sexuality is. This is a difficult idea.

Perhaps we can grasp it by approaching another difficult idea: that infants have a sexual life.

5 Infantile sexuality

In the Interpretation of dreams, Freud sketches a picture of the birth of the human mind.[39] The hungry infant at the mother's breast has a pleasurable experience: not only does she experience the pains of hunger abated, the emotional calm of her mother holding her, but there are also physically pleasurable sensations around her mouth as she sucks on the breast, and physically pleasurable sensations of being filled up (with mother's warm milk). Next time the child gets hungry, or distressed, she will hallucinate the earlier experience of satisfaction. Crucially, the hallucination of satisfaction is itself satisfying. It provides its own gratifications, and in this way imaginative activity starts to take on a life of its own. And so does a life of sucking and swallowing. This is basically Freud's account of how an erotogenic zone is established.[40] It begins around a biological function, such as like feeding, urinating or defecating. Infants experience tension, intensity and pleasure in these activities; and they find ways to recreate these experiences independently of their original biological function. For Freud, the advent of thumb-sucking represents a huge psychosocial achievement. For now the child can recreate some of the intense physical and psychical pleasures he had while at the breast, even when his mother is away, even after he is weaned. His thumb is under his control in a way that his mother's breast is not, and he can bring about not only pleasurable physical sensations around his mouth and thumb, but also the pleasurable imaginative activity which circulates around sucking. For the memories and fantasies will tend to be about having things in the mouth: breast, thumb, food, milk. The fantasies may radiate out from there, but they will provide the core. Imaginings of satisfaction will be imaginings of being full, of sucking, of taste and so on.

If the infant never moved from breast to thumb, we would consider sucking to be an innate aspect of the nutritive instinct. Whatever pleasures were involved would not be a matter of great interest.

But as the infant starts to suck on thumb, blanket or doll, this activity separates itself from the innate pattern of seeking nourishment and takes on a life of its own. So, for instance, in the sucking – and the imaginative activity that surrounds it – the infant is able to take over a calming activity that had previously required a maternal presence. By fantasizing a breast, the infant will be able to calm herself in its absence. In this way the child begins to acquire capacities for independence and creativity; but inevitably memorials are established to these first imaginative stirrings. So, in later life, we find 'comfort food' comforting. From a psychoanalytic point of view, it is no accident that typical comfort foods – ice cream, mashed potatoes, rice – tend to leave a milky coating in the oral cavity.

Erotogenic zones are also important sites of prohibition and social struggle. Our parents will teach us that we *cannot* keep sucking at the breast, we *cannot* keep sucking at the bottle, we *cannot* keep sucking our thumbs. Similarly, we *cannot* keep defecating or urinating into our diapers whenever we want. Nor can we continue to rub our genitals whenever we feel like it.[41] Nor can we openly pick our nose. In this way, parents serve as a kind of *zoning commission*: they enhance the significance of a zone by prohibiting activities that would relieve tension and bring sensual pleasure.[42] These bodily activities become zones of excitement in part because they are forbidden. They also become sites in which basic conflicts between pleasure, imagination and social prohibition get enacted.

As a result, these erotogenic zones can organize the meanings of imaginative activity. And they can survive into adult life. To take a real-life example that will make the point,

- a middle-aged woman came into analysis because she found that she could no longer sit down at the dinner table to eat with her family. If she tried to eat with her family, her teeth would clench and her lips would purse tightly together. In the analysis it emerged that the meaning of her symptom was that she could no longer 'swallow' the life she was leading.

Unbeknown to her, this woman was expressing a fundamental refusal in the language of orality. This example is dramatic, but in our culture eating disorders are common. Freud's point is not merely that in a disorder such as bulimia fundamental conflicts over what I accept and what I reject, what I am and what I am not, get enacted in oral terms; it is rather that gorging and vomiting *provide the paradigms* of what it is for me to accept and what it is for me to reject.[43] To take another example, an adult in a fury might even spit. The fury provides an occasion for the adult to return – or, in Freud's terms to *regress* – to a primal expression of rejection. The spitting isn't just the form of rejection; it is paradigmatic of what it is to reject.

One can see how infantile forms can survive into adult life, but why think of them as forms of infantile *sexuality*? One answer can be eliminated: that the infant is treating his mouth as though it were his genitals. The infant has not yet started his physically pleasurable and imaginatively active life around his or her genitals, so it makes no sense to think of the mouth as in any sense a substitute. It may at some later stage of life become a substitute, but it is not one yet. So, why conceive it as sexual? Freud's argument seems to be an *argument from unification*. The tension, pleasure and imaginative activity that swirl around the oral erotogenic zone can be thought of as a <u>component drive</u> because – in varying degrees; and more or less well – it is eventually incorporated into adult sexual life. 'Sucking at the mother's breast is the starting point of the whole sexual life, the unmatched prototype of every latter sexual satisfaction,' Freud says. It is, moreover, that to which our fantasies return in times of need.[44] Infantile sucking counts as sexual because it is a physical-pleasurable activity that lies on a developmental continuum: in infancy we suck at breasts and plastic nipples, then we suck thumbs and blankets, then we suck on ice cream and candies and other delicious foods, then we kiss, and later we again get to suck on breasts and genitals in overtly sexual activity. In 'normal development,' sucking activity is preserved, taken up and integrated into overt and explicit sexual activity. And even in so-called 'abnormal' development when, say, oral pleasures displace the rest of sexual life, we can recognize them as sexual precisely by their ability to take the place of the rest of sexual life. In this way, the sexual drive is then seen as composed of various component drives that themselves swirl around various erotogenic zones.

This argument looks plausible, but there are two objections to it – one pays homage to disunity, the other to unity. The homage to disunity says that sexuality is a later imposition on the so-called component drives. The infantile drives gain an aura of sexuality only retrospectively.[45] A farmer tilling his fields in the north of England in the first century may well become a Roman citizen – but that does not express his true nature. Being forced to build Hadrian's Wall was not anything he was aiming for. In a similar vein, we can think of the infant's body–mind as inhabited by disparate and dislocated zones of tension and pleasure. Taken in themselves, there is no reason to regard them *as* sexual. Almost a decade after writing his essay on sexuality, Freud realizes that he has been taking the unity of the psyche for granted. The psyche, he comes to see, is itself a psychological achievement. As he puts it, 'a unity comparable to the ego cannot exist in the individual from the start.' A 'new psychical action' is needed, he says, for an ego to be able to relate to itself *as an ego*.[46] But if we think of infant life before this 'new psychical action,' the disparate zones of tension, pleasure and imaginative activity seem to be just that.[47] The homage to unity, by contrast, takes seriously the idea that the psyche does tend toward some kind of unification – and thus agrees that there is reason to think of the component drives as tending toward *some* kind of integration. But then it is a question what the aim of this unification is. For if the so-called sexual drive is itself in the service of some larger force of psychic unification, there may be reason to reconceptualize that drive.

Retrospectively we may come to see that *sexuality* is not the best way to conceptualize this fundamental unifying aspect of human nature.

6 Eros and practical wisdom

This is the route of thinking Freud took. In 1905, when he publishes the *Three essays*, he argues for the sexual drive with vigor; but only fifteen years later, when he publishes *Beyond the pleasure principle* (1920), he expresses doubt and tentativeness about the theory of the drives. 'No knowledge would have been more valuable as a foundation for true psychological science than an approximate grasp of the common characteristics and possible distinctive features of the drives. But in no region of psychology are we groping more in the dark.'[48] And five years later, when he publishes 'An autobiographical study' (1925), he says, 'There is no more urgent need in psychology than for a securely founded theory of the drives on which it might then be possible to build further. Nothing of the sort exists, however, and psychoanalysis is driven to making tentative efforts towards some such theory.'[49] Even at the very end of his career, just before he dies, Freud says that how the drives work remains 'insufficiently understood.'[50] Nevertheless, his tentativeness does not prevent him from trying out bold hypotheses. And in 1920 he proposes a major reconceptualization of his theory of the drives. He comes to see that there is in human nature a <u>funda-mental force for death, destruction and decomposition</u> – and he calls it the death drive (we shall investigate this in Chapter 5). And in the context of this discovery, Freud realizes that he has not thought deeply enough about the drive he has hitherto called sexual. Sexuality is an important phenomenon in human life, but it is itself in the service of a deeper and more encompassing force: a tendency towards <u>unification and development.</u> He called that force Eros, love or the life drive. The sexual drives, he concludes, 'are best com-prised under the name Eros; their purpose would be to form living substance into ever greater unities, so that <u>life may be prolonged and brought</u> to higher development.'[51] This shift in perspective allows Freud to bring the psychoanalytic understanding of the human psyche into line with the philosophical tradition. As we saw in the Introduction, Freud can now say that 'anyone who looks down with contempt upon psychoanalysis from a superior vantage-point should remember how closely the enlarged sexuality of psy-choanalysis coincides with the Eros of the divine Plato.'[52] This is not merely a grasp at philosophical respectability. Nor is it an attempt to distance himself from the teeming mass of bodily, sexual drives he took such pains to discover. Rather, Freud is trying to do justice to the fact that all of these teeming, bodily, sexual drives are, in their own strange ways, *reaching beyond themselves.* Even the infant who sucks his thumb and pleasurably fantasizes that he is at the breast is, in the very act, <u>trying to make sense of the world and</u> his <u>position in it.</u> There are primal gratifications in this urge, to be sure; but there is embedded in this an elemental desire for under-standing and for orientation. This is why the 'sexual' drives should ultimately be understood as erotic drives. What Freud had been calling sexuality, he now tells us, isn't just an urge towards procreation, nor towards pleasurable bodily gratification: rather it has 'far more resemblance to the all-inclusive and all-embracing Eros of Plato's *Symposium*.'[53] Now the Eros in Plato's *Symposium* is meant to explain how philosophy is possible. Socrates, the erotic philosopher par excellence, begins with an erotic attraction to beautiful boys, but there is something in that attraction which reaches beyond itself. Indeed, there is a kind of cooperation between world and psyche that makes philosophical development possible. The beautiful boys are, after all, *beautiful*: that is what makes them attractive. But there is something restless in Socrates' desire: he is not satisfied simply to obtain sexual gratification with a beautiful boy. Nor does satisfaction come by moving from one beautiful boy to the next. Socrates realizes that he is attracted not merely to beautiful boys – although he *is* attracted to them – he realizes that he is attracted to beauty itself. He thus becomes curious to figure out what beauty is. This whole process of sexual attraction, dissatisfaction, realization, thinking and reorientation – all of this, from a Platonic perspective, is a manifestation of Eros.

Freud posits Eros as a fundamental force for he wants to explain how sexuality is itself integrated into the larger project of human development. But in this reconceptualization we can also see the erotic Freud as reaching beyond himself. He is at least dimly aware that in postulating Eros he is trying to understand how psychoanalysis itself works. Psychoanalysis is above all a practical skill – a structured form of conversation aimed at helping the analysand to get better. Of course, what we mean by 'better' is itself a topic for psychoanalytic and philosophical investigation. But whatever we mean precisely, the following question becomes inevitable: what is it about the psychoanalytic situation that makes it therapeutic? One reason for choosing Eros over sexuality as the proper conceptualization of this force in human life is that it helps to provide an answer to this question. Analysands, with all their infantile longings, conflicts and fantasies, are also reaching beyond themselves. Psychoanalysis is structured to enable the analysand to take advantage of this distinctively *erotic* longing to resume the developmental process (we shall look at how this works in Chapters 5, 6 and 7). Sex is Eros and not just sex because, however infantile and regressive and stuck it may be in a given instance, it is also pushing beyond itself. In coming to understand the nature of this pushing – and how it might be deployed in a thoughtful developmental process – we can come to see how psychoanalytic conversation might cure.

Further reading

Readings from Freud

with J. Breuer, *Studies on hysteria*, SE II: 3–309. This is a classic and it is strongly recommended that one read it in conjunction with this chapter. Note especially the case history of Elizabeth von R, pp. 135–81.

Three essays on the theory of sexuality, SE VII: 123–243. Essential reading for Freud's conception of sexuality.

Other readings

C. Bollas, *Hysteria* (London and New York: Routledge, 2000). An excellent contemporary account of hysteria.

J. Laplanche, *Life and death in psychoanalysis* (Baltimore: Johns Hopkins University Press, 1970). An outstanding account of the sexual drive and how it differs from an instinct.

H.W. Loewald, 'On the therapeutic action of psychoanalysis', in *The essential Loewald* (Hagerstown, MD: University Publishing Group, 2000), pp. 221–56.

Plato, *Symposium* and *Phaedrus* (both available in *Plato: Complete Works*, ed. John M. Cooper, Indianapolis and Cambridge: Hackett, 1997). Many editions are fine. These texts provide an introduction to Platonic Eros. The *Symposium* is the text Freud had in mind.

L. Reiser, 'Love, work and bulimia,' in H.J. Schwartz (ed.), *Bulimia: psychoanalytic treatment and theory* (Madison, CT: International Universities Press, 1988), pp. 373–97. An introduction to how eating disorders get entangled in erotic life.

D. W. Winnicott, 'Transitional objects and transitional phenomena,' in *Playing and reality* (London and New York: Routledge, 1996), pp. 1–25. A marvelous account of how erotic-imaginative life spreads out from thumb-sucking to 'transitional' objects such as a blanket or teddy-bear. The creation of an imaginative play space.

Notes

1 Freud, *Three essays on the theory of sexuality*, SE VII: 135.
2 Freud, *Studies on hysteria*, SE II: 30.
3 Ibid, SE II: 27.
4 Ibid, SE II: 29.

5 Ibid, SE II: 35.

6 Quite aside from doctors, it is arguable that the meaning of hysteria is one of the fundamental issues in Dostoyevsky's *The brothers Karamazov*. The narrator describes Alexei's mother thus: 'this unhappy young woman who had been terrorized since childhood, came down with something like a kind of feminine nervous disorder, most often found among simple village women, who are known as shriekers because of it. From this disorder, accompanied by terrible hysterical fits, the sick woman would sometimes even lose her reason. When she died, the boy Alexei was in his fourth year, and, though it is strange, I know that he remembered his mother all his life – as if through sleep of course' (trans. R. Pevear and L. Volokhonsky (New York: Farrar, Straus and Girous, 1990), pp. 13–14). The narrator describes the father Fyodor as suffering from a peculiar kind of 'muddleheadedness' – which he suspects might even be a 'national form of it.' It is arguable that Dostoyevsky's attempt to chart this muddleheadedness as it works its way in different ways through all of the sons is an attempt to work peculiar forms of male hysteria. See also Proust, *In search of lost time*, for example: 'For even if we have the sensation of being always enveloped in, surrounded by our own soul, still it does not seem a fixed and immovable prison; rather do we seem to be borne away with it, and perpetually struggling to transcend it, to break out into the world, with a perceptual discouragement as we hear endlessly all around us that unvarying sound which is not an echo from without, but the resonance of a vibration from within' (trans. and ed., C.K. Scott Moncrieff, D.J. Enright, T. Kilmartin (New York: Modern Library, 2003) Vol. 1, p. 119). And see S. Kierkegaard (writing under the pseudonym of Anti-Climacus) on the role fantasy plays in despair. 'Fantasy is, in general, the medium of infinitization. It is not a faculty like other faculties – if one wishes to speak in this way, it is the faculty *instar omnium* [for all faculties]. What feelings, understanding and will a person has depends in the last resort upon what imagination he has – how he represents himself to himself, that is, upon imagination' (*Sickness unto death: a Christian psychological exposition for edification and awakening*, trans. A. Hannay (New York: Penguin, 1989), pp. 60–61).

7 Freud, *Studies on hysteria*, SE II:6, emphasis in original.

8 Ibid, SE II: 7, emphasis in original.

9 Ibid, SE II: 30.

10 See Peter Gay, *Freud: a life for our time*, p. 67.

11 See D.W. Winnicott's classic essay, 'Transitional objects and transitional phenomena', in *Playing and reality* (London and New York: Routledge, 1996), pp. 1–25. Winnicott makes the marvelous point that it is constitutive for certain types of activity that the question of whether it is real or not *does not arise*.

12 Or it may be the hysterical flavor of the decade or generation. See A. Krohn, *Hysteria: the elusive neurosis* (New York: International Universities Press, 1978). Krohn argues that it is of the essence of hysteria to hide: to mask itself by imitating various human conditions. Thus one should not expect the manifest symptoms of hysteria to remain constant over time. What expresses itself in obvious medical symptoms in one generation may express itself in eating

disorders in the next. For other excellent accounts of hysteria, see C. Bollas, *Hysteria* (London and New York: Routledge, 2000); J.-D. Nasio, *Hysteria from Freud to Lacan* (New York: Other Press, 1998).

13 Freud, *Studies on hysteria*, SE II: 135.

14 Ibid, SE II: 136.

15 Ibid, SE II: 137.

16 Ibid, SE II: 145–47.

17 Ibid, SE II: 156.

18 Thus even the decision to live as a hermit, isolated from the world, counts as ethical on this broad definition. Living in isolation from others is one way of living with them – a limit case.

19 For a discussion of the distinction between ethics and morality, see B. Williams, *Ethics and the limits of philosophy* (Cambridge, MA: Harvard University Press, 1985).

20 Freud, *Studies on hysteria*, SE II: 157.

21 Ibid, SE II: 175.

22 Ibid, SE II: 166–67.

23 See G. Canguilhem, *The normal and the pathological* (New York: Zone Books, 1989).

24 Freud, *New introductory lectures on psychoanalysis*, SE XXII: 120. For a statement of the seduction hypothesis, see 'Further remarks on the neuro-psychoses of defense,' SE III: 164; and 'The aetiology of hysteria,' SE III: 208–9. And for an account of the mechanism of childhood trauma see *Project for a scientific psychology*, SE I: 347–59.

25 See Freud's famous letter to his colleague and friend Wilhelm Fliess of September 21, 1897, in Freud, *The complete letters of Sigmund Freud to Wilhelm Fliess, 1887–1904* (Cambridge, MA: Harvard University Press, 1985), pp. 264–66. For a history of Freud's changing thinking during this period, see Gay, *Freud: a life for our time*, pp. 90–96.

26 So, in 1917, Freud writes: 'Phantasies of being seduced are of particular interest, because so often they are not phantasies but real memories,' *Introductory lectures on psychoanalysis*, SE XVI: 370. And as late as 1938, at the very end of his career, he writes of the effects of sexual abuse of children by adults, which he says 'do not apply to all children, *though they are common enough*,' 'An outline of psychoanalysis,' SE XXIII: 187, my emphasis. For an account of the treatment of adults who were abused in childhood see G. Gabbard, 'Challenges in the analysis of adult patients with histories of childhood sexual abuse,' *Canadian journal of psychoanalysis* 5 (1997), pp. 1–25.

27 It is important to keep in mind that it is this confluence of reasons that influences Freud, for not all the reasons he cites are good ones on their own. It may have been that his patients were not getting better for other reasons. The background assumption of the cathartic method was that if analyst and patient together uncovered the hidden truth in an emotionally meaningful way, the truth would set the patient free. This wasn't happening. On its own, this gives Freud reason to doubt the seduction theory or the therapeutic method or both. But given that he had other reasons for doubting the reality of all reported seductions, he held onto his method at least for the time being, and doubted that what his patients

were 'uncovering' was the truth. In fact, he had grounds for abandoning both the seduction theory and his therapeutic method.

28 Freud, *Three essays on the theory of sexuality*, SE VII: 135. For reasons that will be explained in the next footnote I translate the sexual *Trieb* as sexual *drive*, and not as sexual instinct, which is found in the translation of the *Standard edition*.

29 The effort to get clear on the distinction between a drive and an instinct is not made easier by the fact that the *Standard edition* translates two different German words *Trieb* and *Instinkt* into the same English word 'instinct.' When Freud talks about human sexuality, he is everywhere talking about a *Trieb* – and this I shall translate as 'drive.' The revised version of the *Standard edition* will make this change as well. For further discussion of this difference see J. Laplanche, *Life and death in psychoanalysis* (Baltimore: Johns Hopkins Press, 1970), Chapter 1.

30 Freud, *Three essays on the theory of sexuality*, SE VII: 135–36.

31 The American Psychoanalytic Association has issued the following statement of the treatment of homosexual patients: '1 Same-gender sexual orientation cannot be assumed to represent a deficit in personality development or the expression of psychopathology. 2 As with any societal prejudice, anti-homosexual bias negatively affects mental health, contributing to an enduring sense of stigma and pervasive self-criticism in people of same-gender sexual orientation through the internalization of such prejudice. 3 As in all psycho-analytic treatments, the goal of analysis with homosexual patients is under-standing. Psychoanalytic technique does not encompass purposeful efforts to 'convert' or 'repair' an individual's sexual orientation. Such directed efforts are against fundamental principles of psycho-analytic treatment and often result in substantial psychological pain by reinforcing damaging internalized homophobic attitudes.'

32 Freud, *Three essays on the theory of sexuality*, SE VII: 147–48, my emphasis.

33 Ibid, SE VII: 153.

34 Ibid, SE VII: 150–51.

35 Ibid, SE VII: 153, my emphasis.

36 Ibid, SE VII: 155. See J. Neu, 'Freud and perversion,' in J. Neu (ed.), *The Cambridge companion to Freud* (Cambridge: Cambridge University Press, 1991), pp. 175–208.

37 Freud, *New introductory lectures to psychoanalysis*, SE XXII: 97; '"Civilized" sexual morality and modern nervous illness,' SE IX: 187; *Three essays on the theory of sexuality*, SE VII: 206. Freud never worked out how sublimation actually worked. For a discussion of the problem see H. Loewald, 'Sublimation: inquiries into theoretical psychoanalysis,' in *The essential Loewald* (Hagerstown, MD: University Publishing Group, 2000), pp. 439–525.

38 Freud, *Three essays on the theory of sexuality*, SE VII: 152–53, my emphasis.

39 He calls it a 'theoretical fiction.' See *The interpretation of dreams*, SE V: 604–5, 637, 642.

40 Freud, *Three essays on the theory of sexuality*, SE VII: 182–84. See also, 'On narcis-sism: an introduction,' SE XIV: 84; *Outline of psychoanalysis*, SE XXIII: 151.

41 See, for example, Freud, 'The dissolution of the Oedipus complex,' SE XIX: 174–77.

42 I am indebted to my colleague Candace Vogler for the marvelous phrase 'zoning commission' to describe parental activity.

43 Freud, 'Negation': 'The function of judgment is concerned in the main with two sorts of decisions. It affirms or disaffirms the possession by a thing of a particular attribute; and it asserts or disputes that a presentation has existence in reality. Expressed in the language of the oldest – the oral – instinctual impulses, the judgement is: "I should like to eat this" or "I should like to spit it out"; and, put more generally: "I should like to take this into myself and to keep that out"' (SE XIX: 236–37). For an introduction to a psychoanalytic understanding of eating disorders, see L. Reiser, 'Love, work and bulimia', in H.J. Schwartz (ed.), Bulimia: psychoanalytic treatment and theory (Madison, CT: International Universities Press, 1988), pp. 373–97; S. Ritvo, 'Mothers, daughters and eating disorders,' in H.P. Blum, Y. Kramer, A.K. Richards and A.D. Richards (eds.), Fantasy, myth and reality: essays in honor of Jacob A. Arlow, M.D. (Madison, CT: International Universities Press,1988), pp. 423–34; S. Ritvo, 'The image and uses of the body in psychic conflict – with special reference to eating disorders in adolescence,' Psychoanalytic study of the child 39 (1984), pp. 449–69; P. Hamburg, 'Bulimia, the construction of a symptom,' in J.R. Bemporad and D.B. Herzog (eds.), Psychoanalysis and eating disorders (New York: Guildford Press, 1989), pp. 131–40. One of the pioneers in the psychoanalytic study of eating disorders is Hilda Bruch. See H. Bruch, Eating disorders: obesity, anorexia nervosa and the person within (New York: Basic Books, 1973); The golden cage: the enigma of anorexia nervosa (Cambridge, MA: Harvard University Press, 1978); Conversations with anorexics (New York: Basic Books, 1988).

44 Freud, Introductory lectures on psychoanalysis, SE XVI: 314. See also, Three essays on the theory of sexuality, SE VII: 222: 'There are … good reasons why a child sucking at his mother's breast has become the prototype of every relation of love. The finding of an object is in fact a refinding of it.'

45 See the entry on 'Deferred action', in J. Laplanche and J.-B. Pontalis, The language of psychoanalysis (London: Hogarth Press, 1983), pp. 111–14.

46 Freud, 'On narcissism: an introduction,' SE XIV: 77.

47 See J. Lacan, 'The mirror stage as formative of the I function, as revealed in psychoanalytic experience,' in Ecrits, trans. B. Fink (New York: Norton, 2002), pp. 3–9.

48 Freud, Beyond the pleasure principle, SE XVIII: 51.

49 Freud, 'An autobiographical study,' SE XX: 56–57.

50 Freud, 'An outline of psychoanalysis,' SE XXIII: 148; and see 'Analysis terminable and interminable,' SE XXIII: 243.

51 Freud, 'Two encyclopedia articles,' SE XVIII: 258. See also Outline of psychoanalysis, SE XXIII: 148; New introductory lectures on psychoanalysis, SE XXII: 108; Civilization and its discontents, SE XXI: 108; The ego and the id, SE XIX: 45. I discuss this at greater length in Lear, Love and its place in nature: a philosophical interpretation of Freudian

psychoanalysis (New Haven: Yale University Press, 1990), Chapter 5; and *Therapeutic action: an earnest plea for irony* (New York: Other Press), Chapter 4.

52 Freud, *Three essays on the theory of sexuality*, SE VII: 134.

53 Freud, 'Resistances to psychoanalysis,' SE XIX: 218. See also *Beyond the pleasure principle*: 'the libido of our sexual instincts would coincide with the Eros of the poets and philosophers which holds all living things together' (SE XVIII: 50); and *Group psychology and the analysis of the ego*: 'In its origin, function and relation to sexual love, the "Eros" of the philosopher Plato coincides exactly with the love-force, the libido of psychoanalysis' (SE XVIII: 91).

Three
The interpretation of dreams

Do you suppose that some day a marble tablet will be placed on the house inscribed with these words:

In This House, on July 24th, 1895
the secret of Dreams was Revealed
to Dr Sigm. Freud

At the moment there seems little prospect of it.
(Freud, letter to Wilhelm Fliess, June 12, 1900)

1 The royal road to the unconscious

Freud considered *The interpretation of dreams* to be his greatest work. It took a while for the world to catch on. The first edition, printed in 1900, had a run of only six hundred copies – and it took eight years to sell them. But Freud continued to revise his beloved book for the next thirty years. During his lifetime, *The interpretation of dreams* went through eight editions – and at each one Freud made additions, emendations and comments upon earlier statements. What has been handed down to us is more than one of Freud's books; it is like an archeological excavation. In the standard translation into English the later additions and comments are included as footnotes to the original text (with one notable exception, which I shall discuss). A date is attached to each footnote, so the reader can see the stage of Freud's thinking at which this idea emerges. This is a book that contains layers of commentary about itself. And so, Freud is not merely the author of this book, he is a companion reader; and he is full of advice about how we should read it. The advice stretches out over almost his entire working career. In this way, The interpretation of dreams is like the Talmud of Freudian psychoanalysis: it contains within itself a running commentary about how it should be read.[1] So, the book took a professional lifetime to write; and I suspect it would take a lifetime to read it through to its depths. The aim of this chapter is to give the reader a philosophically engaged way to approach this book. To begin with, it helps to realize that, precisely because the book has many layers, they do not all hang together coherently. Some parts of the book are seriously at odds with other parts – and readers will eventually have to decide for themselves where the heart of this book lies.

In my opinion, the common understanding of what this book is about is mistaken. On the back cover of one paperback edition, it says,

- What do dreams of swimming, falling or flying symbolize?
- What is expressed in dreams about baldness or loss of teeth?

as though the book is going to tell us the meaning of typical symbols in dreams.[2] Alas, Freud does tell about typical symbols – but his discussion gives a misleading impression. In fact, Freud says little about typical dreams in the first edition. What he does say is mostly about the overall meaning of a dream – such as a dream about the death of a parent. Except for a brief discussion of sexual symbolism, there is virtually no discussion of what symbols in a dream typically mean.[3] But after the first edition was printed, a number of Freud's colleagues took up the topic of typical symbols, and Freud treated this as a challenge to develop his own theory. By the second (1909), third (1911) and fourth (1914) editions Freud is writing so much about symbolism and typical dreams that not only was there a significant expansion of the section on 'Typical dreams,' but an entirely new section on 'Symbolism' was eventually added.[4] None of this could be included as footnotes in the English translation – there was just too much of it. So this is the one topic on which the layering of Freud's thought is suppressed from view. This is a shame; for Freud's later thoughts on symbolism seem to me very much afterthoughts: they conflict with what I take to be the most fundamental ideas in the book.

It is common knowledge that Freud thought dreams were the royal road to the unconscious. But what he actually says is: 'The *interpretation* of dreams is the royal road to a *knowledge* of the unconscious *activities* of the mind.'[5] The italicized words have disappeared from the common understanding, but they are crucial to grasping Freud's project. For, as I shall argue in this chapter, it is not dreams that provide the royal road to the unconscious so much as the conscious, waking activity of interpreting dream-memories in the analytic situation. This activity yields a very special kind of knowledge: not theoretical knowledge of a hidden realm, but practical knowledge of how to take split-off aspects of one's own imaginative activity and incorporate them into a living investigation of how to live. And thus what one 'discovers' is not so much hidden contents, but unconscious *activities* of the mind. Call them unconscious thoughts if you will, but the interpretation of dreams is essentially concerned with active mind.

2 Principles of dream interpretation

Obviously dreams have meaning. We wake up and regularly remember dramatic scenarios and vivid images that we dreamt the night before. These are what Freud called the *manifest content* of a dream. Freud's idea is that, in some strange way, these manifest meanings point beyond themselves. They mean more than they seem to be saying. The idea that dreams have a deeper or hidden meaning goes back to antiquity but, in general, ancient dream interpretation assumed that dreams could be treated like oracles: portending a fate or future – if only one could read it. The message was assumed to be coming from an outside, possibly divine, source. One notable exception to this outlook was Plato. He thought dreams manifested desires within us. In the *Republic*, he has Socrates say that all of us are born with unruly desires of which we are for the most part unaware. These are desires

> which are aroused in sleep when the rest of the soul – the rational, gentle and ruling element in it – slumbers, and the bestial savage part, filled with food or drink, suddenly comes alive, casts off sleep, and tries to go out and satisfy its own

nature. In this state, as you know, since it is released and set free from all shame or rational judgment, it can bring itself to do absolutely anything. In its imaginings it has no hesitation in attempting sexual intercourse with a mother – nor with anyone or anything else, man or god or animal. There is no murder it will not commit, no meat it will not eat. In short, it will go to any length of folly and shamelessness.[6]

So it wasn't Freud who first came up with the idea of sons wanting to sleep with their mothers. Now Plato thought that the meaning of these dreams was right on the surface, and thus that they didn't really need interpretation. But he left it unclear what one was to do about them. If Socrates did have a monstrous, Typhonic nature, that truth might be revealed to him in his dreams. But then what?

In effect, Freud brings together these two strains of ancient thought. He takes dreams to be pointing beyond themselves, but he takes them to be revealing sources of desire coming from deep within us. And he tries to formulate a systematic method of uncovering the hidden meaning of dreams – one that enables us not only to understand them, but to do something about them.[7] Freud lays down three principles of dream interpretation. First,

- The interpretation of a dream must take the context of the dreamer's life into account.

'This method takes into account not only the content of the dream,' Freud says, 'but also the character and circumstances of the dreamer; so that the same dream-element will have a different meaning for a rich man, a married man or, let us say, an orator, from what it has for a poor man, a bachelor or a merchant.'[8] That is, we cannot look simply at the content of a dream but must consider how such content is embedded in the overall life of the dreamer. The meaning of every dream, Freud says, 'can be inserted at an assignable point in the mental activities of waking life.'[9] Even more strongly, locating a dream in the overall context of waking life is precisely what interpretation consists of: 'for "interpreting" a dream implies assigning a "meaning" to it – that is, replacing it by something which fits into the chain of our mental acts as a link having a validity and importance equal to the rest.'[10]

The second principle is:

- Dream interpretation must be holistic.

The individual dream must be interpreted as a whole; the individual parts of the dream gain whatever sense they have by their contribution to the whole. In particular, the ancient, atomistic method of decoding the individual elements and thereby building up an interpretation is rejected.[11] From these two constraints one can see right away that it is untenable to assume that a dream of falling, flying, having one's teeth fall out or going bald will always mean the same thing. These images are not fixed symbols, and they do not have only one meaning. To understand any particular occurrence of an image, we need to understand how it fits into the dream as a whole; and to understand that we need to understand how the dream as a whole fits into the dreamer's life as a whole. These tenets go to the heart of Freudian dream interpretation; and Freud should have fought off the latter-day temptation to include an extra symbol decoder.

There is one more principle of dream interpretation:

- The ultimate authority on the meaning of a dream is the dreamer.

Freud expresses admiration for the ancient author of a dream-book, Artemidorus of Daldis who, like Freud, rejected the idea that interpretation could be a simple matter of decoding symbols. He insisted, like Freud, that one must take the context of the dreamer into account. But Freud takes himself to be improving upon Artemidorus by imposing one more constraint: 'The technique which I describe in the pages that follow differs in one essential respect from the ancient method: it imposes the task of interpretation upon the dreamer himself.'[12] This does not mean that no matter what the dreamer says, he must be right. The point is, rather, that ultimately the meaning of a dream must be given by the dreamer. The analyst, then, must be facilitating a process by which dreamers can come to say for themselves what the meaning of the dream is. And so, the analyst should not be in the position of telling analysands what their dreams mean.

Taken together, these three principles imply a remarkable conclusion: that Freud is primarily concerned not with the interpretation of dreams, but the self-interpretation of dreamers. It is for the dreamers to say what their dreams mean, and they do this by explaining (to themselves) how the dream fits into their lives as a whole and why it matters.

3 Freud's self-interpretation

In fact, *The interpretation of dreams* is the self-interpretation of a dreamer – Freud himself. Throughout the book the most illustrative analyses of dreams come from Freud's own experience. Indeed, this book is constitutive of Freud's self-analysis: he is here declaring for himself what his own dreams mean. So while the official rhetoric is that this is a scientific treatise on the nature of dreams, unofficially the book persuades by being exemplary. In effect, Freud is saying 'Here is how I uncover the meaning of my own dreams; follow my example and you will be able to say to yourself who you are.'

Consider Freud's account of one of his own dreams, the dream of the botanical monograph:

> I had written a monograph on a certain plant. The book lay before me and I was at the moment turning over a folded colored plate. Bound up in each copy there was a dried specimen of the plant, as though it had been taken from a herbarium.[13]

Freud begins making associations with the dream – and, again, there is no substitute for reading his own account.[14] But here are some of his associations: he remembers seeing a new book, *The Genus Cyclamen*, in a bookshop window that morning; cyclamens are his wife's favorite flowers; he remembers an anecdote about a husband who forgets to bring his wife flowers on her birthday; this confirms his theory about forgetting; he had written his own botanical monograph: an essay on the coca-plant that influenced Dr. Karl Koller to publish on (and get credit for) the anesthetic properties of cocaine; a realization that he had had a daydream of being operated on for glaucoma, the doctor remarks how easy the procedure has become now that cocaine was used. Freud thinks, 'I should not give the slightest hint that I had a share in the discovery.' He then remembers an actual event: his father was operated on for glaucoma. Dr. Königstein, an ophthalmic surgeon, performed the operation, Dr. Koller administered the cocaine and remarked that 'this case brought together all of the three men who had had a share in the introduction of cocaine.' He had seen another book, a *Festschrift*, which bragged of Dr. Koller's discovery; he had an excited conversation with Dr. Königstein on that occasion (topic not revealed), had met Professor Gärtner [Gardener] and had congratulated him and his wife on their blooming looks. Memories from secondary school: of a herbarium, failure to identify a crucifer in a botany exam, artichokes are his favorite flowers; his wife brings him his favorite flowers.

Freud continues:

> I saw the monograph which I had written lying before me. This again led me back to something. I had had a letter from my friend [Fliess] in Berlin the day before in which he had shown his power of visualization: 'I am much occupied with your dream-book. I see it lying finished before me and I see myself turning over the pages.' How much I envied him his gift as a seer! If only I could have seen it lying finished before me![15]

There follows a memory from medical school of being passionate about monographs, especially those with colored plates – but of not being able to afford them. This takes him back to 'a recollection from very early youth. It had once amused my father to hand over a book with colored plates ... for me and my eldest sister to destroy ... the picture of the two of us blissfully pulling the book to pieces (leaf by leaf like an artichoke, I found myself saying ...).'

Perhaps this is enough to give the flavor of the associations. There are two features that are discernible even in these initial associations: first, they tend to cluster around certain nodal ideas – flowers, books; second, they tend to gravitate towards important life-issues – love and ambition. Freud goes on to other dreams and other topics; but he continues to associate to flowers, and this eventually brings him to two childhood memories:

> The following scene from my childhood has been described to me, and my memory of the description has taken the place of

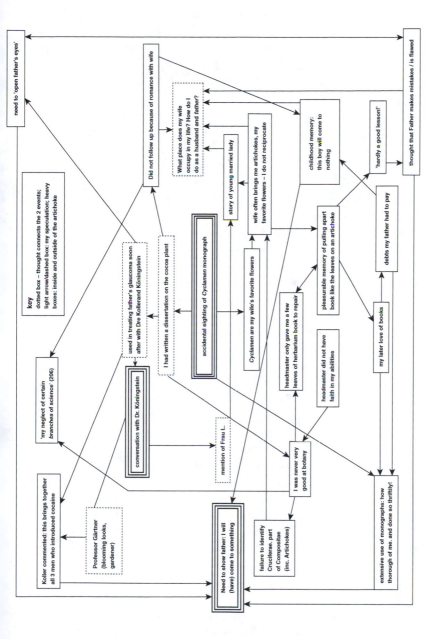

Figure 3.1 Dream material of botanical monograph – done in the manner of an inverted artichoke

my memory of the scene itself. It appears that when I was two years old I still occasionally wetted the bed, and when I was reproached for this I consoled my father by promising to buy him a nice new red bed in N, the nearest town of any size.

When I was seven or eight years old there was another domestic scene, which I can remember very clearly. One evening before going to sleep I disregarded the rules which modesty lays down and obeyed the calls of nature in my parents' bedroom while they were present. In the course of his reprimand, my father let fall the words: 'The boy will come to nothing'. This must have been a frightful blow to my ambition, for references to this scene are still constantly recurring in my dreams and are always linked with an enumeration of my achievements and successes, as though I wanted to say: 'You see, I have come to something.'[16]

Freud's theory of dreams is detailed; but one doesn't have to go into the details to see the broad-scale significance here. Freud begins with a seemingly innocuous dream, and through a series of associations, other dreams, associations to those dreams, he is led to the meaning of his life. Unbeknown to him, he already has an organization and purpose: his life is itself an attempt to say to his father, 'You see, I have come to something.'

Note that the blistering childhood memory is not itself repressed. This has nothing to do with recovering repressed memories. What is missing from Freud's conscious awareness before the dream (and subsequent analysis) is not any particular memory, but a sense of how it all fits together. Psychologically speaking, it may be fascinating to work out how dreams are actually constructed; but philosophically speaking, what matters is that Freud had already organized his life around a fundamental value – to amount to something in his father's eyes – without realizing he had. And he needs a peculiar kind of reflection (analysis), which works its way through dreams for him to be able to realize that his life is *already* an answer to the question of how to live.

It is worth dwelling on this moment, not because we want to psychoanalyze Freud the individual, but because we want to understand the challenge he lays down for anyone who wants to take seriously the Socratic question of how to live. The childhood scene, as best I understand it from his meager description, is that young Freud is urinating in a chamber pot in the parental bedroom in front of his parents. The year is 1863 or 1864, so a chamber pot would not be uncommon. Freud says that he disregarded the rules that modesty lays down, so it seems that the offense was urinating in front of his parents and in the parental bedroom. There is reason at least to wonder whether in that moment little Freud was already 'saying' to his father and his mother, 'You see, I have come to something!' (There was a developmental achievement to be proud of: at two years old he was wetting his bed (and grandiosely reassuring his father he would buy a new bed); now, at seven or eight, he could stand up like an adult male and urinate in an adult chamber pot.) If so, the father's remark would have come as an even more crushing blow.

'The boy will come to nothing.' Note the syntax: the phrase is not directly addressed to the young Freud. Freud père is talking to his wife, it is as though the boy isn't there. The syntax alone betrays that he doesn't see the boy. The utterance has the shape of an oracle. It is not directly addressed to him, and is certainly not conversation, but in an uncanny way it is indirectly addressed to him: it is said openly in his presence, it is explicitly about him, and it predicts his future. It states his fate in negative and unalterable terms: his life will come to nothing. Note too that the utterance links together a crux of issues: young Freud's body (he's urinating), his sexuality (he's holding his penis and perhaps showing it off to his parents), his ambition and the social mores of the day. As we saw in the last chapter on the sexual-erotic, an utterance like this can take Freud back to his most basic bodily functions and link them up with his strongest ambitions and highest ideals.

There are two ways to understand this paternal dictum; as falsifiable and as unfalsifiable. On the first reading, Freud could conceivably achieve some goal in life that would prove his father wrong. On the second reading, nothing Freud achieved in life – authoring a book, discovering psychoanalysis – could possibly count as amounting to something. This is a Kafkaesque reading in which no achievement of the son is anything the father can recognize. Thus the poignancy that in adult life Freud keeps dreaming and daydreaming about his father's blindness. The aged Freud père actually goes blind; Freud actually participates in restoring him to sight and his father still can't see he's amounted to anything (at least, in Freud's imagination). The phrase is haunting in part because it is enigmatic.[17] The eight-year-old boy can only have a dim understanding of what 'coming to nothing' or 'coming to something' means. Indeed, his life is given over to trying to figure it out. And, before the analysis, the project has to be quixotic because, in a confused way, Freud is treating an unfalsifiable fate as though it were a falsifiable prediction. He keeps trying to prove his father wrong – he does well in school, goes into medicine, writes a paper on the coca plant, restores his father to sight – and yet no actual achievement seems to do the trick. The recurrent dreams continue, and so do the efforts to 'come to something.' The enigmatic nature of the utterance facilitates its functioning as a fate. Freud is aware of his memories, aware of his achievements – what remains unconscious is how it all fits together and what it means for him. This requires explanation.

A psychologically sensitive person (who has not had analysis) might well reflect, 'I keep acting as though I wanted to prove something to my father, although it doesn't seem to work. When I was young I did well in school, now I'm successful in my profession … and yet somehow I don't think any of this would count for much with my father.' One doesn't need analysis for this insight; one needs analysis to see how it all fits together. Freud shows that the mind is active, forever making loose associations of which a person is often unaware. These associations can link up a minute detail in life – glimpsing a botanical monograph in a store window – to fundamental life issues. Without analysis, the psychologically sensitive person is not in a position to grasp this fractal quality of life. For it is analysis that teases out the recurring structures – in the microcosmic details of life as well as the macrocosmic structure of one's life.

Moreover, the (merely) psychologically sensitive person would be unlikely to grasp the transformations that Freud showed were a common part of mental life. For example, reversal: In his discussion of that traumatic childhood scene, Freud goes back to another dream in which he is at a railway station, and he hands a blind old man a glass urinal.

This [childhood] scene, then, provided the material for ... the dream, in which – in revenge, of course – the roles were interchanged. The older man (clearly my father, since his blindness in one eye referred to his unilateral glaucoma) was now urinating in front of me, just as I had in front of him in my childhood. In the reference to his glaucoma, I was reminding him of the cocaine, which had helped him in the operation, as though I had in that way kept my promise. Moreover, I was making fun of him; I had to hand him the urinal because he was blind, and I reveled in allusions to my discoveries in connection with the theory of hysteria, of which I felt so proud.[18]

It is difficult enough to recognize the fractal nature of psychological life, but here is an added difficulty: sometimes there are elementary transformations, such as reversal. Even Freud does not grasp all of this, as far as one can tell from the text. He sees that in this seemingly innocuous and trivial dream he has actually reversed positions: now his father is urinating in front of him. And he, Freud, has come to something. But Freud does not seem to recognize another reversal: it is now his father who has come to nothing. Here is a blind old man, incontinent – and in the dream, it is Freud who does not recognize who he is.

The idea of elementary transformations such as reversal opens up another intriguing possibility. Perhaps Freud's feelings are not simply directed towards his father; perhaps there is a structured Father-position in Freud's imagination. Sometimes his father occupies that position; other times Freud himself does – perhaps on other occasions in life someone else will. The Father – as it is structured in Freud's imagination – cannot recognize the accomplishments of the Son. The Son, for his part, will 'come to nothing.' As Freud goes through life he may shift positions, and other people may come to occupy varying positions for him. The question then arises for any particular emotional encounter, who are Freud's feelings *about*? Are they genuinely about the particular person towards whom his emotions are ostensibly directed? Or is that person just the current occupant of some primordial position, say, the Father or the Son? (We shall investigate this idea further in the next chapter on transference.) To continue with Freud, his adult life was marked by a series of broken friendships and professional associations.[19] (He separated or broke with Breuer, Jung, Adler, Rank, Ferenczi, Stekel, among others.) In each case he had high hopes, followed by disappointment. It is as though, in each case, Freud is saying to them, 'You have not amounted to a psychoanalyst.' And he puts his colleagues in a position of saying to him, 'Father, can't you see I've come to something?' Unbeknown to himself, Freud has taken on the paternal role and is re-enacting it over and over again. He longs for male friendship; he longs for colleagueship; and he is fated never to have it. Obviously, we are not in a position to know for sure whether this interpretation is correct; the interesting point is that it could be.[20] For it shows that it is not enough for Freud to discover one of the central meanings of his life – it is not enough to discover it in an emotionally and psychologically vivid way. If this insight is to provide insight, Freud must also acquire a practical ability to recognize this meaning as it arises in the small-scale and large-scale issues in life. The process of acquiring this practical skill Freud would later come to call working-through.[21]

4 Dreams as activity

Twenty-five years after he first published The interpretation of dreams, Freud added this footnote to the end of the chapter 'The dream-work,' his account of how dreams are formed:

> I used at one time to find it extraordinarily difficult to accustom readers to the distinction between the manifest content of dreams and the latent dream-thoughts. Again and again arguments and objections would be brought up based upon some uninterpreted dream in the form in which it had been retained in the memory, and the need to interpret it would be ignored. But now that analysts at least have become reconciled to replacing the manifest dream by the meaning revealed by interpretation, many of them have become guilty of falling into another confusion which they cling to with equal obstinacy. They seek to find the essence of dreams in their latent content and in so doing they overlook the distinction between the latent dream-thoughts and the dream-work. At bottom, dreams are nothing other than

a particular form of thinking, made possible by the conditions of the state of sleep. It is the dream-work which creates that form, and it alone is the essence of dreaming – the explanation of its peculiar nature.[22]

Freud uses the term *latent content* for the hidden meaning of a dream. The *manifest content*, as we have already seen, is the surface-meaning of the dream; what dreamers remember when they wake up. In this footnote, Freud is correcting an error in his own technique. For, as we have seen, if the aim of psychoanalytic treatment is to help analysands move forward, simply telling them the hidden content won't help.[23] Indeed, it may get in the way of genuine self-understanding. Suppose an analyst is eager to teach a patient the hidden content of a dream. And suppose the analysand is eager to learn. The analysand may gain some genuine cognitive insight. He may be able to say with some understanding, 'I realize I've been going through life, achievement after achievement, with a sense of not measuring up. I've got to accept that there is this propensity in me to see myself as falling short. Whatever my father did or didn't say to me in the past, now it is me who is always so self-critical. I've got to take responsibility for that!' The words may be psychologically astute; they may emerge out of heartfelt conversation. But there is nothing in the words themselves that guarantees that they can be used in an understanding-kind-of-way. Indeed, at the extreme, such words can be used as psychobabble: a phony 'self-understanding' that is used to evade any real self-understanding.

The mature Freud comes to recognize that the meaning of a dream cannot be its latent content. Indeed, the latent content only gets its meaning via its location in the whole whirl of psychic activity in which it is embedded. On its own, the content 'You see, I have come to something!' has only an anemic, public meaning; it is abstract and without texture. As such, it doesn't really give the meaning of Freud's dream. Nor need this particular content as such have ever occurred in Freud's mind. The point is not that Freud has this actual thought buried in his mind, hidden from consciousness. Rather, the point is that his dreams and associations can be summed up as having that meaning. The living realization of this is what has been kept hidden from him. To understand the meaning of a dream, we have to know more than what the latent content is, we have to know how that content gets itself expressed in the dreamer's whirl of psychic activity.

The essence of dreaming, says Freud, is the dream-work – and this is the process by which the dream is put together. But if an understanding of the dream-work is going to have therapeutic potential, then it cannot merely be a *theoretical* understanding of the process by which the dream was constructed; it must be a *practical* understanding of the dream-activity as it extends itself into waking life. It is, of course, important for Freud to grasp his myriad associations to the dream of the botanical monograph; important to understand how his dreaming endowed that dream with the meaning it has for him; but all of this can be of use only if it helps him acquire the ability to recognize that very same dream-activity as it is alive in the here-and-now. Only then have we grasped the meaning of a dream in a psychoanalytically appropriate way.

Of course, this is an idealization, for the task of analyzing is never fully complete. It is a condition of life itself that unconscious wishes will forever be finding new ways of expressing themselves.

And so, having the ability to recognize dream-activity will always involve renewing and developing that skill. But, in addition, Freud tells us that every dream plunges down into the unconscious further than analysis can go.

> There is often a passage in even the most thoroughly interpreted dream which has to be left obscure; this is because we become aware during the work of interpretation that at that point there is a tangle of dream-thoughts which cannot be unraveled and which moreover adds nothing to our knowledge of the content of the dream. This is the dream's navel, the spot where it reaches down into the unknown. The dream-thoughts to which we are led by interpretation cannot, for the nature of things, have any definite endings; they are bound to branch out in every direction into the infinite network of our world of thought.[24]

It seems that we have to accept an essential incompleteness to our analyzing activity. However successful we are at interpreting a dream, there will always be a beyond.

Is there significance to the beyond?

5 In dreams begin responsibilities[25]

In the same year that Freud added that footnote about our dream-activity, 1925, he wrote a further essay on dream interpretation.[26] In it, he specifically addresses the question of our responsibility for our dreams. *Obviously* one must hold oneself responsible for the impulses in one's dreams, he says.

> What else is one to do with them? Unless the content of the dream (rightly understood) is inspired by alien spirits, it is part of my own being. If I seek to classify the impulses that are present in me according to social standards into good and bad, I must assume responsibility for both sorts; and if, in defense, I say that what is unknown, unconscious and repressed in me is not my 'ego' then I shall not be basing my position on psychoanalysis, I shall not have accepted its conclusions – and I shall perhaps be taught better by the criticisms of my fellow men, by the disturbances in my actions and the confusion in my feelings. I shall perhaps learn that what I am disavowing not only 'is' in me but sometimes 'acts' from out of me as well.[27]

At first glance it may look as though Freud has missed the point. The impulses that are getting expressed in my dream are largely outside of my conscious awareness; and certainly not under my control. Why should I blame myself for my dreams – even if they express evil impulses? They are, after all, not up to me. Freud would only take issue with the words 'after all.' His point is not about blaming oneself for the dream or for the impulses expressed in it. It is about holding myself responsible for what I do next. I do this in part by coming to recognize these impulses as part of me. And in part I do this by acquiring the practical skill by which I can recognize these impulses as they arise – and by which I can either modify or redirect them. This is not an activity by which I blame myself for impulses not under my control, it is an activity by which I expand my living repertoire and bring these impulses into the domain of my life. (As we shall see in Chapter 6, the former is the activity of the superego, the latter is the activity of the ego.) Freud's point is that if I don't engage in this practical activity of making these impulses my own, if

I leave them split-off and unconscious, they will eventually leak out into public space – and then others will blame me.

The philosopher Martin Heidegger argued that we are creatures that are necessarily born into a culture and age that give us the concepts and categories with which we experience the world. We are always already experiencing the world with concepts we did not choose – we are 'thrown' – and thus the task of evaluating them is far from straightforward. The second division of Being and time is an investigation into what is involved in taking responsibility for our thrown natures. But, for Heidegger, this is an account of what would be involved in taking responsibility for the ethical categories, cultural values, and scientific theories of the age. But if we take Freud's discoveries seriously, the problem of taking responsibility for our thrown natures is radicalized. For now we are thrown into a world of meanings whose significance is pervasive, idiosyncratic and largely unconscious.

What is involved in taking responsibility for that?

6 Primary process

Unconscious mental activity, Freud argues, works according to a different process than the typical thought of conscious life. He called the ordinary activities of conscious thought secondary process:

> here we follow logical connections and plausible reasoning. We are directed by the official meanings of words. The unconscious works according to a different form altogether, which he calls primary process. We see a reflection of it in the loose associations a person makes to a dream: flowers-leaves-books-artichokes-herbarium-cocaine-wife-father-Koller-Königstein-doctor … , and so on. These ideas have various connections in Freud's mind. Some connections are by sound – Koller, Königstein – some by meaning – Koller-Königstein-doctor; some via puns: flowers-leaves-books; some via contingent life events: cocaine-wife; cocaine-father.

Some are by sight: Freud moves from violets → violet trunk → artificial violet → childhood memory where he promises to buy his father a new red bed. And presumably some connections are established arbitrarily: one idea comes into the mind, then another; and a connection is thereby established. These ideas form connecting clusters, and they tend to form around 'nodal points.'[28] So, for instance, it is reasonable to speculate that flower was a nodal point in Freud's mind, with associations radiating out in various directions to other nodal points that themselves radiate out.

Freud is concerned not only with the paths of thought, but with the distribution of psychic intensity. Freud is talking about a psychological phenomenon: human life is pressured and intense. Certain ideas press themselves on our awareness, certain symptoms, such as Ms. von R's thigh-pain, cry out for attention. Sometimes our attention gets stuck on those ideas, sometimes our attention moves on. Obviously, one ought to expect that there will be certain neurological correlates to this phenomenon. Certain parts of the brain may, as they say, 'light up.' But independent of empirical research there is no reason to think that psychic energy is equivalent to neural energy. What Freud is trying to map are the transformations of the pressures of our psychological life.[29] He is trying to make sense of the fact that these transformations can be varied and idiosyncratic.

In unconscious mental activity, Freud argues, psychic energy moves across these loose associations of ideas. Think of the movement of Freud's conscious associations to his dream. Primary process, he hypothesizes, moves something like that. In this way, psychic energy is displaced along the associative paths. Because of this displacement, an important psychological phenomenon becomes possible: an unconscious wish may transfer its intensity onto a conscious or preconscious idea.[30] This is one of Freud's earliest discussions of transference; and in this case it is occurring inside the mind. In some cases there may be a transfer of intensity from various ideas onto a single innocuous idea. In such a case, 'the intensity of a whole train of thought may eventually be concentrated in a single ideational element.' Freud called this process condensation.[31] So, again, flower seems to be a point of displacement and condensation in Freud's mind. His self-analysis revealed that he had a hidden infantile wish: to show off his penis and his grown-up ability to urinate; to win the respect of his parents for 'coming to something.' This infantile striving for sexualized gratification is shattered by the paternal utterance, which serves as a prohibition for young Freud. The wish is not destroyed, but it can no longer seek direct gratification without arousing too much anxiety. And so the intensity of this wish – the psychic energy – radiates out onto associated ideas. We have already traced some of the myriad paths, but we can see them converge on the image of a flower, on the innocuous sighting of a botanical monograph.

This is a simple theory of mental activity, but it has powerful consequences. First, this mental activity has the form of a mechanism. And although the mechanism has a strategic outcome, there is no intentionality. One does not need the workings of an intelligent censor or a homunculus to explain it.[32] There only need to be certain primitive mental mechanisms – for example, the outbreak of anxiety – which keep unpleasant ideas at bay. These ideas then transfer their energy onto innocuous ideas, ideas that can be experienced in dreams and conscious thoughts. This gives indirect expression to the unconscious thoughts, and thereby relieves pressure for their direct expression. On Freud's theory, one way that repression works is simply by relieving the pressure for the expression of the forbidden idea.

Second, this mental mechanism creates symbolic meaning as a byproduct of its functioning. The transfer of psychic energy occurs across associations of ideas. And so, while *flower* may become a charged idea for Freud, it thereby comes to stand for the connected ideas through which intensity flows. As Freud puts it, the unconscious idea gets itself 'covered' by the conscious or preconscious idea. The picture of the psyche is thus of differentiated networks that allow psychic energy to flow through to a particular idea. The idea thus comes to stand for its empowering network. For it is through the lit-up idea that the other ideas in the network gain their expression. There is no inherent symbolization process, the associations need not be through normally recognized paths of meaning; indeed, the connections between ideas can be arbitrary and contingent.

Third, the creation of meaning can thus be idiosyncratic. Flowers have long been symbols of romance, so there is reason to think this is a connection which many of us share. But Freud also goes from flowers to coca to cocaine to Koller to Königstein to father to blind to operation to being seen. For Freud, flowers can come to stand for amounting to something in his fathers' eyes. This is an utterly idiosyncratic meaning that can only be discovered by tracing the routes of Freud's own associations. It is thus a misunderstanding of Freudian psychoanalysis to think of it as primarily concerned with shared symbols of psychic life. Even when he is talking about typical symbols, he reminds us that they 'frequently have more than one or even several meanings, and ... the correct interpretation can only be arrived at on each occasion from the context.'[33] Thus, in Freudian psychoanalysis, one should not expect any symbol to have a fixed, shared archaic meaning.

Fourth, as a byproduct of this process, ordinary events and innocuous ideas take on heightened importance. As Freud puts it, 'the dream-process finds it easier to get control of recent or indifferent ideational material which has not yet been requisitioned by waking thought-activity; and for reasons of censorship it transfers psychical intensity from what is important but objectionable onto what is indifferent.'[34] Obviously, various forms of pathology are possible, but this form of mental activity also allows for the possibility that ordinary life becomes a source of creative vigor. An ordinary event – like seeing a book in a store window, receiving flowers, dipping a cookie into tea – can itself be embedded in a wealth of associations that both lend it intensity and give it meaning.

Finally, it is a byproduct of this mechanism that we may all be taken by surprise by ourselves. In the Poetics, Aristotle said that the hero of a tragedy will undergo a process of reversal and recognition. So, to take the paradigm, Oedipus sets out to discover who is the murderer of King Laius, and in so doing discovers that he is the murderer. According to Freud, it is a fact about the way our minds work that the seemingly innocuous ideas of every day will typically express meanings of which we are unaware. These meanings will spread out over networks, but they will typically reach meanings that are forbidden, repressed. Thus were we to follow these paths we would inevitably come to moments of reversal and recognition, where we uncover aspects of ourselves that had remained out of view.

7 The fulfillment of a wish

Dream-activity thus displays all the variability that is characteristic of human sexuality. Indeed, Freud thinks that dream-activity is erotic activity in a dreamlike form. A dream, according to Freud, is not simply the expression of a wish; it is its gratification. Freud is not entirely clear how this happens, but we saw in the last chapter how the infant hallucinates the breast – and the hallucination is itself gratifying.[35] Freud conjectures that the infantile mind has not firmly distinguished real-life experience from its imaginative creations and thus, speaking loosely, in the imaginative creation of a breast it is as though the child is at the breast. The experience is so vivid that it has a commanding yet pleasurable power. In this way, imagination is selected as a route of gratification. Even after the mind develops, and a sense of reality is in place, imagination remains a locus of variation and gratification.

We can see a pale reflection of this in the conscious daydreaming of adult life. In imagining some pleasurable scene we are not necessarily expressing the hope that that scene should occur (indeed, we may devoutly hope that the scene should never actually occur); nor need we be anticipating the pleasure that might arise from such an occurrence (the real-life scene might be awful). It is the daydreaming itself that is pleasurable, and that is why it is occurring. Of course, many dreams are indifferent, many dreams make us anxious – some of them shock us with anxiety and fear. Freud eventually recognized that anxiety-dreams can have their own function, signaling real psychic danger.[36] In such cases, anxiety is arising independently of any gratification (we shall discuss this in Chapter 5). But in some cases, Freud argues, anxiety arises precisely because a wish is being gratified. The wish is infantile and the process of disguising it by radiating out across loose associations has not gone far enough.

> There is no longer anything contradictory to us in the notion that a psychical process which develops anxiety can nevertheless be the fulfillment of a wish. We know that it can be explained by the fact that the wish belongs to one system, the Unconscious, while it has been repudiated and suppressed by the other system, the Preconscious.[37]

In 1919, Freud adds a fascinating footnote:

> A second factor, which is much more important and far reaching, but which is equally overlooked by laymen is the following.

No doubt a wish-fulfillment must bring pleasure; but the question then arises 'To whom?' To the person who has the wish of course. But as we know, a dreamer's relation to his wishes is a quite peculiar one. He repudiates them and censors them – he has no liking for them, in short. So that their fulfillment will give him no pleasure, but just the opposite; and experience shows that this opposite appears in the form of anxiety, a fact which has still to be explained. Thus a dreamer in his relation to his dream-wishes can only be compared to an amalgamation of two separate people who are linked by some important common element.[38]

At first one might think it a tautology to say that the dreamer dreams the dreams. But Freud has a way of making this truism uncanny. For he points out that our relation to our dreams is so strange that who (or what) the dreamer is becomes problematic.[39] There are two ways one might respond to this situation. One is to valorize it: that is, one celebrates the fact that we are less unified than we take ourselves to be; celebrates the fact that we are regularly taken off guard by our de-centered selves. The other is to respond to this situation as a task. The idea that, metaphorically speaking, a dreamer is 'an amalgamation of two separate people who are linked by some important common element' is a challenge that needs to be addressed and, as far as possible, overcome. It is this latter response that seems to me more in harmony with Freudian psychoanalysis.[40] Let us return to Freud's dream of the botanical monograph. If a dream can both express and gratify a wish, then we need to think not only of the transfer of psychic intensity from one idea to another, we need to think of the transference of gratification. The wish for paternal recognition – 'The boy has come to something!' – has found a deferred, transferred gratification in a dream of a botanical monograph. However, at the time of the dream, Freud had no conscious experience of gratification and he was unaware of the infantile wish that was being gratified. But now consider his analysis of the dream. The fact that there is transference of gratification provides a clue to the pleasures of analysis – even the pleasures of taking responsibility for one's dreams. For in associating to the dream, Freud is taking up the dream-process and resuming it.

The associations of analysis are, as it were, awakening the dream-process – allowing it to flow in conscious life. And one can thus expect that as Freud continues associating, there is a transfer of gratification across the associations. In this way, the analytic process is a resumption and extension of dream-life. It is simultaneously the process by which one builds up a practical ability to recognize dream-activity as it finds expression in waking life.

Freud took himself to be discovering the antecedent causes of the dream, but we need not worry too much about that. No doubt his wish to come to something goes back to childhood – Freud's dreams about it have constantly recurred in his life – and no doubt some of the associations are tracing out well-worn imaginative connections among ideas. But the dream may also be causing new imaginative connections to be laid down. In his associations to the dream, Freud may be forging new imaginative links. All the better. For the ultimate aim of this activity is the self-interpretation of the dreamer. What Freud should have been concerned with – given his own interpretive principles – is not so much the discovery of the antecedent causes of a particular dream, but rather the living form of his own imaginative capacity. No doubt this contains many remnants from the past, and these need to be charted. But what really matters in all the associating is acquiring a practical understanding of how this vibrant imagination is woven into conscious life.

Freud's dream of the botanical monograph expresses and gratifies a wish, a wish to amount to something. As he associates to that dream, he begins to understand it, but he also takes over the process of gratifying it. The gratifications continue in the process of analyzing it, but in such a way that he is able to take it over. That is, in the associations, the form and content of Freud's own imaginative capacity are laid out for him. The question thus arises for him: how does he want to live with it? His own choice is a radical gratification of the original wish. He takes his dream and analyzes it; on the basis of that analysis he devises a theory of dreams; he writes his dream book. He is now the real-life author of a botanical monograph – that is, a monograph about (the dream of) a botanical monograph. And finally, he can say to his father, 'You see, I have come to something!' Ironically, had he analyzed himself well, at the moment when he could say that to his father, he'd no longer need to.

8 The field of dreams

Freud constructs a field of dreams. That is, he lays out a field of possibilities for dream interpretation – an account of what it could possibly mean to interpret a dream. It is within the field that we can go ahead and make sense of our dreams. Still, something is being left out. If psychoanalysis requires not merely that we recognize the hidden meaning of our dreams, but that we also develop the ability to recognize our dream-like activity in the here-and-now of conscious waking life, there is a question of how we do that. Let us go back to the hypothesis that in adult life Freud continually re-enacted his father's role with respect to his younger colleagues, in effect damning them with a variant of 'The boy will come to nothing!' And let us assume that the hypothesis is true.

Then something important would have escaped Freud's self-analysis – even though his analysis of the hidden content of the dream was accurate. Via his analysis he becomes a world-expert on the dream process, yet he still re-enacts the childhood conflicts he claims to analyze.

Consider again the epigraph of this chapter, a comment Freud makes in a letter to his friend shortly after the publication of *The interpretation of dreams*:

> Do you suppose that some day a marble tablet will be placed on the house inscribed with these words:
>
> In This House, on July 24th, 1895
> the secret of Dreams was Revealed
> to Dr Sigm. Freud
>
> At the moment there seems little prospect of it.[41]

Of course, there were reasons for thinking this: the book wasn't selling. But we are now in a position to see that these conscious concerns might be serving as a cover for unresolved unconscious conflicts. At the very moment of his wishful triumph – the publication of a real dream book – Freud is still having the fantasy that he has come to nothing.

What, then, is missing from Freud's analysis? Freud is so busy discovering transferences *inside* the mind, that he ignores transferences *outside* the mind. And for this he may have needed the help of another person, his own analyst. Freud was the unique person in the history of psychoanalysis who did not have the help of another analyst to recognize and analyze his transference. Imagine that were not so: imagine young Dr. Freud going to his analyst, soon after the publication of the *Interpretation of dreams*.

> 'You know, I just wrote this great book on dreams, but at the moment there seems little prospect of being recognized for it.'
> ——'How does that make you feel?'
> ——'You see! Even you aren't willing to spend one minute recognizing my accomplishment! You just turn it back on me and ask me how I feel! Well, how do you feel? Why can't you spend one minute recognizing my accomplishment before asking me how I feel?'

It is at just such a moment that the recurrent childhood protest, 'You see, I have come to something!' would enter the here-and-now; at just such a moment that the analysis could begin in earnest. And it is at just such a moment that coming to grips with one's unconscious motivations in the here-and-now becomes a live option.

Further reading

Readings from Freud

Freud, The interpretation of dreams, SE IV–V: 1–627. Essential reading for this chapter, although the reader can safely skip Chapter 1.

Other readings

H. Kohut, The restoration of the self (Madison, CT: International Universities Press, 1986).
M. Solms, 'The interpretation of dreams and the neurosciences', Psychoanalysis and history 3 (2001), pp. 79–91.

For those interested in how Freud's theory fits with contemporary neuroscience, see as well the following essays:

M. Solms, 'New findings on the neurological organization of dreaming: implications for psychoanalysis,' *Psychoanalytic quarterly* 64 (1995), pp. 43–67.
——'Freudian dream theory today,' *The psychologist* 13 (2001), pp. 618–19.

Notes

1 There is one new translation of *The interpretation of dreams* that only gives us the original edition (trans. J. Crick, Oxford and New York: Oxford University Press, 1999). It is a fine translation of that original edition; but it seems to me a shame to leave out all the marvelous commentary of the later editions.

2 This is the Avon edition: Freud, *The interpretation of dreams* (New York: Avon Books, 1965).

3 For the relevant sections of the first edition, consult the Crick translation of *The interpretation of dreams*, pp. 185–210, 259–62.

4 There is an account of these changes by the editors: see Freud, *The interpretation of dreams*, SE IV: xiii; xxvii; V: 350n.

5 Freud, *The interpretation of dreams*, SE V: 608; my emphasis.

6 Plato, *Republic*, trans. G.M.A. Grube and C.D.C. Reeve (Indianapolis: Hackett, 1999), IX: 571 c–d.

7 A comparison with Plato is in order. The Socrates in the early dialogues uses the method of cross-examination, or elenchus. But this can only test for inconsistency in a person's beliefs. If a person discovers an inconsistency he may try to do something to rectify the situation. But insofar as it is a therapeutic method, it is directed solely at beliefs. The Socrates of the later period of the *Republic* discusses the unruly desires that are disclosed in dreams, but he has given up on any particular therapeutic method with adults. According to the psychological theory of the *Republic*, by adulthood one's character is largely formed; and it is basically too late for a fundamental therapeutic endeavor. Instead, Socrates concentrates on an account of how to bring up children in the right sort of way. He concentrates on the proper formation of the psyche in the first place. In a way, Freud goes back to the earlier project of Socrates: continuing to talk to adults in the hope of making a fundamental psychic change. Freud does not want to give up on helping adult individuals in their actual situations. It is with this end in view that he devises a method of interpreting dreams.

8 Freud, *The interpretation of dreams*, SE IV: 98–99. And see IV: 105: 'I ... am prepared to find that the same piece of content may conceal a different meaning when it occurs in various people or in various contexts.'

9 Ibid, SE IV: 1.

10 Ibid, SE IV: 96.

11 Ibid, SE IV: 99.

12 Ibid, SE IV: 98n.

13 Ibid, SE IV: 169.

14 Ibid, SE IV: 169–83, 190–91, 215–18.

15 Ibid, SE IV: 172 (**bold** = my emphasis; *italics* = Freud's emphasis).

16 Ibid, SE IV: 216, my emphasis.

17 The importance of enigmatic phrases in childhood has been argued to great effect by Jean Laplanche, 'The unfinished Copernican revolution.' See also J. Lacan, 'The subversion of the subject and the dialectic of desire in the Freudian unconscious,' in *Ecrits*, pp. 281–312. I discuss the role of enigmatic signifiers in Lear, *Happiness, death and the remainder of life*.

18 Freud, *The interpretation of dreams*, SE IV: 216–17.

19 See P. Gay, *Freud: a life for our time*, pp. 140, 213–14, 221–24; 225–43, 470–81, 578–85.

20 And if it is true, then Freud needed a better analyst!

21 See Freud, 'Remembering, repeating and working-through,' SE XII:147–56.

22 Freud, *The interpretation of dreams*, SE V: 506–7n.

23 In the next chapter we shall see that Freud's treatment of the patient he called Dora was fatally marred by this technique.

24 Freud, *The interpretation of dreams*, SE V: 525, my emphasis. See also SE IV: 111n.

25 See W.B. Yeats, *Responsibilities and other poems* (New York: Macmillan, 1916); and D. Schwartz, *In dreams begin responsibilities* (Norfolk, CT: New Directions, 1938).

26 Freud, 'Some additional notes on dream interpretation as a whole,' SE XIX: 127–38.

27 Ibid, SE XIX: 133.

28 Freud, *The interpretation of dreams*, SE V: 595.

29 See, for example, 'On narcissism: an introduction,' SE XIV: 78–79. In fact, contemporary brain research is uncovering fascinating findings for psychoanalysis. For an introduction see M. Solms, 'The interpretation of dreams and the neurosciences,' *Psychoanalysis and history* 3 (2001), pp. 79–91; M. Solms, 'Freudian dream theory today,' *The psychologist* 13 (2001), pp. 618–19; M. Solms, 'New findings on the neurological organization of dreaming: implications for psychoanalysis,' *Psychoanalytic quarterly* 64 (1995), pp. 43–67. See also M. Solms and O. Turnbull, *The brain and the inner world: an introduction to the neuroscience of subjective experience* (New York: Other Press, 2002), pp. 181–216; M. Reiser, 'The dream in contemporary psychiatry,' *American journal of psychiatry* 158 (2001), pp. 351–59; M. Reiser, *Mind, brain, body: towards a convergence of psychoanalysis and neurobiology* (New York: Basic Books, 1984); J. Le Doux, *The emotional brain: the mysterious underpinnings of emotional life* (New York: Simon and Schuster, 1996).

30 Freud, *The interpretation of dreams*, SE V: 594–96, 589; 562–63, 553–56, 604–5.

31 Ibid, SE V: 595.

32 This account of Freudian psychoanalysis avoids the criticisms that Sartre made of it. See J.P. Sartre, *Being and nothingness: a phenomenological essay on ontology*, trans. H. Barnes (New York: Washington Square Press, 1956), pp. 86–116. For an excellent critique of Sartre's argument see S. Gardner, *Irrationality and the philosophy of psychoanalysis* (Cambridge: Cambridge University Press, 1993), pp. 40–58.

33 Freud, *The interpretation of dreams*, SE V: 353.

34 Ibid, SE V: 589.

35 Ibid, SE IV: 122–33; S.E. V: 550–72. See J. Hopkins, 'The interpretation of dreams,' in J. Neu (ed.), *The Cambridge companion to Freud* (Cambridge: Cambridge University Press, 1991), pp. 86–135.

36 Freud, *Beyond the pleasure principle*, SE XVIII: 32.

37 Freud, *The interpretation of dreams*, SE V: 580.

38 Ibid, SE V: 580n–581n.

39 This is a theme taken up to great effect by Jacques Lacan. See, for example, *The four fundamental concepts of psychoanalysis* (New York: Norton, 1998), Chapter 1, 'The unconscious and repetition.'

40 This is another reason why I think it a mistake to think of the unconscious as a 'second mind' with its own rational structure of propositional attitudes (see Chapter 2). Such a conceptualization not only makes the unconscious look more rational than it is; it makes the picture of there being 'two people' more static than it should be. The aim of psychoanalysis is not to help a person realize that she is actually two people – a kind of acquiescence – but to help a person bring what had hitherto been split-off aspects of herself into active communication. We shall discuss this in more detail in Chapter 7.

41 Freud, *The interpretation of dreams*, SE IV: 121n.

Four

Transference

1 Introduction of the concept

Transference is one of the fundamental concepts of psychoanalysis – and it has had its own developmental history. Freud introduces the idea at the beginning of his career, in the *Studies on hysteria* (1895).

'Transference onto the physician,' he says, 'takes place through a false connection.' A patient experienced a desire that Freud should give her a kiss. 'She was horrified at it, spent a sleepless night, and at the next session, though she did not refuse to be treated, was quite useless for work.' In the analysis Freud discovered that the patient had in the past experienced that same desire towards another man – and that desire was being re-experienced in the analytic situation.

> What happened therefore was this. The content of the wish had appeared first of all in the patient's consciousness without any memories of the surrounding circumstances which would have assigned it to a past time. The wish which was present was then, owing to the compulsion to associate which was dominant in her consciousness, linked to my person, with which the patient was legitimately concerned; and the result of this mésalliance – which I describe as a 'false connection' – the same affect was provoked which had forced the patient long before to repudiate this forbidden wish. Since I have discovered this, I have been able, whenever I have been similarly involved personally, to presume that a transference and a false connection have once more taken place.[1]

Transference is introduced to explain an apparent abnormality in the doctor–patient relationship. But what is the abnormality? I don't think it's all that uncommon for patients to find their doctors attractive. And certainly it is not uncommon for a patient to have a passing erotic thought. After all, when patients visit doctors, they regularly take off their clothes. They then have their body inspected – often in more detail than at any other time of their lives. And even when they don't take off their clothes, it often remains a possibility.

distinction here between sexual and medical

The social situation is structured to minimize embarrassment to both parties. There is a tacit understanding that doctor and patient are to keep passing erotic thoughts to themselves.

What is abnormal about the situation Freud describes, then, is not that the patient has a passing erotic thought; it is that she is obliged to confess it to her doctor as part of her treatment. She has experienced erotic wishes before, but she has never before had to speak her desire to the object of her desire.

Freud conceptualizes transference in such a way as to preserve the standard image of the doctor–patient relationship. Note that this is a clinical moment that might well cause anxiety in a young doctor. Before Freud has figured out what the problem is, all he knows is that he has a patient who is 'quite useless for work.' This is a new form of treatment, and it does not seem to be working well. The concept of transference looks tailor-made to quell that anxiety. The moment at which it looks as though the method isn't working is revealed as actually being the disease manifesting itself. It is a psychological disease, but a disease nonetheless. And, whatever is happening precisely, it is all happening in the patient. The concept of transference, as Freud first introduces it, allows Freud to localize the relevant happenings inside the patient. And this allows him to preserve a conceptualization of himself as taking part in a doctor–patient relationship as normally understood. The patient is the person who has the disease; the doctor is the person who is there to cure her.

So while Freud introduces a treatment-method that inevitably disrupts the normal doctor–patient relationship – 'say whatever comes into your mind' – the concept he introduces to explain that disruption legitimates the normal doctor–patient relationship. Among other things, it absolves the doctor of a certain kind of responsibility. On the surface it looks as though the patient is starting to fall in love with her doctor. The concept of transference reassures the doctor that, really, this has nothing to do with him. Moreover, we now know that this conceptualization is formulated in the wake of a spectacular breakdown in the treatment of Anna O.[2] Anna O underwent a hysterical labor and named her doctor as the father. It is worth noting that this conceptualization of transference serves to absolve the doctor of any responsibility for 'paternity.' In each of these cases a woman patient is becoming erotically involved with her doctor, in each of these cases the patient wishes the doctor to abandon his normal role – give me a kiss!, have a baby with me! – and Freud responds by introducing a concept that reinforces that normal role.

Let us consider in simple terms the very idea of a transfer. For something to be a transfer there must be a stable background against which the transfer occurs. For instance, I want to transfer myself from my apartment to my office. I get up and walk to work. For this to be possible there must be a fairly stable environment – streets, buildings, stairs – in which I take my walk.

For transference to be conceptualized *as a transfer* one must presuppose a stable background across which the transfer occurs. In the case Freud discusses, a wish is transferred across space and time: it originally occurred in the patient's past with one gentleman; it emerges again in the clinical present, directed onto Freud. Is there anything more we can say about the stable background Freud presupposes? It seems that it must also include the social world of both patient and doctor. In this case, the social world is turn-of-the-century Vienna, with its mores, artifacts and other manifestations of European culture. The social world must be included in the assumed background because the possibility of Freud recognizing this moment as transference requires that he see it as abnormal. If wishing to kiss one's doctor had been the accepted norm for doctor–patient relations, neither he nor the patient would have been puzzled or troubled. There would then have been no pressure to explain it in a special way. To be able to recognize an event as abnormal requires a background of norms against which this moment is seen as not fitting in. Thus the problem for which transference purports to be an answer necessarily arises from an apparent disruption in the normal social order.

2 Dora

Freud's most significant discussion of transference was written approximately a decade after he first introduced the concept – in the postscript to the case study of a young woman he called Dora.[3] And he invokes transference to explain the failure of the analysis. We ought then to be attentive to the possibility that the concept is being formulated in ways that focus the blame on Dora. Our concern is not to reassign blame; it is to inquire whether the conceptualization of transference might serve defensive functions.

Freud sees Dora at about the same time as he is completing *The interpretation of dreams* (1900). In the last chapter, we saw that his dream of the botanical monograph expressed a wish to amount to something. There is another important dream he discusses – the dream of Irma's injection – in which he uncovers in himself two powerful wishes: a wish to get rid of recalcitrant women patients and a wish to be vindicated.[4] These wishes were thus alive at the time Freud was treating Dora. He tells us that he first thought of writing up the Dora case under the title 'Dreams and hysteria,' for it supported his theory of dreams.[5] The postscript is written a few years later and, however magnificent his insights into transference are, it is also true that Freud is trying to vindicate himself for a patient he actually did get rid of. He reports that fifteen months after Dora abruptly broke off analysis, she came back and asked Freud to resume treatment. 'One glance at her face, however, was enough to tell me that she was not in earnest over her request.'[6] Ironically, it is Freud who taught us to be suspicious of anyone who thinks he can grasp another's psychological state with a single glance. He concludes with the most disturbing sentence in the Freudian corpus: 'I do know what kind of help she wanted from me, but I promised to forgive her for having deprived me of the satisfaction of affording her a far more radical cure for her troubles.'[7] It seems that Freud's account of transference is being written by an angry man seeking justification.

In the case history, Freud interprets Dora as having gone through her own hysterical pregnancy.[8] Nine months after her suitor, Herr K, made a seductive proposal, Dora came down with stomach cramps, which at the time were diagnosed as appendicitis. Freud suspected that this was a hysterical labor. Freud knew about Anna O's hysterical pregnancy with her doctor. If he is thinking of transference as that which is coming around again – that which is about to be transferred *onto him* – might he not have been dimly aware that, if he hung on for nine months, he might be named as the father in another hysterical birth? From the dream of Irma's injection, we know that Freud is dreaming about injecting a dirty syringe into his woman patient. Is it any wonder that he in effect said, 'Get rid of this patient! I'm not the father! It's only transference!' There is certainly room to wonder whether Freud re-enacted Breuer's flight. And there is also room to wonder whether this flight from allegations of paternity isn't recurring in the conceptualization of transference.

Let us go back to the scene. Dora, a bright eighteen-year-old in a Viennese bourgeois family, was treated by her adult world as an object of exchange. Her father was having an affair with a family friend, Frau K, and Dora was indirectly encouraged to receive the attentions of the husband, Herr K. For a while she collaborated with this arrangement, but there came a moment when she broke this social world apart. Herr K propositioned her during a walk around the lake, she slapped him, complained to her father – and the adults ganged up and insisted that Dora invented the story. Dora wrote a suicide note, fainted, and her father brought her to Freud – perhaps in the hope that Freud would help restore the earlier adulterous harmony.

After three months of treatment, Dora delivered a metaphorical slap to Freud. She announced abruptly that she was going to end the treatment. 'I did not succeed in mastering the transference in good time,' Freud explains. He was aware that Dora was treating him like her father, but that blinded him to an association she was making between him and Herr K.

> In this way the transference took me unawares, and, because of the unknown quantity in me which reminded Dora of Herr K, she took her revenge on me as she wanted to take her revenge on him, and deserted me as she believed herself to have been deceived and deserted by him. Thus she *acted out* an essential part of her recollections and phantasies instead of reproducing them in the treatment.[9]

Freud is describing a situation in which he was unable to see Dora's imaginative activity unfolding in the here-and-now of the analytic situation.

3 A special class of mental structures

Freud's failure with Dora provokes him to rethink the concept of transference. With hindsight, we can see him moving towards a more holistic conception. He says that transferences are 'new editions or facsimiles' in which old impulses and fantasies are transferred onto the doctor. But, he continues, '*a whole series of psychological experiences are revived*, not as belonging to the past, but as applying to the person of the physician at the present moment.'[10] He now calls transference 'a special class of mental structures.'[11] Freud is no longer talking about an isolated desire – say, for a kiss – but about a framework of experience. He seems to have abandoned the idea that transference is simply the transfer of a single emotion or desire. It is not that a brute desire to give Herr K a slap is transferred across space and time onto Freud. Rather, Dora is coming to experience Freud in Herr-K-like ways, and that is why she wants to give him a slap. That is, Freud is getting entangled in a web of meanings that had, for Dora, previously been experienced towards Herr K. Let us say that Freud is coming to occupy a Herr K position in Dora's overall orientation to the world. Obviously, work will need to be done to make this idea precise. But, roughly speaking, the idea is that in addition to the shared meanings of the social world – which help to orient all members of society – there is also an idiosyncratic layer of meanings that orient Dora in particular ways. So, to say that in Dora's world there is a Herr K position is simply to say that, as Dora organizes her life and outlook, there will tend to be an older male figure who is at once charming, seductive, attentive, manipulative and self-centered – in relationship to whom she organizes her own complicated emotional responses.

Dora's world is not something that exists solely inside her mind. Dora's world includes Freud and Herr K, her family, fin de siècle Vienna, and so on: it's just that all these people and cultural artifacts have been elaborated with structured yet idiosyncratic meanings that help shape Dora's response to the world she inhabits. This is what

Freud means by a 'mental structure,' a 'whole series of psychological experiences.' Until we understand the whole structure of Dora's world, naming any position in it – such as a Herr K position – must remain tentative. For all we yet know, Herr K was himself assigned a 'narcissistic father position.' It may also be possible that, while Herr K was originally assigned such a position, her particular experiences of Herr K and various aspects of her own growth helped her to transform her orientation into something that was more specifically suited to Herr K. This would be what Freud called a 'revised edition': she now has a distinctly Herr K position in her orientation to the world.[12] Freud seems to be working his way towards a conception of transference as an idiosyncratic world coming into view. Dora orients herself to some older men in Herr-K-like ways. As she enters a new environment – the analytic situation – a question arises: how is she going to relate to Dr. Freud? There are probably several positions he could have taken up – a maternal or paternal figure, Herr K or Frau K positions, the role of her younger brother, and so on – and perhaps she did fleetingly try out various positions on him. But it is a hallmark of Dora's predicament that she has a relatively limited, although idiosyncratic, set of roles in terms of which she experiences people and events. She quells her own anxiety, calms herself, by experiencing the world in a familiar pattern. She thus has a tendency to experience people as though they are occupying fixed positions.

Freud is tentatively developing a new conception of transference. And while he wouldn't use these terms himself, I think it's fair to say that in the original conception, transference is a transfer of a desire or emotion *across a world* (a world that is largely taken for granted); while in the new conception transference is *an idiosyncratic world coming into view* in the analytic situation. This world is no longer taken for granted; it becomes the primary focus of inquiry and treatment. What makes transference a *special* class of structures is that in the analytic situation the idiosyncratic world can come into view as such. In ordinary life, people approach others in structured, idiosyncratic ways – and although that may lead to break-ups in personal relations, fights, misunderstandings, normally people do not recognize the extent to which the catastrophe was the outcome of a clash of structured approaches to life. The challenge, then, is to devise a form of interaction in which people can come to recognize their own activity in creating structures that they have hitherto experienced as an independently existing world.

4 Transference as the breakdown of a world

I now want to consider an interpretive possibility Freud overlooked. The point is not to second-guess Freud about what was actually going on with Dora; rather, it is to open up the field of interpretive possibilities. Again, our aim is not to determine what *really* was happening with Dora, nor to determine definitively what treatment would have been best for her. She is not our patient and we do not know. Our aim, rather, is to inquire what *might* have been happening with her and what treatment *might* have helped her. We thereby can develop our conception of what transference is as well as develop possibilities for psychoanalytic treatment. But what follows is an imaginative exercise, a thought-experiment. Imagine this scenario:

> Dora is a bright but emotionally immature teenager. Her feelings for Herr K are a confused jumble. She has an active imagination, but little experience of incorporating her fantasies into daily life. When Herr K propositions her by the lake, she is overwhelmed. She does not have the developed emotional capacity to react to that proposal as she saw fit; rather, she is flooded with anxiety, reacts abruptly and breaks the situation up with an angry slap.

In short, Dora's slap is a manifestation of an *anxiety defense*. This is similar to the imagined case in Chapter 1 of Mr. R jumping from the couch. And it is worthwhile to review this basic structure to see what contribution it can make to our understanding of transference.

The point of paying attention to transference is that one can focus on the here-and-now: patterns of emotions, reactions and behavior occurring in the analytic system also occur elsewhere in life. The analytic situation supposedly provides us with a fractal microcosm – a repetition that we can then discover in other microcosms and macrocosms in the analysand's life. But if the transference is to yield genuine insight, the repetition must be captured at the right level of generality.

Consider Dora's angry departure from her analysis. Let us assume Freud was right to think of it as transference and that it was an angry repetition of her slap of Herr K. Now let us imagine that, instead of what did happen between them, Freud was able to see Dora's act as transference in the moment it was occurring. How should he have thought of it? And what should he have done? Freud's answer would be that he should invite Dora to consider what reasons she has for linking him to Herr K; and ask her also to consider what reasons she had for slapping Herr K. Perhaps in the course of the inquiry they would find earlier events of which the slap to Herr K was itself a repetition.

In some circumstances this might be the right way to go. Were Dora an emotionally mature young woman, she would have had good reason to slap Herr K. She might well have been furious that Herr K had made a similar proposal to the governess. Anger is an emotion that tends to make a claim for its own rationality: we tend to believe that our anger is directed towards someone who deserves it. And it might make sense for Dora to get clearer on all the reasons she had for being angry. And she might similarly investigate her reasons for being angry with Freud. She might then break off the treatment in confidence that she was making a good, if angry, decision. Or she might decide to give Freud another chance. But in each case Dora would be investigating her reasons for anger.

But in the imagined scenario, the situation is not so straightforward. As in the case of fear that we examined in Chapter 1, anger is an emotion that has a developmental history. Infants are prone to angry outbursts, though they lack the rationalizing structures of the mature adult. In healthy development, angry reactions become embedded in thoughtful reactions. An angry adult is not just experiencing a feeling, she is *making a claim*. She claims to have been unjustly wronged; she claims that the person at whom she is angry *deserves* to be the object of her anger. Obviously, there is a continuum of intermediate stages between the infantile outburst and the mature angry adult. But precisely because anger has a developmental history, it is possible for that development to be disrupted or inhibited in various ways. One form of developmental failure is of particular interest. A child may experience her own angry outbursts as frightening, overwhelming.

They are experienced by her as too powerful, and she is flooded with anxiety.

Unpleasant as this experience is, it has one strategic advantage for her. In the angry-anxious outburst, she disrupts herself – and thereby disrupts her angry feelings. The disruption is painful; but it is a disruption; and in the disruption there is a certain relief. In this way, the angry-anxious outburst gets selected. And it has paradoxical outcome: every time the young child starts to feel angry – and thus becomes anxious about being overwhelmed by her own emotions – she disrupts this process by overwhelming herself with anxiety. In this way she also disrupts her own emotional development.

This is what is happening in the imagined scenario: Dora has been reacting to anxiety since childhood with angry outbursts. This has had the unfortunate consequence of inhibiting the development of anger as a mature emotion. So, at eighteen, she still has few emotional resources with which to respond to anxiety. As anxiety rises, she still tends towards (immature) angry outbursts. And thus while one can say 'She slapped him because she was angry at him' and 'She was angry at him because he propositioned her,' it does not follow that his propositioning her is the reason for her anger. Rather, his proposition is the occasion for the outbreak of over-whelming anxiety, and the anxiety triggers a massive, angry reaction. The reaction is strategic – it breaks an anxiety-provoking situation apart – and thus we can consider it a defense. But the anger is not mature enough to make a real claim for its own reason-ableness. She lacks the thoughtful resources through which she can experience her own emotions as warranted. Biologically speaking, Dora is eighteen years old, thus it can be difficult for us to see that she has the angry reactions of a three-year-old. In a completely non-mysterious way, the three-year-old emotions have been preserved in the young woman.

This is crucial for understanding what is happening in the trans-ference with Freud.

As Freud is making ever more interpretations of the hidden meaning of Dora's dreams, Dora is starting to feel overwhelmed. Again there is a rising sense of anxiety and Dora lashes out and abruptly ends the treatment.

In this scenario, Dora does break off her relation to Freud in much the same way as she previously broke off her relation to Herr K.

There is a repetition – but there need be no content or thought linking these two repetitions. The salient fact for Dora is that when she is made anxious, she has a limited repertoire of psychological responses. Herr K made her anxious; Freud made her anxious. In each case she defended herself. The repetition occurred not because she unconsciously connected Herr K and Freud through some shared meaning, but because each of them triggered one of her only defense mechanisms. Of course there is a repetition of an angry, disruptive outburst: what else is she going to do? The squid squirts its ink, and it squirts again: not because it has made a deep association between the two moments, but rather because, when threatened, it has only one available defense. On this imagined scenario, Dora's reaction is the opposite of Freud's official account of transference. Dora's problem is not that she is transferring an emotion, desire or meaning from Herr K onto Freud, but that she is so anxious that she is unable to do any such thing. The moment Freud calls transference is actually an anxious moment of breakdown in the ability to carry out transference as Freud understands it.

This is of both clinical and theoretical importance. Clinically this is important because what Dora needs is to calm down. And yet it is precisely Freud's search for hidden meanings that provokes her anxiety. If Freud had a better understanding of this conceptualization of transference, he would have realized that his technique was provoking a therapeutic breakdown.[13] Moreover, there is a danger that, had Dora stayed in treatment, the search for reasons would have facilitated the creation of a false sense of self. No doubt there were plenty of good reasons for her to be angry at Herr K and at Freud. But were these good reasons her reasons? If one assumes from the beginning that Dora has reasons, but we just don't know what they are, there is a danger we shall attribute to her more emotional maturity than she has. What she needs, on this imagined scenario, is an occasion to mature. This will be frustrated if we assume from the beginning that she already has reasons for her anger, she just doesn't yet know what they are.

Theoretically, this imagined scenario is important for it suggests that there are at least three distinct species of transference. There is

1 transference of meaning from a significant figure in the analysand's world onto the analyst.

This is transference as Freud originally understood it: transfer across
a world. This would be the situation in which Dora transferred her
angry feelings for Herr K onto Freud. There is also

2 transference as an idiosyncratic world coming into view.

This would be the situation in which Dora needs someone to
occupy a Herr K position in order to maintain a stable, if limited,
orientation to the world. This is more like Freud's 'special class
of mental structures' coming into view in the analytic situation.[14]
Finally, there is

3 transference as the active disruption of the capacity to carry out
   transference in either of the first two senses.

This is what happens to Dora in the imagined scenario.

5 Transference and the interpretation of dreams

Freud originally planned to publish this case history to confirm his
theory of dreams.[15] In retrospect, one can see that his desire to
uncover the hidden meaning of Dora's dreams provoked a therapeutic disaster. He assumes that if he reveals the latent content of
her dreams, this will have a salutary effect. And he thus ignores
Dora's inability to appropriate the material that emerges in the
analytic situation. With hindsight it seems that Freud's search for
hidden sexual meanings was experienced by Dora as an intrusion
and it led to her abruptly terminating the analysis. Given that the
analysis ended in such a spectacular failure, it is striking that Freud
thinks the case nevertheless shows how well dream interpretation is
woven into treatment.

By searching for hidden sexual content – especially having to do
with Herr K, her father and mother – Freud turns away from
any transference-meaning the dreams might have. Conversely,
one might well wonder: had Freud concentrated on possible

transference-meanings of Dora's dreams, might he not have altered his therapeutic technique? Let's take another look at one of Dora's dreams with the idea of transference in mind. An interested reader should compare Freud's analysis. The following disclaimers are important: first, I do not pretend to know what was going on in Dora's mind. These are just thoughts, focused on the transference, that would come into my mind as I listened to a patient such as Dora. Second, these thoughts would occur in my mind in the form of questions that the dream provokes. I would not necessarily say anything to the patient. Here is the first dream Dora reported in her analysis:

> A house was on fire. My father was standing beside my bed and woke me up. I dressed myself quickly. Mother wanted to stop and save her jewel-case; but Father said: 'I refuse to let myself and my two children be burnt for the sake of your jewel-case.' We hurried downstairs, and as soon as I was outside I woke up.[16]

And here are some transference-associations that might be occurring as the analyst listens:

• *A house was on fire.*

Is this Dora's representation of the analytic situation? There is an ambiguity: It might mean: 'I am burning up, being consumed by the flames rising around me – and I need the analysis to help me damp down the flames.' Or it might mean: 'The analysis is burning me up! You're going too fast! This is getting too hot for me to handle!' It might mean both: an expression of her ambivalence about the analysis and whether it can help her. On the whole, I would be concerned about Dora's rising anxiety about the analysis. Freud reports that this was a recurrent dream for Dora, and thus an analyst might wonder whether it is a recurrent anxiety dream.[17] Thus it might be among her last attempts to represent her anxiety in dreamlike, representational form. The danger would be that, if the anxiety is not calmed, she will disrupt the dream-process, as well as the analytic process.

• *My father was standing beside my bed and woke me up.*

In the analytic situation, Dora is lying on a couch and Freud is sitting near her. It is reasonable to assume that he ends a session by standing up: he then 'wakes her up' out of the analytic hour in which she has been 'dreaming.' This seems like an expression of a paternal transference. And the dream seems to have a question: are you going to be a good paternal father who awakens me to a danger and protects me? Or are you going to be a self-absorbed, narcissistic father, who uses me for his own ends? Is the analytic situation an occasion for me to wake up from the dream-like fog in which I've been living my life? Or is it the panicked wake-up call of a fire alarm?

- *Mother wanted to stop and save her jewel-case; but Father said: 'I refuse to let myself and my two children be burnt for the sake of your jewel-case.'*

We don't know much about the mother from the case history. But in terms of the transference, we seem to have a maternal figure who wants to stop and rescue something she thinks is important – her 'jewel-case'; and a paternal figure who is in a rush, who has a sense of impending danger, who is protective of himself and his children and who, by comparison with the perceived danger, considers the jewel-case unimportant. The question is: which of these positions will the analyst come to occupy? Is the analyst going to be a self-absorbed mother, dawdling over her jewel-case? Is the analyst going to be preoccupied with rescuing his own theories? Or might he be a protective father who will rescue Dora from the dangers, from the anxiety, she feels emerging inside herself? (Note that even here there is an expression of ambivalence: the father is himself in an anxious rush.)

- *We hurried downstairs, and as soon as I was outside I woke up.*

The father gets his way – suggesting that the analyst has been put in the position of the paternal figure. In the manifest content, Dora is rescued from the burning house, and that is an encouraging sign in terms of the analysis. But there is something sufficiently anxiety-provoking about the situation that she wakes up. That is, she breaks off the dream abruptly. Might she not similarly break off abruptly from a dreamlike analysis?

In short, one can listen to the dreams as providing a visual commentary on the analytic process itself. In the dream Dora expresses fear, anxiety and ambivalence about the analytic process – but she also expresses some hope. I leave a transference-analysis of Dora's second dream as an exercise for the interested reader. If you try, you will see for yourself that by the time of the second dream, all hope is gone.

6 From repeating to remembering

Freud invokes the concept of transference to explain the breakdown of Dora's analysis. It takes a genius to extract from this failure a solution to the problem of psychoanalysis. How does it cure? From the beginning of his career, Freud lived with a sense that the truth shall make you free; but he had little idea how. By now he had learned that it was not enough simply to uncover and communicate the hidden contents of a person's mind. Even if what Freud said to his patients was true, the manner of the communication was not of the right sort to make that truth liberating. But then, what is the right sort of communication? What is the nature of the therapeutic word? To answer this question, Freud looks to the transference. In some way transference got in the way of Freud's attempts to tell Dora the unconscious contents of her mind. Although he does not explicitly conceptualize the three senses of transference, he does recognize that the situation is ambiguous: Psychoanalytic treatment does not create transferences, it merely brings them to light, like so many other hidden psychical factors ... all the patient's tendencies, including hostile ones are aroused; they are then turned to account for the purposes of the analysis by being made conscious, and in this way the transference is constantly being destroyed. Transference, which seems ordained to be the greatest obstacle to psychoanalysis, becomes its most powerful ally if its presence can be detected each time and explained to the patient.[18] Freud now sees that all the resistance and disruption that he had blamed on the transference is in fact the unconscious, invading the analytic situation in all its living recalcitrance. If Freud can learn to address people in such a way that they can learn to recognize the transference *as* transference, then they will begin to acquire the practical skill of recognizing their own unconscious mental activity in the here-and-now. In this way they can begin to acquire the practical ability to intervene. It is the acquisition of this practical ability that facilitates therapeutic change.

The question now is one of technique: what is the form of addressing patients that will help them to recognize the transference – and in such a way as to develop an active, self-conscious capacity to intervene and shape one's mental life? Again, simply naming the transference is unlikely to help. Just as a patient can feel bombarded and intruded upon by another presuming to tell her the unconscious contents of her mind, so too with a simple declaration of the transference, however accurate. Interpretation is itself a practical skill – and Freud is in the process of acquiring it. Freud lived with this problem for another decade, and in 1914 published 'Remembering, repeating and working through,' which is his deepest meditation on transference. In my opinion, it is the most significant article Freud wrote: if all of his works were lost except for this one, we would be able to reconstruct what is valuable in psychoanalysis.

He begins by announcing 'far-reaching changes' that have occurred in psychoanalytic technique. In stark contrast to the way he treated Dora,

> the analyst gives up the attempt to bring a particular moment or problem into focus. He contents himself with studying whatever is present for the time being on the surface of the patient's mind, and he employs the art of interpretation mainly for the purpose of recognizing the resistances which appear there, making them conscious to the patient.[19]

Freud here officially renounces his role as the detective of the unconscious. He is no longer on the prowl for the key to some mystery hidden in the unconscious. Patients themselves determine what they are going to talk about by speaking whatever comes into their minds. Freud will point out resistances to their free speech, but his aim is to help them resume their speech. He is no longer the suspicious cross-examining magistrate of a hostile witness. At least, those are the new ideals Freud articulates. Of course, patients have been asked to speak their minds since the beginning of psychoanalysis;

but now Freud is willing to linger with what they are saying, rather
than immediately move on to what they are not saying. Analysands
will thus have an enhanced sense that, in the analysis, *they* are speaking. Moreover, what the analysands are talking about is immediately
present to conscious awareness. Indeed, their conscious awareness is
precisely that which they are speaking.

Equally important, Freud restricts himself to using interpretation
'mainly for the purpose of recognizing the resistances which appear
there.' This is a revolutionary change in technique. If unconscious
wishes and fantasies really are alive, trying to get themselves
expressed, there must be counteracting forces holding them away
from conscious awareness. Thus what appears on the 'surface'
of conscious awareness ought to be what Freud calls a *compromise
formation* – an expression of these conflicting forces. What is being
said by the analysand is, in an inverted way, a manifestation of what
is not being said. And if one can help analysands recognize the ways
in which their conscious thoughts function as resistances, one can
expect aspects of unconscious mental activity to rise to the surface of
their own accord. One does not need to delve into the analysand's
unconscious to tell them what's there; analysands will become able
to speak aspects of their own (hitherto) unconscious mental life for
themselves – precisely because it will be rising to the surface of their
conscious experience. 'From this there results a new sort of division
of labor: the doctor uncovers the resistances which are unknown to
the patient; when these have been gotten the better of, the patient
often relates the forgotten situations and connections without any
difficulty.'[20] Think of the difference between an archeological excavation and surface archeology. In the latter, an archeologist may walk
along a ploughed field and note the frequency with which, say,
ancient Roman coins can be found in the furrows. Such a person has
faith in the upward pressure of the earth's crust. Certain artifacts
from deep below the surface will be pushed upwards – of course,
always against the resistance of the earth above. Still, coins, other
artifacts from the ancient world, as well as human bones will rise to
the surface. And on the basis of various forms of analysis, the surface
archeologist can sometimes give quite a sophisticated account of
the ancient civilization. In a similar way, Freud is now relying on the
upward thrust of unconscious mental activity.

This new technique is designed to address the problem of appropriation: what is involved in people being able to take up their own
psychological states in ways that genuinely make them their own.
This is a difference that makes a therapeutic difference. It is all too *suggestion*
easy for an analyst to say, 'You have an unconscious desire to … ' and
the analysand might willingly agree, 'Yes, I have an unconscious
desire to … ,' and it might even be true that he does have such a
desire. The analysand might even grasp all the reasons the analyst has
for thinking he has this unconscious desire – and they might well be
good reasons. Thus the analysand comes to have a sincere, justified
true belief about his own unconscious mental state. And yet this
belief cannot make the right kind of therapeutic difference – because
it does not connect with the mental activity it purports to name.

How then to make the connection? Freud made a crucial discovery: that in the analytic situation there tends to be an inverse
correlation between remembering and repeating. In the analytic
situation, 'the patient does not *remember* anything of what he has
forgotten and repressed, but *acts* it out. He reproduces it not as a
memory but as an action; he *repeats* it, without, of course, knowing
that he is repeating it.'[21] So, for instance, the analysand does not
remember that he used to be defiant towards his parents, but he acts
defiantly now toward the analyst. He doesn't remember having been
embarrassed and confused by his early sexual researches, but he is
embarrassed and confused now in the analytic situation. 'As long as
the patient is in treatment he cannot escape from this compulsion
to repeat; and in the end we understand that this is his way of remembering.'[22] Transference, then, is a repetition that cannot (yet) be
remembered in the right sort of way. Freud seems to suggest that it
is a repetition of an entire orientation to the world. 'Transference,'
he tells us, 'is itself only a piece of repetition, and the repetition is a
transference of the forgotten past *not only on to the doctor but also on to all
other aspects of the current situation.*' In the analytic situation, the analysand '*repeats everything* that has already made its way from the sources
of the repressed into his manifest personality – his inhibitions and
unserviceable attitudes and his pathological character-traits. He also
repeats all his symptoms in the course of the treatment.'[23] In other
words, the analytic situation becomes a microcosm in which a
person's enduring unconscious conflicts are re-enacted.

Freud's aim now is to structure the analytic situation so that the repetition will not remain simply one more repetition in this person's life. The repetition, Freud says, should be allowed to assert itself in the analytic situation. 'We admit it into the transference *as a playground* in which it is allowed to expand in almost complete freedom and in which it is expected to display to us everything in the way of pathogenic instincts that is hidden in the patient's mind.' In this playground, Freud is able to assign a new 'transference meaning'.

> The transference thus creates an intermediate region between illness and real life through which the transition from the one to the other is made. The new condition has taken over all the features of the illness; but it represents an artificial illness which is at every point accessible to our intervention.[24]

This would seem to be transference of type (2): allowing an idiosyncratic world to come into view.

There are two aspects of this technique that are crucially important: first, it treats the emotion or behavior as it is occurring in the here-and-now. The analyst treats the illness, Freud says, 'not as an event of the past, but as a present day force.'[25] Thus what is being addressed by both analyst and analysand is an emotionally vivid present. (Even if the analysand feels bored or sleepy, that is the emotionally vivid present.) Second, however powerful the emotions are, the analyst is also treating it as though they were unfolding in a play space, an intermediate region. A unique blend of reality and unreality is accorded to the experience: and this allows the analysand to experience his emotion in a vibrant way *and* to begin to play with it.

Let us imagine how this might have worked in Freud's treatment of Dora. Assume Herr K was a seducer; and that he did proposition Dora just as she reported. Assume too that there were earlier experiences in her life – say, with her father – in which an attractive older male figure used her for his own purposes. On the basis of these experiences – as well as certain features of her own psychological makeup – she establishes a fairly fixed orientation towards a Seducer figure. We shall call it a Herr K position, because he is the latest occupant and features of his personality may now come to shape the position in various ways.

Freud's technical mistake at this early stage of his career was to bombard Dora with interpretations – of allegedly hidden meanings in her unconscious. The meanings were sexual and seductive, and they concerned Herr K. There is thus reason to suspect that she began to experience Freud in Herr-K-like ways – and with some justification. It is arguable that Freud was more concerned with justifying his theories than with helping her. With so much talk about her sexuality and so little concern for her, she might well come to feel that she is again being used by an older male authority figure. But precisely because there is real justification for her experience, it is difficult for her to see that she is also imaginatively active in assigning certain roles to certain figures.[26] What is needed is a transformation of technique that will allow the analytic situation to become a 'playground,' an 'intermediate region.'[27] In the revised technique, the analyst foregoes normal forms of engagement with another. The analyst renounces normal social forms – even the normal social form of the doctor–patient relationship – as well as familiar forms of erotic, competitive or aggressive engagement. The aim is to provide an environment in which the transference can unfold, but that nevertheless facilitates the analysand's ability to recognize her reactions *as* transference. So, had Freud refrained from indulging his own desire to prove his theory, had he inhibited his own impulse to tell Dora what is really going on in her unconscious, it is at least possible that as she began to experience Freud as another Herr K, she would also be in a position to experience a certain unreality of that experience. That is, as she orients herself towards him as an older man, out to use her for his own purposes, she might also be able to experience something uncanny. After all, Freud would be sitting there in a non-intrusive way, not fighting back, allowing her to experience him that way.

Instead of saying, 'You're now treating me just like Herr K,' the analyst would primarily listen and allow the Herr K transference to develop. On this revised technique, a quick interpretation like this, even if correct, is serving a defensive function *in the analyst*. It is as though the analyst cannot take the transference, and is naming it to bring it to a halt. Perhaps the analyst might at some point ask an interpretive question: 'You seem to be treating me as though I am going to use you. Is that your feeling? If so, in what ways am I going to take advantage?' The question would be in the service of allowing the transference to grow and, as it is growing, have it articulated in conscious, verbal thought and communication.

Freud says that while the transference is 'a piece of real experience,' it has a 'provisional nature.' In the imagined scenario, we can see why. On the one hand, since transference is a real psychological phenomenon, it is likely that at some point in the analysis, Dora will put Freud in a Herr K position. Indeed, it is likely she will do so over and over again. But, on the other hand, Freud's non-seductive response would not be something Dora could easily experience as 'Herr K again.' For there is one thing a seducer-figure such as Herr K can never allow: for his intended prey to experience him as a seducer. The seducer does not say, 'I am here only for my own purposes. I shall gratify my desires and be gone. You mean nothing to me beyond the gratification of my desire.' He says, rather, 'You are my true love; this is really serious,' and so on. In the imagined scenario, it is just at the moment when Dora is experiencing Freud as an older, male seducer that – rather than denying it – he invites her to describe in detail what he is like.

This would facilitate the process by which conscious 'remembering' takes the place of repeating. Although Dora may have been experiencing Freud as 'another Herr K,' she was not yet in a position to express it to herself that way. This is her repetition. The analysis encourages her to appropriate that very experience by taking it over in conscious thought and verbal expression. This is what it is to remember.

The symptoms of the illness, Freud says, are given a new 'transference meaning,' and the analysand's ordinary neurosis is replaced by a 'transference neurosis.' As Dora is coming to experience Freud in Herr-K-like ways, she is also asked to describe her thoughts and feelings as best she can. In the actual Dora case, the analysis broke down over the transference. But in this imagined scenario, Dora experiences a different kind of breakdown: a breakdown in her ability to experience reality unproblematically in certain ways. As she is trying to describe Freud in Herr-K-like ways – or, as she is experiencing Freud in Herr-K-like ways – she also experiences that there is something about her experience that doesn't ring true. This experience of breakdown in one's standard modes of interpretation makes it possible for the analysand to recognize her own transference. This experience of breakdown is a psychological luxury. In normal social circumstances one is too busy coping; and the breakdown in one's ability to cope hardly seems like a luxury. The psychoanalytic situation is structured to offer an existential Sabbath: a benign environment that does not provoke too much anxiety, in which one takes an hour's rest from normal life in order that one has the liberty to experience an interpretive breakdown. Only when Dora can experience that Freud both is and is not Herr K can she begin to recognize her own mental activity. By the time she can sincerely tell Freud, 'You know, I am experiencing you in these ways,' she is also not experiencing him in these ways. For part of her earlier experience was that it remained unnamable and utterly real. Her current experience is being named and experienced as somewhat uncanny. This is what it is to give a new transference meaning to her experience.

In the transference neurosis, Dora's world starts to come into view. Rather than simply experiencing Freud in Herr-K-like ways, the analyst and analysand jointly come to recognize that there are a structured set of responses that orient Dora's emotional life. When done well, this is not an intellectual exercise; it is an emotionally vivid reality that analyst and analysand are trying to grasp as such. But in this emotionally vibrant experience, something comes to light that one might conceive as a Herr K position. Once one has the idea of a structured position, one can inquire into other positions to which it is structurally and dynamically linked. With Dora, perhaps there was also a position of the absent mother, the benign brother, the seductive father. We don't know. But we would expect these positions to come to light in the transference, in part by the shifting roles Dora assigned to her analyst. As Dora herself comes to recognize these various positions and their interrelations, she begins to grasp the world of meanings that she has hitherto used to interpret experience and orient herself. This is what it is for that world to start to open up. For in grasping the constricted nature of the possibilities that she has mistaken for reality, she opens up new possibilities for life.

With hindsight, Freud's actual analysis of Dora looks like a war of two worlds. As we hypothesized the previous chapter, Freud's own life is oriented around an attempt to overcome the paternal curse, 'The boy will come to nothing.' Freud offers Dora interpretations again and again in his own attempt to come to something, a psychoanalyst. This is his repetition. For her part, Dora's world seems to be organized so as to reinforce a sense that she is really alone. In this context, Freud's relentless interpretations were experienced by her as more evidence for her isolation. In an important sense her experience was accurate; she was alone. But she was thus denied the opportunity to see how active she was in the organization of her experience. She experienced Freud in a Herr K position without being able to experience the Herr K position as a position.

In the imagined scenario, by contrast, the war of worlds is avoided, and Dora's world slowly comes into (her) view. Although in an introduction we must omit the complexity of an actual analysis, in broad outline an analysis is structured around four crucial moments: first, a person typically enters analysis because she is in pain and has a sense that things are not going well. For Dora there was fainting, and a suicide note, and an angry slap. Her world is already breaking down, although she does not recognize it as such: her ability to cope is under pressure. Second, the analytic situation provides a safe environment to enact the breakdown. The familiar forms of experience are acted out in the transference. This opens up, third, the possibility of a special form of communication. In the imagined scenario, as Dora places Freud in a Herr K position, the analyst must recognize that anything he says will most likely be heard in a Herr-K-like way. He has to figure out what, if anything, to say that will be heard from a Herr K position, but will nevertheless undermine attempts to weave him into this structure. He cannot say, for instance, 'I am not a seducer like Herr K was; you are just trying to put me in that position'; for that is precisely what a seducer would say. That is what Herr K himself might have said to Dora, if Dora had told him about a previous lover. By contrast, the analyst might well say nothing, or ask a genuine question. It will be his non-aggressive, non-erotic openness that will help Dora recognize the falsity of her experience. This is the true communication. It is what we *ought* to mean by the interpretation of the transference.

Further reading

Readings from Freud

Fragment of an analysis of a case of hysteria (Dora), SE VII: 7–122. Essential reading for this chapter.
'Remembering, repeating and working through,' SE XII: 145–56. In my opinion this is Freud's most important essay.
'The dynamics of transference,' SE XII: 99–108. An interesting discussion of transference not only as a manifestation of erotic life but as an active resistance to treatment.
'Observations on transference-love,' SE XII: 159–71. Further discussion of transference – and erotic life in general – as a resistance to genuine intimacy.

Other readings

C. Bernheimer and C. Kahane (eds.), *In Dora's case: Freud, hysteria, feminism* (New York: Columbia University Press, 1985). A fine collection of feminist essays on the Dora case.
B. Bird, 'Notes on transference: universal phenomenon and hardest part of analysis,' in A.E. Esman (ed.), *Essential papers on transference* (New York: New York University Press, 1990), pp. 331–61. Outstanding clinical account of transference – and of how transference differs from the so-called transference neurosis.
H. Decker, *Freud, Dora and Vienna 1900* (New York: Free Press, 1991). Fascinating account of the cultural milieu in which Freud's treatment of Dora took place.
B. Joseph, 'Transference: the total situation,' in *Psychic equilibrium and psychic change* (London and New York: Routledge, 1989), pp. 156–67.
J. Lacan, 'Intervention on transference,' in Bernheimer and Kahane (eds.), *In Dora's case*, pp. 92–104. This essay is obscure, but it provides a remarkable account of Dora as in search of the meaning of femininity.
H. Loewald, 'The transference neurosis: comments on the concept and the phenomenon,' in Esman (ed.), *Essential papers on transference*, pp. 423–33. Shows how the concept fits with clinical reality.
S. Marcus, 'Freud and Dora: story, history, case history,' in Bernheimer and Kahane (eds.), *In Dora's case*, pp. 56–91. Excellent account of the narrative and rhetorical structure of a case history.
J. Strachey, 'The nature of the therapeutic action of psychoanalysis,' in Esman (ed.), *Essential papers on transference*, pp. 49–79. Classic paper on use of transference in psychoanalytic therapy.

Notes

1 Freud, *Studies on hysteria*, SE II: 302–3.
2 See Chapter 3.

3 Freud, *Fragment of an analysis of a case of hysteria*, SE VII: 1–122. There are a stunning number of discussions of the Dora case. For an introduction to the secondary reading, see C. Bernheimer and C. Kahane (eds.), *In Dora's case: Freud, hysteria, feminism* (New York: Columbia University Press, 1985); H. Decker, *Freud, Dora and Vienna 1900* (New York: Free Press, 1991); P. Mahony, *Freud's Dora: a psychoanalytic, historical and textual study* (New Haven: Yale University Press, 1996); J. Lacan, 'Intervention on transference,' in Bernheimer and Kahane (eds.), *In Dora's case*, pp. 92–104.

4 Freud, *The interpretation of dreams*, SE IV: 106–21.

5 Freud, *Fragment of an analysis of a case of hysteria*, SE VII: 10.

6 Ibid, SE VII: 120.

7 Ibid, SE VII: 122.

8 Ibid, SE VII: 101–3.

9 Ibid, SE VII: 119.

10 Ibid, SE VII: 116, my emphasis.

11 Ibid, SE VII: 116.

12 In the contemporary literature on psychoanalysis there is a tendency to assume (1) that a phrase like 'Dora's world' must mean Dora's subjective world; and (2) that a subjective world must be 'inside the mind' or intrapsychic. Dora's world is then taken to be an internal world. But then how could Freud be part of Dora's world? It would seem that Dora would have to project her internal image of Herr K out onto Freud and then introject this new figure. But these assumptions of projection and introjection are being dictated by an understanding of 'subjective world' that is itself unexamined. Before we can understand transference, we need to re-examine what we could mean by a 'subjective world.' To do this we need to put aside the (Cartesian) assumption that by 'subjective' we must mean inner, intrapsychic, and by 'objective,' outer. For the purposes of this discussion, I assume that Dora's world is her subjective world, in the sense that it reflects her orientation to the world. But Dora's world is the shared social world, although embellished by idiosyncratic meanings and orientations. Thus Sigmund Freud, the doctor, was very much part of Dora's world; he lived in Vienna, not inside her mind; although in Dora's dealings with him, she did orient herself towards him in idiosyncratic ways.

13 Moreover, in seeing both the abrupt termination and the slap as anxious disruptions, it becomes possible to link them to other anxious events in Dora's life: for example, her fainting spell and suicide note. Here again is an anxious disruption of a social world that has become too much to bear. And one may only be able to make these links if one sees them as the anxious disruptions they are.

14 Elsewhere I called this an *idiopolis*: an idiosyncratic polis. See Lear, 'An interpretation of transference,' in *Open minded: working out the logic of the soul* (Cambridge, MA: Harvard University Press), pp. 56–79.

15 Freud, *Fragment of an analysis of a case of hysteria*, SE VII: 4.

16 Ibid. S.E. VII: 56.

17 Ibid, SE VII: 56.

18 Ibid, SE VII: 108, my emphasis.
19 Freud, 'Remembering, repeating and working through,' SE XII: 147.
20 Ibid, SE XII: 147.
21 Ibid, SE XII: 150, emphasis in original.
22 Ibid, SE XII: 150, emphasis in original.
23 Ibid, SE XII: 151, my emphasis.
24 Ibid, SE XII: 154–55.
25 Ibid, SE XII: 151. As Freud later puts it, 'one cannot overcome an enemy who is absent or not within range' (XII: 152).
26 And, in general, even when people distort their experience of others, they are so erotically or aggressively or competitively engaged, they do not have the psychological freedom to step back and see how active they are in shaping what they take to be an experience of reality.
27 The idea of an intermediate region and play-space has been marvelously developed by D.W. Winnicott, 'Transitional objects and transitional phenomena,' in *Playing and reality* (London and New York: Routledge, 1996), pp. 1–25. The literature on transference is enormous, but there is a collection of classic essays on the subject in A.E. Esman (ed.), *Essential papers on transference* (New York: New York University Press, 1990). All the essays are excellent, but the reader who wishes an introduction might begin with the following essays: S. Freud, 'The dynamics of transference' and 'Observations on transference love'; J. Strachey, 'The nature of the therapeutic action of psychoanalysis'; B. Bird, 'Notes on transference: universal phenomenon and hardest part of analysis'; D. Winnicott, 'On transference'; H. Loewald, 'The transference neurosis: comments on the concept and the phenomenon.' Another volume with excellent essays on the subject of countertransference – that is, transference in the analyst – is B. Wolstein (ed.), *Essential papers on countertransference* (New York: New York University Press, 1988).

Five
Principles of mental functioning

1 The pleasure principle and reality principle

Freud tried to formulate principles of how the mind works. He was of course influenced by the scientific theories of his day, but basically he was drawing on clinical experience. He wanted to explain the neurotic life of his patients, and he saw neurosis as an expression of psychological conflict. Might there then not be conflicting principles of mental life?

For the first half of his career, he thought there were two. Overall, the mind – or 'psychical apparatus' as he put it – aims to reduce tension. Tension is experienced as unpleasure; thus the mind tends towards pleasure. When the mind is under the sway of the pleasure principle, the diffusion and discharge of tension is the only issue.

Perhaps there is no pure instance in adult life of the mind working according to the pleasure principle, but Freud thought one could see it pretty clearly in dream activity (see Chapter 3). The mind is pressured by an unconscious wish; it distributes that tension across the loose associations of primary process – associations that bear no particular relation to reality – and it discharges that tension in a hallucination of satisfaction. Freud thought that dreaming was a remnant of infantile mental life, and thus he formed a mythical account of the development of mental life. He himself called it a 'fiction.'[1] The newborn infant experiences hunger – a tension – and is fed and comforted at the breast. An experience of satisfaction is laid down in memory, and at the next experience of hunger, the infant mind hallucinates the breast.

the state of psychical rest was originally disturbed by the pre-emptory demands of internal needs. When this happened, whatever was thought of (wished for) was simply presented in a hallucinatory manner, just as still happens today with our dream thoughts every night.[2]

The hallucination is itself gratifying.

The problem is that hallucination does not provide lasting satisfaction – it does not fill the infant's tummy – and thus the mind must start to take reality into account. The mind starts to form a conception of external reality and of how to bring about a real change. 'A new principle of mental functioning was thus introduced; what was presented in the mind was no longer what was agreeable but what was real, even if it happened to be disagreeable. This setting-up of the *reality principle* proved to be a momentous step.'[3] On this account, the reality principle has the same basic aim as the pleasure principle – the reduction of tension – but it takes a detour through reality in order to provide lasting satisfaction. Thus, when the mind is operating according to the reality principle, it associates among ideas according to the logical connections of secondary process; it pays attention to perception of the world; and it aims at action that will bring real-life satisfaction.

Taken literally, this developmental account makes no sense. How could a mind operating according to the pleasure principle make a (realistic) decision to operate in a different way? At the very least, we need an account of how realistic mental functioning comes to be selected on the basis of infantile experience. But it is worth noting that one could tell a very different story of the origins of the mind – one that moves in the opposite direction. At birth, the mind is oriented towards the world and trying to comprehend it. It is trying to think realistically as best it can; but part of its own developmental process is learning how to do this. It tries to think of the breast, and as a byproduct has an experience of satisfaction. Because of this satisfaction, imaginative activity gets selected and starts to take on a life of its own. On this story, it is the pleasure principle that develops out of the reality principle.

The point is not to rule in favor of either story, but to bring out their mythological status. Freud's hypothesis is based not on the observation of infantile development, but on the analysis of adult neurotic patients. He is working backwards from his own clinical experience. Adult neurotics *never* display a pure culture of the pleasure principle or a pure culture of the reality principle. Neurotic behavior and imaginative activity are always conflicted. And Freud wants to see these conflicts as the outcome of conflicting principles. In this way he purports to provide an *analysis* of the psyche.[4] The heuristic value of his myth of the origins of the mind is that one can supposedly see each of these principles at work in isolation. Thus one can get a clearer idea of what each principle is. In actual human reality, one never sees these principles at work on their own.

2 Turning away from reality

It is tempting to get lost in the details of Freud's theory of the mind. Therefore, it is worth reminding oneself that everything valuable in his account is an extrapolation from his clinical experience. And the central feature of his experience is what he called the neurotic's tendency to turn away from reality. At the beginning of 'Formulations of two principles of mental functioning,' Freud says that '*every* neurosis has as its result, and probably therefore as its purpose, a forcing of the patient out of real life, an alienating of him from reality.'[5] Neurotics 'turn away from reality,' he says, because they find it unbearable. What does this mean? Let us briefly reconsider some moments from the case studies:

- *Ms Elizabeth von R* thinks she must stay at home and tend to her father. It looks like, and to some extent it is, an accurate perception of social reality. By doing so she effectively avoids the social and erotic challenges of entering the adult world. She avoids having to think about her newly available brother-in-law (although she may well be taken up with him in her unconscious imaginative life); she turns away from the challenges of separating from her parents, leaving home, becoming a marriageable, sexually available woman. Instead, her life is organized around hidden gratifications in staying at home with her father, nursing him, and looking after her own 'painful' leg. She can certainly perceive reality in the sense she has a basic sense of the social and physical world she inhabits. On the other hand, she has isolated herself socially, and this in turn gives her space to be taken up with her own imaginative life. Her life becomes a swirl of idiosyncratic meanings – often unconscious – organized around the pain in her thigh. As she gets ever more absorbed with her illness, she is ostensibly being responsible, but in fact she is ever more taken up with her own imaginative life.

- *Anna O's and Dora's hysterical births*: A hysterical wish is getting acted out in social space. Anna O is conscious that she is enacting a labor, but it is unlikely that she actually believed Dr. Breuer had sexual intercourse with her and that she was in the process of giving birth to a real-life baby (if she did, she would be suffering a psychotic delusion, an altogether more serious break with reality than a neurotic turning away).[6] Rather, her waking life is taken over by dreamlike activity: she is having cramps, feeling contractions, going through the motions of labor. All this serves to distract her from the real-life task of experiencing the disappointment and anger at Dr. Breuer's decision to end the treatment. Dora is not aware that her cramps are psychosomatic, expressing a hysterical labor. But they serve to absorb her attention and provide a focus for her own imaginative life. In this way her life becomes absorbed in her own imaginative activity.
- Mr. R may remove and replace a stone to express his love and hate, but in so doing he keeps himself busy with his own imaginative life. He remains unaware of his hate, and in his business he distracts himself from the fact that his father is dead, and that he has no hope with his lady-friend. He drives himself to distraction trying to pay back money to someone to whom he doesn't owe money, but the whole drama keeps him at a distance from the central dilemma of his life.

In each of these cases, the individual has not lost all touch with reality; rather, there is a perturbation in their reality-testing. Each of these people grasp, up to a point, the physical and social world they inhabit. What they don't understand is that their perception of the world is getting distorted in wishful ways. As one sees its effects in adults, the pleasure principle exerts a gravitational pull on reality-testing and practical life. There is a kind of *swerve* towards wishfulness in ordinary life.[7] Freud's case studies are dramatic. It is thus important to recognize that the neurotic turn away from reality is a fairly common feature of everyday life. We all, Freud thought, have the task of negotiating our erotic impulses with the mores and customs of society. He described some classic deformations of erotic–social life, but the variations are endless:[8]

1 The man who is (over and over) attracted to women who are already going out with (married to) someone else.
2 The woman who is sexually indifferent to her husband, even frigid, but finds sexual satisfaction in a secret affair.
3 The man who admires his wife, but is sexually unattracted to her. He is excited by prostitutes, slutty types and pornography.

The man who is only attracted to women who are unavailable (1) takes himself to be the unlucky victim of fate: if only she were free, he would at last be happy. As it is, he is wistful, jealous of the other man, absorbed with thoughts of his unavailable love. What he does not recognize is that the woman's unavailability is not an accidental fact about her; it plays an essential role in his attraction to her. Were she to become available, he would lose interest – but of this he is unaware. Freud pointed out that such a person is recreating the triangular structure of childhood where the woman he loved (his mother) is in an important sense unavailable to him (with another man). Over and over he recreates the frustrations of the incest taboo. And while he suffers the pangs of jealousy, the intense pain of unrequited love, he is oblivious to the gratifications that keep him absorbed. For in being attracted to the unavailable woman, this is his way of holding onto her *as unavailable*. He holds onto the forbidden figure as the object of his erotic imagination. So, in terms of 'turning away from reality,' the point is not that he should fit in with social norms and find a woman of his own. Rather, it is that in his attraction to this particular (unavailable) woman, he is in fact absorbed in his own fantasy life. Unbeknown to him, this woman is functioning (for him) as little more than a place-holder for the fixed position of the Unavailable Woman. He takes himself to be attracted to a particular person; what he doesn't realize is that his attraction flows in large part from the position she occupies in his imaginative life.

The woman involved in the extramarital affair (2) does not recognize the role that secrecy and prohibition play in her erotic life. Consciously, she is bored with her husband, feels she has outgrown him, feels sexually turned off; she finds her lover exciting, interesting, what she really wants. What she doesn't recognize is that she has created a secret space in which officially forbidden sexual activity can occur – and that plays an essential role in her excitement. She may sincerely tell her lover that she is getting up the courage to leave her husband – it is as though she is taking realistic considerations into account, but as she gets close to acting she can't quite do it. What she does not recognize is how important it is to her to maintain her lover *as forbidden*. Perhaps in childhood she was prohibited from various erotic–sexual activities, and she came to experience prohibition itself as exciting. Again, the point is not that she should shape up, accommodate herself to social norms and get back into her marriage. Nor is it that she should end her marriage and go out with her lover. Rather, she 'turns away from reality' in the sense that she uses real-life people as though they were figures in a fixed fantasy-world. For her, exciting sex must occur in a secret space with a forbidden lover – and that structure is re-enacted again and again. Unbeknown to her, her current lover functions for her as a place-holder in a fairly rigid imaginative structure.

Finally, in case 3, Freud pointed to a typical difficulty we have in bringing together the affectionate and erotic currents in our life. Little boys tend to idealize their mothers and, as they become more sexually aware, they keep at a distance the idea that their beloved mothers actually participate in this messy, strange sexual activity. What can emerge in adult life is a person who finds it difficult to be sexually attracted to women he admires; and difficult to admire women to whom he feels attracted. This may distort his perception of most women. The point, again, is not that he should fulfill the social ideal of admiring and being attracted to the same woman; it is that he is likely to over-idealize some, and unfairly disparage others. He is forcing women to fit into specific roles in his imaginative life; and in this way he distorts reality.

3 Virtue and neurtue

Our ability to inhabit social reality can be disturbed by the gravitational pull of wishful forces – and this is of ethical significance.

In broadly Aristotelian approaches to ethics, ethical life is based on excellences of character, or virtues. On this approach there is a distinctive conception of human flourishing – the virtues are those aspects of character that enable a person to flourish. In every case, this is – to adapt Freud's terminology – a turning *towards* reality. To take a psychoanalytically salient example, consider the virtue of courage.[9] We are not concerned here only with bravery on the battlefield, but courage in everyday life. Courage requires an accurate understanding of the world one inhabits; and an accurate understanding of one's place in it. Courage is a kind of truthfulness. And it is on the basis of one's self-and-world understanding that one is able to act courageously.

A virtue like courage is a perceptual-and-motivational unity: one sees the world and understands oneself in certain ways and is thereby motivated to act. As such, courage is a source of creative repetition. No matter how varied experience is, no matter the peculiarities of the moment, a courageous person will be alive to the salient aspects of the situation that call for courage; and she will have the capacity to engage in an appropriately creative response. Yet her creativity will always be brought back to the question of how to live courageously, and thus her acts will form a structure of repetition.

A neurosis, by contrast, will express itself in a structure of repetition that is more rigid and limited. Nevertheless, *one can get good at being neurotic!* That is, one can develop a character that displays a certain skill, mastery, even creativity in being neurotic. It becomes difficult to recognize a structure of repetition precisely because there are so many creative variations on a theme. Such people seem to display an uncanny excellence in being neurotic. I shall call this a *neurtue.* This is more than a rigid neurotic structure of repetition. Let us go back to Dora, and imagine that she has the neurtue of isolation. That is, in addition to the fact that people in her social world really do use her for their own purposes, Dora is also unconsciously active in structuring her life so as to experience herself as fundamentally alone. Real-life disappointments will be attributed an enhanced significance – as though her father's real self-absorption told her who she was and what was possible for her in life. She will also develop skills of cutting herself off from others – fainting and suicide notes in the family, slapping Herr K and running away, breaking off treatment with Freud. Again, whatever real-life provocations there might have been in each of these cases, she will turn them to her own purposes. Finally, she will be a master in interpreting the myriad ambiguous events in life as though they confirm her sense that she is really alone in the world.

Dora's neurtue, so we imagine, is creative – she makes marvelous and varied use of her life experience – but her creativity is ultimately used in the service of reinforcing a fairly rigid structure of life-possibilities. All of her possibilities are ones in which she experiences herself as on her own. She uses her neurtue in ingenious ways to reinforce her sense of herself as isolated. The crucial point is that all roads lead to alone.

By now it should be clear that Freud's principles of mental functioning – the pleasure principle and the reality principle – *are essentially ethical in nature*. To be sure, this is not how it looks on the surface of Freud's writings. He writes in the scientific style of his day. And when he talks about how the 'psychic apparatus' works, it is as though he is charting mental functioning in much the same way as he would chart brain functioning, if only he could observe a brain.[10] The mind working according to the reality principle is treated as though it were straightforward perception of the empirical world. But the basis of Freud's theorizing is his observation of neurotic patients within a psychoanalytic setting (and his own self-analysis). What Freud is trying to explain are pathological perturbations in how these people are living. That is, he sees people who are failing to flourish, and he sets out to give a psychological account of why that is. On his account, neurotics fail to live well because they themselves 'turn away from reality.' Freud never sees a pure case of the pleasure principle or the reality principle at work. Rather, they are theoretical posits, whose joint and conflicted workings are supposed to explain what he does see: people living structured unhappy lives. The pleasure principle and reality principle are there to explain why people are doing such a poor job answering the question of how to live.

4 Beyond the pleasure principle

In the devastated aftermath of World War I, Freud was brought up short by the so-called war neuroses. Soldiers came back from the front traumatized: their minds would be flooded with horrific memories of war, they would wake up night after night terrified by dreams of the same atrocity. Such patients present a dramatically different profile from a person suffering neurotic conflicts.[11] In particular, their terrifying dreams cannot reasonably be interpreted as the disguised gratification of a wish. Nor can one understand their tortured daily lives as the outcome of a conflict between the pleasure and reality principles. These people were being overwhelmed by trauma over and over again. There is no way one could understand that as a neurotic turning away from reality.

On the basis of one symptom – traumatic dreams – Freud is willing to make a fundamental revision in psychoanalytic theory. 'Dreams occurring in traumatic neuroses,' Freud says, 'have the characteristic of repeatedly bringing the patient back into the situation of his accident, a situation from which he wakes up in another fright (*Schreck*). This astonishes people far too little.'[12] What ought to astonish us? The German word *Schreck* is somewhat misleadingly translated as fright, for Freud's point is not that the person is frightened in his dreams over and over again. Freud distinguishes *Schreck* from fear and anxiety.[13] Fear and anxiety are states of fearful preparedness for danger: anxiety is a generalized preparedness; fear is directed toward a specific threatening worldly object. *Schreck*, by contrast, is what happens when one is unexpectedly overwhelmed by dread. Freud emphasizes the factor of surprise. The normal defenses against danger do not have time to operate, and one is overwhelmed by dread.

It is one thing for this to happen on the battlefield; it is quite another for it to happen night after night in dreams. What is the mind doing? It looks like the mind is inflicting the same traumatic damage on itself, over and over again. What could the function of such dreams be, given that they are not wish-fulfillments?

At this point, Freud makes a remarkable theoretical leap: he argues that traumatic dreams are not simply dreams; they also contain active disruptions of the dream-process.[14] What is most astonishing about the dreams of the traumatic neuroses, then, is not that people repeatedly dream about frightful scenes; it is that they repeatedly *wake up* overwhelmed by dread. In the so-called traumatic dream, the mind seems actively to disrupt the dream-process, and traumatize the person all over again. In such a traumatic repetition, Freud tells us,

> the pleasure principle is for the moment put out of action. There is no longer any possibility of preventing the mental apparatus from being flooded with large amounts of stimulus, and another problem arises instead – the problem of mastering the amounts of stimulus which have broken in.[15]

Freud now sees the dream part of the traumatic dream as an attempt to restore the capacity to dream. The dreaming mind is in effect attempting to master the trauma retrospectively. Thus these dreams are not operating according to the pleasure principle, nor are they aiming towards wish-fulfillment. Rather, Freud says, the traumatic dreams

> are endeavoring to master the stimulus retrospectively, by developing the anxiety whose omission was the cause of the traumatic neurosis. They thus afford us a view of a function of the mental apparatus which, though it does not contradict the pleasure principle, is nevertheless independent of it and seems to be more primitive than the purpose of gaining pleasure and avoiding unpleasure.[16]

There are two important aspects of the traumatic dream. First, the dreaming part of the traumatic dream is attempting to restore the (damaged) capacity to dream. If one could only keep on dreaming – even if it were a scary dream – then the capacity to dream would be up and running again; and dreaming could take on its normal function. But, second, this attempted restoration fails: the mind seems to disrupt the dream-process by inflicting on itself yet another traumatic awakening.

It is precisely at this moment that Freud makes a theoretical move that, in my opinion, is extravagant. He starts with the recognition that there are some dreams that do not operate according to the pleasure principle, and do not seek gratification in wish-fulfillment.

But he moves to the conclusion that there must be some more primordial principle of the mind that has hitherto lain hidden. He calls it the *compulsion to repeat*. And he makes a major revision to his theory in *The interpretation of dreams*: 'This would seem to be the place, then, to admit for the first time an exception to the proposition that dreams are the fulfillments of wishes.'[17] Wish-fulfillment, Freud now thinks, is not the 'original function' of dreams. Originally, dreams operated 'beyond the pleasure principle' – expressing this brute compulsion to repeat. Only later do they acquire the function of wish-fulfilling gratification.[18] But why assume that a mind that has been so damaged by trauma is operating according to a more original function? Why not simply assume instead that the mind has been damaged? As such, it may have difficulty operating according to any principle. On this interpretation, there is no primordial principle *beyond* the pleasure principle; there is mental breakdown.

Freud talks about a compulsion to repeat – as though repetition were the aim of the compulsion. If this were a primordial principle, it would be an alternative to the pleasure principle, and it would explain the repetitive traumatic dreams. But one does not need a new principle of mental functioning to explain the phenomena. What Freud sees is compulsive repetitiveness. This is what needs explaining. But he helps himself to the assumption that repetition is the *aim* of the compulsion. This extra assumption has wide-ranging consequences. Freud did not think his discovery was restricted to traumatic dreams. Rather, he thought that traumatic dreams were so dramatic that they enabled him to see this strange phenomenon; but once he saw it, he could see it everywhere. He comes to think that the compulsion to repeat pervades the psychoanalytic situation. All sorts of behavior that he had earlier explained in terms of a clash between the pleasure principle and reality principle are now to be explained as a manifestation of this primordial compulsion. 'Patients repeat all of these unwanted situations and painful emotions in the transference and revive them with the greatest ingenuity,' Freud tells us. 'None of these things can have produced pleasure in the past, and it might be supposed that they would cause less unpleasure today if they emerged as memories or dreams instead of taking the form of fresh experiences.' In the past Freud told us that these acts had hidden gratifications; that they were disguised wish-fulfillments and compromise formations. Now he tells us that they lead only to unpleasure; and that they are performed under the primordial compulsion to repeat.[19] In effect, Freud is saying that much of an analysand's behavior in the transference must be understood in a new way. But if his theory of transference needs to be revised, so does his account of therapy and cure. For, by this point in Freud's career, psychoanalytic therapy consists in the proper handling of the transference. And yet the revision has to be carried out in the light of a fundamental force that Freud admits he doesn't really understand. 'If a compulsion to repeat does operate in the mind,' Freud says, 'we should be glad to know something about it, to learn what function it corresponds to, under what conditions it can emerge and what its relation is to the pleasure principle – to which, after all, we have hitherto ascribed dominance over the course of the processes of excitation in mental life.'[20] This is tantamount to an admission that Freud does not yet understand the fundamental principles of psychoanalysis.

5 Compulsive repetition

'What follows,' Freud says, 'is speculation, often far-fetched speculation which the reader will consider or dismiss according to his individual predilection.'[21] But the issue ought not to be a matter of personal taste, but of the best way to conceptualize the clinical phenomena. I would like to try out a more austere hypothesis than the one Freud put forward. Let us avoid Freud's assumption that the compulsive repetitiveness we see is a manifestation of a compulsion to repeat. We abandon the teleological assumption that repetition is the aim of the compulsion. How, then, might we understand it? It seems there are two possibilities, each of which might occur in different circumstances.

First, we might be witnessing a repeatedly failed attempt to master a trauma. The mind keeps trying to dream the event through, but is repeatedly overwhelmed. In this case, there would be no basic psychological principle – no 'repetition compulsion' – whose aim needs to be explained. Rather, the compulsive repetitiveness would be an epiphenomenal manifestation of the mind's failure to keep functioning. In war neurosis, the soldier is brought back to the traumatic scene not because there is an elemental insistence that the scene be repeated, but because mental efforts to lend meaning to this traumatic disruption miscarry again. By way of analogy, in some polluted lakes, frogs are producing monstrosities when they try to reproduce. The pollution has, as it were, traumatized the ecosystem, and the outcome is frogs producing monstrous miscarriages over and over again. Clearly, the aim of all this repetitive activity is not to re-enact the traumatic scene and produce another monstrosity. The frogs are trying to reproduce just as they have always done; it's just that for the time being their capacity to do so has been disrupted.

The second possibility is that the mind becomes active with respect to traumatic disruption. It disrupts itself. This is the formation of a primitive defense that I earlier called the *anxiety defense*: when the mind becomes anxious, it overwhelms itself. In this case, as the dreamer approaches the horrifying memory, rather than tolerate the anxiety of dreaming it, he actively disrupts his own dream-activity. This is not a healthy response: the mind avoids anxiety by disrupting its own ability to function.

If this is correct, then two different kinds of phenomena can show up as repetitions. First, there is the neurotic creation of an idiosyncratic and limited world. This is the repeated gratification of a fantasy – under conditions of repression – in which the same basic structure gets acted out again and again. So, to continue with our imagined example, Dora behaves and experiences the world so as to re-enforce an overall sense that she is alone. One should expect this to recur inside the transference. Here the transference is manifesting itself as an idiosyncratic world coming to light – and one does not need a new theoretical principle to explain this. But there is a second kind of repetition in which a person induces a break in her own mental functioning. Traumatic dreams provide a vivid example: the dreamer disrupts her own capacity to dream, waking up in dread. Other examples may be less dramatic. In the psychoanalytic situation, think of the difference between the elaboration of the transference as an idiosyncratic world coming into view, and the active and abrupt disruption of that process. Consider in this light of Mr. R's jump from the couch.[22] Here is an abrupt, disruptive act that serves to break the flow of the analytic process. It is also a disruption of Mr. R's mental processes: in the moment, his own reflective capacity to say what he is doing breaks down.

Or, consider again Dora's slap. Obviously, such an act could have been a thoughtful and well-deserved response to a seducer. It could also have been a neurotic repetition of the first sort: part of a well-developed repertoire of responses in which she reinforces an overall sense of being alone. But consider another interpretive possibility: that the scene is so overwhelming for her that she anxiously acts to disrupt it. In so doing, she disrupts herself. Her own mental activity becomes flooded and confused. And although this anxiety attack is painful, it does have strategic value: it distracts her from thinking about how she wants to react to Herr K's proposal. And now let us suppose that it is this active disruption that is repeated in the psychoanalytic situation. Dora disrupts the flow of her imaginative life by abruptly ending the analysis. Note that repetition is not the aim of the repetition. If there is an aim here, it is to avoid facing up to the looming situation by inducing disruption and anxiety.

This suggests that two different kinds of phenomena can show up in the transference: transference as the elaboration of a world, and transference as the disruption of that world. Freud cannot see this distinction because he thinks he has discovered a primordial principle that explains all repetition. Even worse, this principle gets in the way of a real explanatory account. Freud cites some familiar examples of neurotic repetition: the benefactor who is abandoned time after time by each of his protégés; the man whose friendships all end in betrayal; the lover who passes through the same stages in a love affair over and over again.[23] In the past, Freud would have explained these phenomena as dynamic outcomes of attempts to achieve wishful gratifications under the constraints of the external world. The repetition would itself be explained in terms of other complex forces – the pleasure principle and the reality principle. Now repetition is 'explained' in terms of itself: these are all cited as instances of the compulsion to repeat. Freud thinks he is achieving a theoretical unification; in my opinion he is turning away from a diversity of phenomena.

6 The death drive

Freud now argues for the existence of a distinct primordial drive, which he calls the death drive. The argument has two steps. First, he argues that the compulsion to repeat reveals that the drives in general are essentially conservative. The fact that we are driven to repeat indicates 'a drive is an urge inherent in organic life to restore an earlier state of things which the living entity has been obliged to abandon, under the pressure of external disturbing forces.'[24] This seems strange, he says, because we tend to think of drives as driving us forward in life; but when we meditate on the fact of repetition we realize we are being driven backward. This argument depends on the idea that repetition is the aim of the compulsion: otherwise there is no ground for the claim that the compulsion seeks to restore an earlier state of things.

Second, Freud argues from the conservative nature of the drives to the death drive. 'It is,' he says, 'possible to specify the final goal of all organic striving.'

> It would be in contradiction to the conservative nature of the drives if the goal of life were a state of things which had never been attained. On the contrary, it must be an old state of things, an initial state from which the living entity has at one time or another departed and to which it is striving to return by the circuitous paths along which its development leads. If we are to take it as a truth that knows no exception that everything living dies for internal reasons – becomes organic once again – then we shall be compelled to say that 'the aim of all life is death.'[25]

The conclusion of the argument is dramatic. But the argument depends on the questionable premise that the aim of repetition is repetition.

This is a critical moment in the development of psychoanalysis. It has yet to be resolved satisfactorily. On the one hand, Freud is correct to pick out certain disruptive psychic activities that do not fit his model of mental functioning according to the pleasure principle and reality principle. On the other hand, his attempt to rethink the mind is compromised by his teleological assumption that a repetitive compulsion is a compulsion to repeat. It is not just that his solution to the problem is invalid; he is not clear about what the problem is. He focuses on repetition; but, in my opinion, the new and puzzling phenomenon he discovered is the mind's active disruption of its own functioning. Freud's question was 'Why does the mind aim at repetition?'; it ought to have been 'Why and how does the mind disrupt itself?'

Perhaps the most unfortunate aspect of Freud's speculation is that he uses the death drive to explain human aggression. For Freud, the death drive is an entropic tendency in every living organism – a tendency to fall apart. Aggression is this tendency deflected outwards. Aggression is thus understood as a secondary, defensive phenomenon. On this account people are aggressive towards others because they deflect outwards an internal tendency to decompose. Aggression towards others is only a way of postponing the day when one undergoes self-destruction. Perhaps there is something to be said in favor of this picture. But in the short run it lulls one into thinking one has a theory of aggression when that is what is missing. What is needed is a psychodynamic account of the role of aggression in psychological and social formation. Moreover, on this derivation, humans are not essentially aggressive; it is just their tragic fate, the price of (temporary) existence. Are we not thereby encouraged to turn our gaze away from our own aggressive natures? About a decade after writing *Beyond the pleasure principle*, Freud expresses astonishment that psychoanalysis so long 'overlooked the ubiquity of non-erotic aggressivity and destructiveness and can have failed to give it its due place in our interpretation of life.'[26] In my opinion, Freud never succeeded in giving aggression its due place in the psychoanalytic interpretation of life; and it is the death drive that got in the way. It is a challenge for future generations to develop a distinctively psychoanalytic account of human aggression and destructiveness.[27]

Further reading

Readings from Freud

'Formulations on the two principles of mental functioning,' SE XII: 218–26. Important formulation of the difference between the pleasure principle and the reality principle.

'The loss of reality in neurosis and psychosis,' SE XIX: 183–87. Gives an account of the very different senses in which there is a loss of reality in neurosis and in psychosis.

'A special type of object choice made by men. (Contributions to the psychology of love I),' SE XI: 165–75; 'On the universal tendency to debasement in the sphere of love. (Contributions to the psychology of love II),' SE XI: 176–90. These articles explore the tendency in some men to split apart sexual attraction to women and idealization of them.

Beyond the pleasure principle, SE XVIII: 1–64. Freud's argument for the death drive.

Other readings

M. Klein, 'Envy and gratitude,' in Envy and gratitude (London: Hogarth Press, 1984), pp. 176–235. Introduces the concept of envy in a distinctively psychoanalytic way: a tendency toward destructiveness, especially directed against creativity. The following four essays are also on this topic.

B. Joseph, 'Envy in everyday life,' in Psychic equilibrium and psychic change (London and New York: Routledge, 1989), pp. 127–38.

E.B. Spillius, 'Varieties of envious experience,' International journal of psychoanalysis 74 (1993), pp. 1199–1212.

M. Likierman, '"So unattainable": two accounts of envy,' in Melanie Klein: her work in context (London and New York: Continuum, 2001), pp. 172–91.

R. D. Hinshelwood, 'The death instinct and envy,' in Clinical Klein (New York: Basic Books, 1994), pp. 135–43.

Notes

1 Freud, The interpretation of dreams, SE V: 604–5, 637, 642.

2 Freud, 'Formulation on the two principles of mental functioning,' SE XII: 219.

3 Ibid, SE XII: 219.

4 See Chapter 1, 1 'Analysis of the psyche.'

5 Freud, 'Formulation on the two principles of mental functioning,' SE XII: 218, my emphasis.

6 See Freud, 'The loss of reality in neurosis and psychosis,' SE XIX: 183–87.

7 I discuss this in Lear, Happiness, death and the remainder of life, pp. 114–16.

8 See Freud, 'A special type of object choice made by men (Contributions to the psychology of love I),' SE XI: 163–75; and 'On the universal tendency to debasement in the sphere of love (Contributions to the psychology of love II)', SE XI: 179–90.

9 See Aristotle, Nicomachean ethics, III.6; Plato, Laches.

10 See, for example, Freud, Project for a scientific psychology, SE I: 281–397.

11 During my training as a psychoanalyst, I had the opportunity to spend two years on the staff of the Psychiatric Unit at the Veterans Hospital in West Haven, Connecticut. There I had the occasion to treat patients suffering from

severe cases of post-traumatic stress disorder (PTSD), which derived from their experiences in the Vietnam War. It was that experience that enabled me to read *Beyond the pleasure principle* with some understanding. There was such a difference between those patients and my other psychoanalytic patients, I could see why Freud was compelled to offer another theory.

12 Freud, *Beyond the pleasure principle*, SE XVIII: 13.

13 Ibid, SE XVIII: 12.

14 Ibid, SE XVIII: 13–14.

15 Ibid, SE XVIII: 29–30.

16 Ibid, SE XVIII: 32.

17 Ibid, SE XVIII: 32–33.

18 Ibid.

19 Ibid, SE XVIII: 21–22.

20 Ibid, SE XVIII: 23.

21 Ibid, SE XVIII: 24.

22 See Chapter 1.

23 Freud, *Beyond the pleasure principle*, SE XVIII: 22.

24 Ibid, SE XVIII: 36.

25 Ibid, SE XVIII: 37–38.

26 Freud, *Civilization and its discontents*, SE XXI: 120.

27 One place to begin looking is in the work Melanie Klein and her followers have done in formulating a psychoanalytic conception of envy. See M. Klein, 'Envy and gratitude,' in *Envy and gratitude* (London: Hogarth Press, 1984), pp. 176–235; E.B. Spillius, 'Varieties of envious experience,' *International journal of psychoanalysis* 74 (1993), pp. 1199–1212; B. Joseph, 'Addiction to near death,' in *Psychic equilibrium and psychic change* (London and New York: Routledge, 1989), pp. 127–38; B. Joseph, 'Envy in everyday life,' in *Psychic equilibrium and psychic change*, pp. 181–91; H. Rosenfeld, 'On the psychopathology of narcissism: a clinical approach,' in *Psychotic states* (London: Hogarth Press, 1965), pp. 169–79; H. Rosenfeld, 'A clinical approach to the psychoanalytical theory of the life and death instincts: an investigation into the aggressive aspects of narcissism,' in E.B. Spillius (ed.), *Melanie Klein today: developments in theory and practice*, Vol. 1, *Mainly theory* (London and New York: Routledge, 1988), pp. 239–55. See also W. Bion, 'Attacks on linking,' in *Melanie Klein today*, Vol. 1, pp. 87–101, and 'A theory of thinking,' *Melanie Klein today*, Vol. 1, pp. 178–86; and E. O'Shaughnessy, 'W.R. Bion's theory of thinking and the new techniques in child analysis,' in *Melanie Klein today*, Vol. 2, *Mainly practice* (London and New York: Routledge, 1988), pp. 177–90. The Kleinians themselves look back to Freud's account of the *negative therapeutic reaction* (*The ego and the id*, SE XIX: 49–50; *From the history of an infantile neurosis*, SE XVII: 68–69; 'The economic problem of masochism,' SE XIX: 165–66; *New introductory lectures on psychoanalysis*, SE XXII: 109–10). There are some patients, Freud says, who in response to a good psychoanalytic interpretation get worse rather than better. This isn't just the analysand complaining about getting worse – which may simply express his jealousy of the analyst. It is something more malign. The analyst makes a thoughtful interpretation and the analysand is overtaken by stomach cramps, has

to run to the bathroom with diarrhea, has a headache, starts coughing uncontrollably, becomes dissociated, falls asleep. There is a disruption that makes it impossible for the analysand to take in what the analyst is saying. The analysand is active in disrupting his own capacity to metabolize the words of another. His capacity for learning and growth is subjected to a primitive attack: and he is the author of the attack. He is actively attacking his own ability to function as a psychological being. This is an outstanding question: whether there is some malign and paradoxical 'principle' of mental functioning by which the mind attacks its own existence.

Six

The structure of the psyche and the birth of 'object' relations

1 Mourning And Melancholia

Freud discovered the psyche had structure through his study of the distorted ways in which people relate to themselves. He was particularly interested in cases in which a person would suffer a dramatic loss of self-esteem or would subject herself to incessant self-criticism. Freud warns that he is not giving an account of all forms of depression; and he suggests that the diagnosis called melancholia might not pick out a real clinical unity. Some forms of depression flow from purely somatic causes, he says, and he will only focus on one psychological configuration that expresses itself in depression.[1] He takes his cue from depression that is typical of mourning. The mourner's sadness and withdrawal of interest in the normal goings-on in the world are unsurprising; not just because it is a common occurrence, but because we think we understand what is happening. The mourner is taken up with emotion-filled memories of the lost loved one. This is his way of trying to maintain a connection to the dead loved one; and it is a way of coming to accept the loss. But this process, at least in principle, has a culmination. In healthy circumstances, a person over time achieves an emotional reorientation: he may live with fond, happy and sad memories, but comes to accept that this is his new way of living with his loved one. And 'when the work of mourning is completed the ego becomes free and uninhibited again.'[2] Melancholic depression in some ways looks like mourning, although there are two asymmetries: first, the person need not have lost a loved one in the external world; second, the melancholic can be devastatingly critical of himself. He finds that he does not measure up in any dimension. Freud discovered that these asymmetries were related. 'In mourning it is the world which has become poor and empty; in melancholia it is the ego itself.'[3] Although by normal standards, the melancholic's self-assessment is distorted, Freud argues that it is nevertheless giving us an accurate account of his psychological condition. To explain this condition, he had to give an account of how the self could judge itself. How could a person simultaneously take up two positions, that of the judge and the judged?

Freud thought there had to be a split in the personality: 'one part of the ego sets itself over against the other, judges it critically and, as it were, takes it as its object.'[4] Freud would come to call this the superego. It earns the title *ego* because it exercises the authority and critical judgment of the subject. And it earns the title *superego* because it exercises critical judgment over the ego itself. A word about translation: Freud writes in colloquial German, and thus the phrase translated as 'the ego' is simply 'Das Ich' – literally, 'the I' or simply 'I.' Freud's German can at times make it ambiguous whether he is talking about a person – with an expression that draws attention to the first-person perspective – or about a psychic agency of the person. This is a fruitful ambiguity. For we are trying to understand a condition of a person/ego – namely, depressed melancholia – which we understand as arising from a certain kind of split in herself (ego), in which one part of herself (ego) sets itself against another part of herself (ego). Only when we inquire into how these parts interact is there reason to conceptualize the ego as a particular psychic agency in the overall psychic structure of the self (ego). The reason this particular agency is conceptualized as ego is that it is the agency that puts itself forward as the self, and exercises authority and judgment – functions associated with being a self. Since 'ego' has by now become an English word, and is the commonly accepted translation, I am going to use it.

When the ego is split like this, there is a real question of where I am located. If I am in the superego position, I will take up the role of the accuser. I might even speak to myself in the second person:

'You shouldn't have done that!' Or: 'Jonathan, what an idiot!' Here the accent will be on unleashing criticism. If I am in the ego position, I may feel embarrassed or ashamed; I may just feel depressed with no clear idea why. That is, I may have no conscious awareness of any criticism; I just feel low, fatigued. Freud's point is that this generalized depression is the manifestation of an internal criticism of which I am unaware. It is also striking that my position can vary: at one moment I am full of cruel self-criticism; at another, I am abject and low.

But perhaps Freud's most astonishing discovery is that the focus of blame can shift from another onto oneself. If one listens carefully to the self-criticisms of the depressed person, Freud tells us, one will sometimes come to realize that the criticisms actually fit someone else. There may be some modifications to fit circumstances − and disguise what is going on − but basically the criticism reflects feelings the person has for a loved one, or some other important person in his life. 'So we find the key to the clinical picture: we perceive that the self-reproaches are reproaches against a loved object which have been shifted away from it on to the patient's own ego.'[5] (The phrase 'loved *object*' can seem cold, infelicitous. After all, Freud is talking about a person, a *subject*, who is loved. Still, Freud's point is that this subject, is nevertheless the object of *emotion*. It is a formal point. She is the person to whom the emotion is directed.) One can see straightaway how pathologies of self-assessment can arise. Suppose I hold myself responsible for falling short of an ethical ideal: I am less generous than I ought to be. But at least I have located myself in ethical space; I know the truth about myself, even if it isn't very pretty. Perhaps I can now do something about it. Freud's point is that this image of honest self-confrontation can be deceptive. What this ethical self-examination may cover over is my rage with my father for having been so ungenerous with me. My anger has been lost − or, rather, it has been displaced onto me. And as a result I am confused in my attempt to understand myself, and assess how to live with others. I take my core issue to be about generosity and selfishness, whereas my real problem is how to live with a fury and disappointment I do not understand. According to Freud, then, thinking that one is not doing a good job in taking up the question of how to live might itself be a symptom of disease. Just because one is taking ethics seriously does not at all mean that one is on the road to well-being. Note that, in this scenario, there is a strategic economy of rage. We can analyze it as having structural moments, although there is no need to suppose it must actually develop this way.

Stage one: I experience my father as being unkind to me, and feel anger arising.
Stage two: anxiety.

Perhaps I fear that my anger will cause my father to withdraw his love even more. Perhaps I fear that he will retaliate in some way. In each of these cases, I have what philosophers call propositional attitudes: I fear *that* something might happen. As we saw in Chapter 1, these are the kinds of fears that are located in what Freud called the preconscious. I may nevertheless be unaware of them – and they may be kept from consciousness in various ways. However, there is no need to suppose that the transition from stage one to stage two must be based on anything as sophisticated as propositional thought. It may simply be that having angry feelings towards my father generates anxiety. These can be elemental mental operations that occur below the level of propositional thought.

Stage three: my anger and anxiety disappear. Instead, there is an angry voice directed at me.

The anger is now finding a route of expression that feels at once safe and justified. The threat of retaliation from others is gone, and I feel I deserve the (self-) criticism. (I deserve to be punished for being angry at my father.) This is a strategic outcome that I did not choose or intend. It has the painful consequence that I am now harshly self-critical. Still, the transposition removes the threat from the external world – I no longer have to fear my father will retaliate – and that is why it has been selected.

Stage four: the angry voice disappears. All that is left is depression and low self-esteem. The anger is still getting expressed, but it is no longer recognized as such.

2 Self and other

Freud noticed that as the depressed person blames himself (rather than his father) for being ungenerous, he actually becomes ungenerous himself. In a strange way *he becomes worthy* of his self-criticism. Freud's point goes deeper than the by now familiar observation that if a person grows up in an ungenerous environment he is likely to imitate the behavior, and thus develop an ungenerous character.[6] He argues that this imitative, character-forming behavior is itself motivated by powerful fantasies, not simply to be *like* his father but to *be* him. These fantasies can be remarkably efficacious. The person can actually succeed in shaping his ego in his father's image (and thus when a person blames himself for his selfishness, it can be radically unclear where the blame is directed). Freud called this process *identification*.[7] We need to know more about what identification is and how it works. In particular, how do people's fantasies of being their mother or father actually shape who they are?

But, first, notice the ethical confusion this situation generates. To continue with the imagined example: a person blames himself for being ungenerous; and in a strange way he becomes who he takes himself to be. One might think that self-criticism could be an occasion for growth; but he is stuck in depression. And his attempts at ethical reflection only reinforce the self-criticism: as he purports to 'step back' in reflection he finds more reasons to be critical. His reflection turns out to be a repetition of, not a solution to, the problem. His problem is that he is mistaken about what the problem is. His problem is not ultimately about his lack of generosity; it is about the extent to which he is going to live his father's life. Most psychological talk won't help either. Even if one correctly comes to believe that one's unkindness is linked to certain attachments he still has towards his father, there is no reason to think that this correct insight on its own will somehow reach down to those attachments and start to undo them. This is not the place to discuss psychoanalytic technique. But it is worth noting that the peculiarities of psychoanalytic conversation are designed to facilitate a process by which psychological insight and speech is itself efficacious in reshaping the psyche. Psychoanalytic conversation is meant to bring about a fundamental change in the structure of the psyche.

How any conversation could do this is a topic worthy of philoso-phical reflection.[8]

3 The psychological birth of the infant

The psyche, Freud came to see, is itself a psychological achieve-ment. The point is not merely that the psyche develops over time, but there are distinctly psychological processes that guide and facil-itate that development. There are, to be sure, fascinating things to be learned about how the brain and neurons develop; fascinating things to learn about the relationship between brain-development and the nature of experience. But there is a further crucial issue. If we want to understand how the human psyche develops we also need to know what experience is like for *the person* whose psyche is developing. We must take the subjective nature of her experience systematically into account.[9] Psychoanalysis aims to give a rigorous account of how the psyche develops on the basis of what experience is like for the subject.

The pediatrician and psychoanalyst D.W. Winnicott, writing a generation after Freud, once said, 'There *is no such thing as a baby.*'[10] He was trying to capture the nature of infantile experience. While we are looking on from a third-person point of view we see two people in the room – a mother and her baby – from the baby's point of view there is a sea of experience. A newborn at the breast, Freud hypothesizes, does not yet have a clear sense of self and other. Infants will feel bodily excitations, as well as sensations of being held, sucking at the breast, being filled up. Slowly, the infant will give texture to an inchoate sense of inside and outside. From experiences of feeding, and then of rest and separation from the mother, the infant will gradually develop a sense that mother exists separately. 'In this way,' Freud says, 'there is for the first time set over against the ego an "object," in the form of something which exists "outside" and which is only forced to appear by a special action.'[11] One way to capture this state of affairs is to say that really a mother and infant are in the room – that is, after all, what we see from a third-person perspective. It's just that the infant is not yet in a position to grasp this reality. But what if we observers are trying to see what is really there in the room *subjectively* speaking? It is misleading to say there are two subjects in the room. Rather, we are trying to capture the subjectivity *from which* two subjects will emerge. It thus makes sense to say that there is a field of experience, a mother–infant field.[12] This is schematic as it stands; but the idea is that a sense of self and world develop correlatively from the earliest bodily and mothering experiences. An infant needs to develop her sense of where she ends and the rest of the world begins. The infant does not start with a clear sense of herself and her mother as distinct people; that sense is, rather, built up on the basis of myriad interactions. 'In this way,' Freud tells us, 'the ego detaches itself from the external world. Or, to put it more correctly, originally the ego includes everything, later it separates off an external world from itself.'[13] That is why, if we are trying to capture the reality of subjective experience, 'There is no such thing as a baby.'

The way Freud puts it is that 'a unity comparable to the ego cannot exist in the individual from the start; the ego has to be developed.'[14] A 'new psychical action' is required for the infant to develop a sense that her experiences are *her* experiences. What is the nature of this new psychical action? Before trying to answer this question, we must admit that any answer must be hypothetical. We are not able to get detailed answers from a pre-linguistic infant as to the nature of her experience. Basically, we try to answer this question by a process of triangulation.

First, Freud thought that certain aspects of adult life should be understood as a *regression* to an earlier form of experience. Precisely because the adult ego is a psychological achievement, there are possibilities for return. For instance, when some adults fall in love they have an experience that the boundaries separating them from each other have melted away, that they are immediately in touch with each other's feelings, that they can read each other's mind. Thus the intense experience of having found one's 'other half.' In this sea of experience, the question 'Whose experience is it?' loses salience. It is easy to miss the power of Freud's point. The experience is not merely one in which I daydream that I have found my 'other half.' Rather, the experience of falling in love is so powerful that I actually regress to earlier forms of mental functioning; my sense of self and other starts to melt away. Fantasy is not just a daydream with imagined content; it is a powerful form of mental activity by which the boundaries of the ego start to come undone. So, for Freud, the fact that there are occasions in adult life in which we experience the boundaries between self and other melting away is evidence that earlier in life these boundaries were not as firmly fixed as they later become.[15] Second, Freud's daughter Anna Freud, as well as Melanie Klein and D.W. Winnicott, developed techniques of psychoanalyzing children that significantly involved play. If one plays with young children who have recently acquired language, they will play games that involve swallowing or being swallowed by monsters, giving birth to babies that are inside one's tummy, and so on.[16] We take these verbal and play-acted fantasies to give us insight into the pre-linguistic infant's mind. Freud worked almost exclusively with adults, but he did advise parents on how to deal with problems their little boy was having – and obtained detailed reports on the child's experience.[17] He also made astute observations about the behavior of an infant who was just in the process of acquiring language.[18] Third, detailed empirical studies of pre-linguistic infants – for instance, turning their heads away as a form of rejection, approaching and avoiding a new object, feeding, changes in facial reactions in response to changes in the mother's face – can give us insight into the movement of the infant's emotions.[19] We know much more about infant development than Freud did, but research supports his basic account of the 'new psychical action' by which the infant develops a sense of self. 'The ego,' Freud says, 'is first and foremost a bodily ego.'[20] What he means is that the original experiences of the self are formed around experiences of bodily functions. Imagine an idealized scene of the infant at the breast. With only a rudimentary, yet emerging, sense of self, she feels a hungry, gnawing feeling. This gives her an elemental sense of inside; it is as though there is a restless, gnawing painful presence inside of her. Mother envelops her in her arms – and the baby is bathed in a calm, loving environment. The infant is now sucking at the breast; her oral cavity is filled with warm, milky, mother-stuff: and she can feel it travel down inside her, fill her tummy and extinguish the pain. She is now full of mother-stuff; it is inside her, part of her; and she falls into a quiet dream-filled sleep.

It is around such experiences that the infant develops a fantasy of actually taking mother inside. The fantasy is facilitated by the fact that the infant doesn't have a clear sense of where mother begins or ends. And in some sense the infant is right: she *does* now have some of mother inside her. Freud called this bodily fantasy of taking mother inside *introjection*.

Around this fantasy, certain elemental narratives can be formed. So, if the child experiences hunger pangs, it can come to seem like there is a creature inside her, gnawing away. Taking mother inside calms this creature down, makes it go away − at least, for a while. But the hunger pains come back − as will other distressing feelings of anxiety, etc. − and there will be a tendency to imagine that there is an enduring creature − a 'monster' − living inside that can be calmed down or defeated or killed by a mother who is also inside.

There is another aspect of this fantasy that is crucial: in taking mother inside, I can fantasize not merely that I am *like* her, but that I *am* her. In this idealized scenario, mother is a calm figure; and because she is calm she is calming. I am hungry, distressed, in pain; mother comes and envelops me in a sea of calming words, feelings of being held, familiar smells, and as I am fed I calm down. In calming down, I become like her. But I am like her because I now have her inside: I *am* her. At least, so the fantasy goes. Freud called this *identification*. Identification is a fantasy that I *am* someone else, or that I have the essence of that person inside me. It is not merely a fantasy that I am like the other person. It can occur at varying levels of sophistication throughout development, but its core rests on an oral fantasy of taking a substance − physical as well as mental − inside.

This account of psychic formation suggests that the pre-linguistic infant has an archaic, oral 'theory' of mind.[21] She forms a rudimentary sense of self via a sense of having taken mother inside her. And in an important sense the fantasy is correct. For it is around the fantasy-activity of having mother inside her that a sense of self − a sense of inside versus outside develops. In this way, the fantasy of introjection has real efficacy. And Freud thinks that the infant is thus capable of expressing a precursor to linguistic judgment. Once we have language, we use it to affirm and deny things; but

in the language of the oldest − the oral − instinctual impulses, the judgment is: 'I should like to eat this' or 'I should like to spit it out'; and, put more generally: 'I should like to take this

into myself and to keep that out.' That is to say: 'It shall be
inside me' or 'it shall be outside me.'[22]

Basically, the infant is motivated to take pleasurable things inside,
and to fantasize getting rid of bad things by spitting, vomiting,
urinating and defecating. This is a fantasy Freud called *projection*.

Because these bodily fantasies are primordial, in times of psychological stress people will return to them. From a psychoanalytic
point of view, it is no surprise that as children go through puberty,
or leave home to go off to college, they begin to suffer from eating
disorders.[23] Nor is it surprising that throughout life, anxiety is
expressed in an upset stomach, an irritable bowel or an urgent need
to urinate. Moreover, even in psychic health, we find that our language of emotions is laden with corporeal metaphors. So, a person
is made to 'eat his words,' 'cough up a confession,' 'spit it out.' We
get things off our chests, out from inside us, and so on.

4 Identification

Freud says that identification is 'the earliest expression of an emotional tie with another person.'[24] The first identificatory fantasies, as
we have seen are oral; but more sophisticated fantasies of identification occur throughout childhood. And as the child gains a more
independent sense of herself, the possibility opens of relating to her
parents in two different ways. As she comes to see herself as one
person in the world among others, she can relate to a parent either
as someone else in the world, whom she loves or hates or desires;
or she can relate to the parent as though she were that person.
In the former case, Freud says, the child is choosing the parent as
an object; the parent is whom she would like *to have*. In the latter
case, the child is identifying with the parent; the parent is whom
she would like *to be*. And this is not just a daydream: identification
can have real efficacy. As Freud tells us, 'identification endeavors to
mould a person's own ego after the fashion of the one that has been
taken as a model.'[25] Freud gives an example of how an identificatory symptom can emerge. A little girl will develop a cough in
imitation of her mother. Note how easy it is to develop a cough. She
can come by it honestly – as when she catches a cold – and then

hold onto it by continuing to cough. The coughing will keep her throat raw, and she'll feel a continued need to cough. Or she might feel a faint tickle in her throat. Or she might just spontaneously try out a cough. Once she's started, the coughing will tend to maintain itself. There is no need for her to have any propositional thought, 'I want to be just like mommy; she has a cough, therefore I'll cough just like her.' She has just started coughing; and in coughing she is like mommy. Once the cough is in place, it becomes a magnet for personal meanings:

- In coughing, I am not just like mommy, I am mommy. This is mommy's cough and I am coughing mommy's cough.
- In having the mommy-cough, I can take mommy's place. I put myself in the mommy position and now I will be attractive to daddy in the way that a mommy is (we shall discuss the Oedipus complex in the next section).
- In having the mommy-cough I express my love and admiration for mommy by imitating her.
- In having the mommy-cough I express my resentment for mommy, by getting rid of her and making her superfluous.
- In having the mommy-cough I am also punished for having all these bad desires.

As Freud puts it, 'You wanted to be your mother, and now you are – anyhow so far as your sufferings are concerned.' Freud said this was 'the complete mechanism of the structure of a hysterical symptom.'[26] Thus might a girl develop into a young woman who experiences herself as an ill person. Through identification with her mother, she experiences illness as that special something that makes her attractive. And she is right, at least to the extent that through illness she commands the attention of those around her. But the illness also serves as punishment for her rivalrous ambitions. And it is a means through which she inhibits herself: she can use her illness to constrict her life in all sorts of ways.[27] This is what Freud means when he says that 'the shadow of the object falls on the ego.' The young neurotic woman – who suffers illness after illness – is suffering in the shadow of her mother, although she has little understanding that this is her situation.[28]

5 The Oedipus complex

On the basis of his own analysis and the analysis of others, Freud came to think that there was a childhood crisis that was constitutive of the human condition. He called this crisis the Oedipus complex, and he thought it had a profound effect in structuring the psyche. It was on the basis of the Oedipus complex and its fate that he thought he was justified in making universal claims about the structure of the human psyche. Freud has been criticized for not taking sufficient account of the wide variation in family structures across cultures. And it is true that his specific formulation is especially appropriate for the nuclear families of bourgeois modernity. However, I think it a mistake to conclude that he was only tracking a local cultural problem. But to get to the formulation of a problem that is at least a candidate for being a human problem, we need to find the right level of generality. We need to describe a condition that will remain constant over variations in family structure. In its most general formulation, the relevant conditions are:

1 Helplessness: humans are born dependent on (some kind of) parenting and nurturing to survive. And infants have elemental experiences of dependency.
2 Ambivalence: whatever the parenting situation is, the infant will form loving and aggressive feelings towards the parenting figures.
3 Prohibition: as children begin to enter society – that is, as they enter social relations with parenting figures – they will be forced to abandon certain aspirations of acting on their feelings of love and hate.

When the parenting figures are in fact biological parents, this third condition is acquiescence to the incest taboo. Freud considered the incest taboo as constitutional of society.[29] Even when the parenting figures are not biological parents, one should expect a counterpart of the incest taboo to hold. For society tends to require that children eventually separate from their parenting figures, and form significant attachments to other members of the larger group. This facilitates the survival of the society, in part by encouraging reproduction, in part by fostering emotional ties amongst the members.

So, in its most general form, the Oedipus complex is a challenge each child confronts, which might be expressed thus: how do I, as a psycho-sexual being, enter society?

The paradigmatic Oedipus that concerned Freud was the hero of Sophocles' *Oedipus the tyrant*: a man fated before he was born to marry his mother and kill his father and who, in adult life, discovers that, unbeknown to himself, he has already lived out his fate. Freud argues that on the right interpretation, this myth describes us all, man and woman, boy and girl. But he calls his interpretation a 'simplification,' a 'schematization,' which he admits does not likely occur as such in human beings.[30] In its 'simplified form' the child will be attracted erotically to the parent of the opposite sex; and will identify with the same-sex parent. The little boy wants to have his mother and be his father; the little girl wants to be her mother and have her father. For a while these emotions coexist, but eventually the child sees the same-sex parent as an obstacle to having the other parent. At this point, the child develops hostile feelings towards the same-sex parent. Overall, then, the child's relation to the same-sex parent is ambivalent.

This is the familiar structure of the Oedipus complex – and Freud *basically admits that it never occurs*. What actually occurs, Freud thinks, is more complicated. For the child will also typically have erotic feelings towards the same-sex parent and will form identifications with the parent of the opposite sex. He called this the *negative* Oedipus complex. In this version the little boy would like to be his mother and have his father (or let his father have him). The little girl would like to be her father, and have her mother. But if a child wants to be both parents *and* wants to have both parents – and as a result of inevitable frustrations feels ambivalently towards them both – what is left of the thought that this has anything particularly to do with Oedipus?[31] The crucial feature of the childhood emotional predicament Freud describes is absent from the Oedipus myth: *emotional ambivalence towards all the important people in one's environment*. Typically there will be mother-loving feelings as well as mother-hating feelings (for getting in the way of one's desires); there will be father-loving feelings as well as father-hating feelings (for getting in the way of one's desires). And there will be mother-fearing and father-fearing feelings: perhaps they will withdraw their love or find some other way to retaliate in the face of one's hate-filled feelings. The so-called Oedipus complex – which occurs in all sorts of variations – is a childhood florescence of ambivalence towards the important people in one's life. It is an emotional crisis because the conflicting feelings are strange to the child, and the child does not have the mature resources to negotiate it.

6 The superego

The superego is an infantile solution to an infant's problem. Freud calls it the heir to the Oedipus complex.[32] It is a little difficult to follow the developmental story because both the ego and the superego are built up out of layers of identifications. The 'simplified case' (which Freud says never exists as such) is based on a nuclear family with heterosexual parents. As we have seen, such family structures can vary, and even within this family structure myriad variations are possible. Still, the 'the simplified case' sheds light on the broad structure of superego formation. Again, we can think of it in terms of structural moments.

- The child has already built up a sense of ego identity based on a series of identifications with the same-gendered parent. The little boy has a sense of himself as like his father; the little girl has a sense of herself as like her mother.
- As a result of these ego-identifications, the child begins to experience an increased sense of longing for the parent of the opposite sex. 'Since I am the mommy, the daddy is who I want to have.' 'Since I am the daddy, mommy is who I want to have.' Note that such desires only become possible after the child has a more differentiated sense of self and other.
- The child now experiences the same-gendered parent as getting in the way. 'I can't have mommy (daddy) because daddy (mommy) won't let me.'
- Fury at the same-gendered parent. And a desire to get them out of the way.
- Anxiety. (Perhaps also fear of retaliation or loss of love.)
- Identification with the same-gendered parent: but now at a level that is differentiated from the original identifications that created the ego.

This is the creation of the superego. There are three important points to note about this process. First, identification is a basic unconscious fantasy that is triggered by anxiety. In response to a threat, the child resorts to age-old mental mechanisms of taking the threatening object inside. Taking it inside is a way of containing it, gaining control over it, removing it from the external world. (This is a mental tropism of the type we discussed in Chapter 1. It is psychological activity, but it is occurring below the level of choice or intention.) Second, the outcome of this activity has strategic value. The angry feelings towards the same-gendered parent vanish. And with the angry feelings gone, the anxiety also disappears. But, third, the angry feelings find their own way to re-emerge: in the form of a critical internal voice set over against the ego: 'it confronts the ego as an ego ideal or superego.'[33] This voice is sometimes consciously heard; often it works unconsciously.

As with infantile solutions in general, they solve an immediate problem, but they create others. Thus Freud says that unconscious mental processes tend to have a fate. In this case, the ambivalence towards a loved figure in the external world is momentarily dealt with, but in its place ambivalence emerges inside the psyche. On the one hand, there are ideals set up in the ego associated with the qualities of the parent. Freud tends to call this the ego ideal. On the other hand, there is often also a terrible punishing voice, holding the ego accountable for falling short of those ideals. And there is an internal voice of prohibition: while the child ought to live up to some ideals, she is not allowed to take on all the prerogatives of the parent.[34] In short, the child starts to demand of herself that she abandon her own wishes.

We now have in place all the ingredients for Freud's famous structuring of the psyche into id, ego and superego. The id is the repository of unconscious wishes and angers. The ego, according to Freud, is in a doubly conflicted position. The first conflict is in relation to the id. The ego is charged with perception, reality testing, satisfying one's desires under the constraints of accurate beliefs about the world. But it is formed via identifications with the parents that reflect the id's wishes. The infant has wishes to have/be the parent: and reacts by introjecting the figure. Freud suggests that this is the way the ego achieves control over the id. 'When the ego assumes the features of the object,' Freud says, 'it is forcing itself, so to speak, upon the id as a love-object and is trying to make good the id's loss by saying: "Look, you can love me too – I am so like the object."'[35] Because of the ego's dependence on the id, reality testing will always be liable to wishful distortions.

The ego's second conflict is in relation to the superego, which confronts the ego for falling in too much with the id's wishes. The poignant irony is that the child has reacted to wishes for one parent, by internalizing the other parent's prohibitions – and these prohibitions now become self-imposed. And because the superego now offers a new outlet for the child's angry feelings, pathologies of self-rage can arise. All the fury that would have been directed onto the outside world is now directed onto the self.

7 Genealogy

Freud thought that he had given an account of how the moral sense emerges in humans: 'the differentiation of the superego from the ego is no matter of chance; it represents the most important characteristics of the development both of the individual and of the species.'[36] Philosophically speaking, there is a question of what significance, if any, this account has. One might think that it simply does not matter how a sense of values emerges in a person, all that matters is that it arises. We can then assess our capacity to live with these values in its own terms. Freud thinks otherwise.[37] For him, there is a question of how we ought to value our capacity to live with values – and that question cannot be adequately addressed without knowing how the capacity comes to be. We shall assess Freud's genealogical account of large cultural formations, like morality and religious belief, in the next chapter. In the remainder of this chapter, we shall focus on the consequences for the individual.

Freud thought that the ways values come to be established make them legitimate objects of suspicion. For three reasons: first, to the extent that values are internalized in order to repress angry and wishful impulses of the id, they keep a person in the dark about what his feelings are. A person may sincerely consider himself to be a kind person, and he thereby keeps himself from an awareness of his cruel impulses.

Second, Freud argued that there were hidden, dynamic relations between the forbidden id-impulses, and the forbidding superego commands. The commandment 'Thou shall not be cruel' – or, more benignly, 'Always be kind' – can have its own cruelty in it. In this way, cruelty finds a distorted way of getting itself expressed. 'Thus the superego is always close to the id and can act as its representative vis-à-vis the ego. It reaches deep down into the id and for that reason is farther from consciousness than the ego is.'[38] What is 'highest' and what is 'lowest' in humans are, Freud argues, intimately related.

Third, because of this intimate relation between id and superego, our values can make us ill. Remember, the superego arises in the first place because the child is threatened by his own angry feelings directed at one or other parent. These angry feelings disappear but – via identification and establishment of the superego – they are redirected onto the ego. And, in a cruel twist, this makes a person ever more subject to his own aggression. 'The more a man controls his aggressiveness,' Freud says, 'the more intense becomes his ideal's inclination to aggressiveness against his own ego. It is like a displacement, a turning round upon his own ego.'[39] This is the pathological self-criticism one finds in depressive melancholia: 'the excessively strong superego which has obtained a hold upon consciousness rages against the ego with merciless violence, as if it had taken possession of the whole of the sadism available in the person concerned.'[40] A person is spared the consequences of inflicting his sadism on people in the external world; he is spared the consequences of seeing himself as a sadistic person, but only at the cost of inflicting that sadism on himself. Obviously, this is pathology. But Freud challenges us to confront this question: to what extent is this an account of our acquisition of a moral capacity going badly wrong? Or to what extent does this admittedly pathological case shed light on the normal case? (We shall look into this in the next chapter.) At the least, Freud's account of the formation of psychological structure requires a significant revision of his conception of neurosis and psychoanalytic therapy. For neurosis can no longer simply be conceived in terms of repressed ideas in the unconscious. Similarly, the aim of therapy can no longer be understood simply as 'making the unconscious conscious.' Neurosis must now be understood in terms of structural conflict: the parts of the psyche are at odds with each other. It would seem that if we are going to make the unconscious conscious, what needs to be made conscious is the overall structure and dynamic interactions of the psyche. And that needs to be made conscious, not as an intellectual achievement, but as a structure-changing insight. It would seem that therapy ought to aim at overcoming the belligerent relations. And that would seem to require a basic change in the structure of the psyche. For the psychic parts were originally identified by their oppositional relations to each other. If the aim of therapy is to facilitate benign and constructive communications between the various psychic parts, what is left of the idea that there are distinct parts? How are we then to conceptualize psychic structure? And how can any talking cure succeed in bringing about such fundamental psychic change?

These are questions which Freud's account of psychic structure raises – but Freud does not answer them. Freud says that 'Psychoanalysis is an instrument to enable the ego to achieve a progressive conquest of the id.'[41] Elsewhere he lays down the goal of psychoanalysis as '*Wo Es war, soll Ich werden*' – which can be translated either as 'Where id was, there ego shall become' or as 'Where it was, there I shall become.'[42] But these phrases remain enigmatic. Freud does not say what it would be to live up to these psychoanalytic values. He talks both about the repression of the Oedipus complex and about its 'dissolution': but he never spells out the difference between the two.[43] And this does create a problem, both psychoanalytically and philosophically.

We are by now familiar with the problem that a person who raises an ethical question of how to live may in fact be doing nothing more than inflicting (yet another) cruel superego punishment upon himself. But there is a new layer to the problem. Suppose such a person went into psychoanalytic therapy – and suppose that in the course of the treatment the person gives up his cruel superego and, in its place, takes on a more benign and accepting one.[44] Suppose the person was thereby relieved of her pathological guilt. She could now face her wishes and desires in less self-condemning ways. Let us even suppose that she could start to question her values in creative ways. There remains a question: how did this transformation of superego come about? Suppose it came about in more or less the same way as the superego was originally formed: during the course of the analysis, the analysand identified with her benign analyst. The old, cruel superego is modified via some new identifications, and an internal correlate of the analyst is now set up as a new, benign superego. Such an occurrence is compatible with all the genuine gains listed in the previous paragraph. And yet, this is still an infantile solution to an infantile problem. Psychoanalytically speaking, the defensive function of superego formation is getting overlooked.[45] Even if the outcome is a benign superego, to what extent is this a defense against aggressive feelings the analysand might still harbor towards the analyst?[46] After all, the superego was originally formed via unconscious processes of identification in order to avoid angry feelings towards the parent. To what extent is this getting repeated in the analysis, and being labelled a therapeutic success? And if the overall goal of the analysis is to make the unconscious conscious, to what extent does this 'success' still rely on unanalyzed unconscious processes? Is this not just a repetition of the same old infantile unconscious drama all over again?

Philosophically speaking, how can we think of this as a genuine increase in a person's psychological freedom, rather than as the rote substitution of one valuing system for another? Even if there is a genuine increase in a person's psychological flexibility, isn't the question of genealogy still relevant? For if what we see as flexibility is really just the analyst's superego implanted in the analysand, how can this be freedom? This question is not unanswerable; but it remains unanswered. It is a question that Freud's account of psychological structure raises.

Further reading

Readings from Freud

'Mourning and melancholia,' SE XIV: 237–58. A classic. It shows how Freud gained insight into psychological structure and object relations by a differential study of depression and mourning.

Group psychology and the analysis of the ego, SE XVIII: 69–143. An interesting study of group formation. It argues that the psychological structure of individuals is fluid and variable. An attempt to give a psychoanalytic account of group phenomena.

The ego and the id, SE XIX: 13–66. Freud's definitive account of psychological structure.

'The dissolution of the Oedipus complex,' SE XXII: 173–79. Freud's account of life after Oedipus.

'On narcissism: an introduction,' SE XIV: 73–102. This is not so much an introduction of narcissism to the reader as the introduction of narcissism into
psychoanalytic theory. Freud argues that, contrary to first appearances, psychoanalysis can account for narcissism.

Civilization and its discontents, Chapter 1: SE XXI: 64–73. Crucial discussion of the
cruelty of the superego. Freud begins to face up to the problem of non-erotic
aggression and hatred.

Other readings

J. Lear, Therapeutic action: an earnest plea for irony (New York: Other Press, 2003).
My attempt to show how a conversation can actually alter the structure of
the psyche.

H. Loewald, 'Instinct theory, object relations and psychic structure formation,'
in The essential Loewald (Hagerstown, MD: University Publishing Group, 2000),
pp. 207–18. A Freudian account that takes seriously the idea that the psyche is
a psychological achievement.

———'The waning of the Oedipus complex,' in The essential Loewald, pp. 384–404.
Fine account of the deeper meaning of the Oedipus complex, and its passing.

Plato, Republic IV, VIII–IX. There are many good translations and editions.
A remarkably well-worked out account of psychological structure.

H. Segal, 'Notes on symbol formation', in E.B. Spillius (ed.), Melanie Klein today,
Vol. 1, Developments in theory and practice (London and New York: Routledge, 1988),
pp. 160–77.

D.W. Winnicott, The piggle: an account of the psychoanalytic treatment of a little girl
(Harmondsworth and New York: Penguin, 1983). A gripping case history of
the vicissitudes of child development.

Notes

1 Freud, 'Mourning and melancholia,' SE XIV: 245.
2 Ibid, SE XIV: 245.
3 Ibid, SE XIV: 245–46.
4 Ibid, SE XIV: 247–48.
5 Ibid, SE XIV: 248.
6 Plato, Republic II–III; Aristotle, Nicomachean ethics I–IV.
7 Freud, 'Mourning and melancholia,' SE XIV: 249.
8 I address this question in J. Lear, Therapeutic action: an earnest plea for irony (New York:
Other Press, 2003). See also, H. Loewald, 'On the therapeutic action of psychoanalysis,' in The essential Loewald (Hagerstown, MD: University Publishing Group,
2000), pp. 221–56; G. Gabbard and D. Westen, 'Rethinking the concept of
therapeutic action,' International journal of psychoanalysis 84 (2003), pp. 823–41.
9 J. Lear, Love and its place in nature: a philosophical interpretation of Freudian psychoanalysis
(New Haven: Yale University Press, 1990), p. 1.

10 D.W. Winnicott, 'Anxiety associated with insecurity,' in *Through paediatrics to psychoanalysis* (London: Hogarth Press, 1982), p. 99.

11 Freud, *Civilization and its discontents*, SE XXII: 66–67.

12 See M. Mahler, F. Pine and A. Bergman, *The psychological birth of the human infant* (London: Karnac, 1975); D.W. Winnicott, 'The depressive position in normal emotional development,' in *Through paediatrics to psychoanalysis*, pp. 262–77; D.W. Winnicott, *The child, the family and the outside world* (Harmondsworth and New York: Penguin, 1984); D.W. Winnicott, 'Mirror-role of mother and family in child development,' in *Playing and reality* (London and New York: Routledge, 1996), pp. 111–18; H. Loewald, 'Ego and reality,' in *The essential Loewald*, pp. 3–20; 'Instinct theory, object relations, and psychic structure formation,' in *The essential Loewald*, pp. 207–18.

13 Freud, *Civilization and its discontents*, SE XXII: 68.

14 Freud, 'On narcissism: an introduction,' SE XIV: 77.

15 Freud thought that one experienced similar feelings of boundaries melting away in certain kinds of religious experience. Thus he explains the oceanic feeling of being at one with the world (*Civilization and its discontents*, SE XXII: 64–73). See also his discussion of the formation of groups in *Group psychology and the analysis of the ego*, SE XVIII: 69–143. (In terms of the psychopathology of everyday life, part of the pleasure of being a sports fan is the pleasure of playing with the suspension of boundaries. I regularly hear television watchers of a game grunt, breathe heavily, speak out loud to the player: it is as though their grunt could help the player edge over the touchdown line/catch the pass/hit the ball, etc. Of course, no sane fan actually believes this; but they are acting as though the exercise of their will could make an immediate difference to the act itself. This is the basis of magical thinking: and one can find a remnant of it in the fan's experience of watching a game. For as every fan knows, there is no such thing as just watching a game.)

16 See, e.g., D.W. Winnicott, *The piggle: an account of the psychoanalytic treatment of a little girl* (Harmondsworth and New York: Penguin, 1983); M. Klein, *The psychoanalysis of children* (London: Hogarth Press, 1980); M. Klein, *Narrative of a child analysis* (London: Hogarth Press, 1984).

17 Freud, *Analysis of a phobia in a five year old boy*, SE X: 5–149.

18 Freud, 'Beyond the pleasure principle,' SE XVIII: 14–17. I discuss the child's 'fort–da'-game in Lear, *Happiness, death and the remainder of life*, pp. 90–105.

19 See, e.g., L.C. Mayes and D.J. Cohen, 'The development of a capacity for imagination in early childhood,' *Psychoanalytic study of the child* 47 (1991), pp. 23–48; P. Fonagy, *Attachment theory and psychoanalysis* (New York: Other Press, 2001); P. Fonagy, H. Steele, G. Moran, M. Steele and A. Higgitt, 'The capacity for understanding mental states: the reflective self in parent and child and its significance for security of attachment,' *Infant mental health journal* 13 (1991), pp. 200–17; M. Main, N. Kaplan and J. Cassidy, 'Security in infancy, childhood and adulthood: a move to the level of representation,' in I. Bretherton and E. Waters (eds.), *Growing points of attachment theory and research: monographs of the Society for Research in Child Development* (Chicago: University of Chicago Press, 1985), pp. 66–104;

A. Slade, 'Quality of attachment and early symbolic play,' *Developmental psychology* 17 (1987), pp. 326–35; A. Slade, J. Belsky, L. Aber, and J.L. Phelps, 'Mothers' representations of their relationships with their toddlers: links to adult attachment and observed mothering,' *Developmental psychology* 35 (1999), pp. 611–19. See also, D.W. Winnicott, 'String: a technique of communication,' in *The maturational process and the facilitating environment* (London: Hogarth Press, 1982), pp. 153–57; D.W. Winnicott, 'On the contribution of direct child observation to psychoanalysis,' in *The maturational process and the facilitating environment*, pp. 109–14.

20 Freud, *The ego and the id*, SE XIX: 26.

21 See R. Wollheim, *The thread of life* (Cambridge: Cambridge University Press, 1984), pp. 130–61.

22 Freud, 'Negation,' SE XIX: 236–37.

23 See Chapter 2, note 43 for an introduction to literature on eating disorders.

24 Freud, *Group psychology and the analysis of the ego*, SE XVIII: 105.

25 Ibid, SE XVIII: 106.

26 Ibid, SE XVIII: 106.

27 See for example the discussion of Elizabeth von R in Chapter 2.

28 Freud, *Group psychology and the analysis of the ego*, SE XVIII: 109.

29 Freud, *Civilization and its discontents*, SE XXI: 104; *Moses and monotheism*, SE XXIII: 82, 120. See also R. Paul, *Moses and civilization: the meaning behind Freud's myth* (New Haven: Yale University Press, 1996); and C. Lévi-Strauss, *The elementary structures of kinship* (Boston: Beacon Press, 1969).

30 Freud, *The ego and the id*, SE XIX: 31–33. See pp. 31–39 for an extended account of the Oedipus complex.

31 Freud says that the negative Oedipus complex occurs because of a child's inherent bisexuality. 'It is this complicating element introduced by bisexuality that makes it so difficult to obtain a clear view of the facts in connection with the earliest object-choices and identifications, and still more difficult to describe them intelligibly' (*The ego and the id*, SE XIX: 33). This way of looking at the situation assumes that there are determinate facts about these early object-choices and identifications, and our problem is getting a clear view. Another way to look at it would be to assume that, at this early stage of emotional development, identifications and object-choices emerge out of a less differentiated emotional field. The infant is in some sense object-related from the beginning and in some sense forming identifications. There may then be no determinate facts – object-choice or identification? – to get a clear view of. Thus it is misleading to describe the child as bisexual – as though there were two distinct currents of sexual attraction in the child, one directed towards women, the other towards men. The child is emotionally attached to both of his parents – and it just happens that they tend to be of two sexes. If the child had three parents of three sexes, he or she would be tri-sexual (not because of three distinct sexual currents inside her, but because she was emotionally involved with all her parenting figures). If we take bisexuality seriously as a distinct attraction to both sexes, then it seems more in accord with Freud's account to say that bisexuality can arise out of the Oedipus complex; it is not a precondition for it.

32 Freud, *The ego and the id*, SE XIX: 36.

33 Ibid, SE XIX: 34.

34 Ibid, SE XIX: 34.

35 Ibid, SE XIX: 30.

36 Ibid, SE XIX: 35.

37 And in this he resembles his philosophical contemporary, Nietzsche.

38 Freud, *The ego and the id*, SE XIX: 48–49.

39 Ibid, SE XIX: 54.

40 Ibid, SE XIX: 53.

41 Ibid, SE XIX: 56.

42 Freud, *New introductory lectures on psychoanalysis*, SE XXII: 80; Lear, *Love and its place in nature*, p. 168.

43 See Freud, 'The dissolution of the Oedipus complex,' SE XIX: 173–79. See also, H. Loewald, 'The waning of the Oedipus complex,' in *The essential Loewald*, pp. 384–404.

44 See J. Strachey, 'The nature of the therapeutic action in psychoanalysis,' in A. Esman (ed.), *Essential papers on transference*, pp. 49–79. Freud occasionally uses the term *ego ideal* to designate a model or paradigm to which a person attempts to conform. It is formed via narcissistic identification by the parents. Freud does not develop his theory of the ego ideal in any detail. But it seems to function as that part of the superego that holds out an ideal for a person to aspire to fulfill as an ego-identification. See, for example, Freud, 'On narcissism: an introduction,' SE XIV: 94–95; *Group psychology and the analysis of the ego*, SE XVIII: 116, 129; *The ego and the id*, SE XIX: 34. The suggestion here is that in the analysis – via a series of narcissistic identifications with the analyst – the analysand is able to exchange what had been a punishing superego for a benign ego ideal. That is, this benign ideal would now play a central role in the analysand's superego functioning.

45 Paul Gray, '"Developmental lag" in the evolution of technique', in *The ego and analysis of defense* (Northvale, NJ: Aronson, 1994), pp. 29–61.

46 See L. Levenson, 'Superego defense analysis in the termination phase,' *Journal of the American Psychoanalytic Association* 46 (1998), pp. 847–66.

Seven
Morality and religion

1 The case against morality

Freud is famous for offering a psychoanalytic critique of morality and religious belief. It is as though he puts Western civilization itself on the couch. His aim is 'to make the unconscious conscious' – that is, he wants to show that morality and religious belief have different origins and serve different purposes than they claim. These are grand reflections about the meaning of civilization. In my opinion, they are – or, more accurately, they *have become* – the least valuable aspect of Freud's work. Perhaps in their time they served as a moment of critique. They do show ways that people can make use of moral or religious systems to gratify unconscious needs. But it is quite a stretch from that claim to the claim that this is the hidden meaning of religion and morality. To justify this latter claim, Freud would need an argument that the possibilities he uncovers are all the possibilities there are when it comes to morality and religion. Freud gives no such argument. Rather, he puts forward two paradigms – and invites readers to join him in thinking that this is all morality and religion amount to. The problem is not just a flaw in Freud's argument. There have been terrible human costs in going along with him. For generations, psychoanalytic institutes refused to train people who admitted to religious belief, on the grounds that they were fixated on unresolved infantile wishes. We do not know how many religiously oriented people – who might otherwise have benefited from psychoanalytic treatment – stayed away because they feared that analysts would try to talk them out of their commitments. We have reports from analysts that analysands found it difficult to talk about their religious beliefs, assuming ahead of time that their analysts must be atheists. They also report that analysands who were atheists assumed a kind of 'knowing alliance' with the analyst – and one can only wonder how often that went unanalyzed.[1] But the harm is not just what these individuals have suffered. As a result, the psychoanalytic profession deprived itself of a nuanced understanding of what the analysis of religiously committed individuals might look like. In a similar vein, it deprived itself of an opportunity to contribute to a robust conception of a flourishing ethical life – because it assumed that morality must be a system of repression and discontent. The aim of this chapter is ground-clearing.

In introducing the reader to Freud's critiques of morality and religion, I will show the limits of their validity. Seeing how Freud's arguments fall short will, I hope, open up possibilities for a deeper psychoanalytic understanding of the meanings of moral and ethical commitments in human life. This ought to make possible a more robust moral psychology.

Freud's critiques of morality and religious belief have the form of a genealogy. In general, genealogies are stories of origins that are meant to have evaluative force. There are two dimensions along which a genealogy can be classified. First, genealogies can be either *legitimating* or *de-legitimating* in intent.[2] That is, a genealogy can seek either to valorize or to undermine via its account of how something comes to be. Second, the account can be broadly naturalistic or supernatural. Either it limits itself to an account of how something could come to be as a phenomenon of nature; or it draws on a source transcending nature as part of the account of origin. In principle, a legitimating genealogy could be either naturalistic or supernatural, and similarly for a de-legitimating one. But the original genealogies tended to be legitimating and supernatural. So, for example, the first recorded use in the *Oxford English Dictionary* is from 1300: 'Tuix Abraham and king daui, Yee herken nov be geneologi.'[3] This genealogy is intended as a pedigree that reveals divine sanction. It valorizes Daui, and legitimates his reign, by claiming that he descends from Abraham. And Abraham is chosen by God.

By contrast, Freud's argument claims to be naturalistic and de-legitimating: if we come to understand how morality arises as a natural phenomenon – as a set of institutions and practices in which human beings come to participate – we shall see that its own claims to legitimacy are false. Even worse, we shall discover that morality's actual aims run counter to its purported aims, and that morality is actually inimical to human well-being. As was said at the beginning of this book, Freud was not a philosopher. He seems ignorant of the ancient Greek approaches to ethics, in which the virtues – or excellences of character – are seen as contributing to a happy life.[4] And although he does mention Kant's categorical imperative, he is not concerned with its place in the overall Kantian approach to practical reason. It is cited more as a moral dictum, along the lines of the golden rule. Freud is concerned with morality as it is lived in society – or, as it was lived in early twentieth-century Europe. These were a normatively governed set of practices and understandings of how one ought to behave with respect to others. Insofar as justification was invoked, it was by appeal to the Ten Commandments and the teachings of Jesus – in particular, his teaching to love thy neighbor as thyself. In Freud's view, society's justification for its moral practices is a legitimating, supernatural genealogy. In response, Freud is going to offer a naturalistic, de-legitimating genealogy of those same practices. Freud's account of the rise of a moral capacity in humans is broadly Darwinian in structure: he gives an account of how the moral capacity comes to be selected in humans. Such an account shows how a phenomenon – such as the capacity for morality – can arise even though no one chose or designed it.

As we saw in the last chapter, Freud thinks the human capacity for morality arises largely as a solution to the problem of aggression. On the one hand, aggression has been selected in humans: our non-aggressive predecessors tended to get killed off before they could reproduce. On the other hand, if humans were merely aggressive animals, they would kill but they would also be under constant threat of being killed. A better solution to the problem of survival is that humans should be able to form societies that can protect their members from the aggression of other societies as well as from the menaces of nature. Society thus needs to be a way of minimizing the aggressive impulses of members of society against each other. So far, Freud's genealogy is similar to various accounts that have been given in the philosophical tradition.[5] What makes Freud's case distinctive is his account of *how* human aggression is deployed in the service of curbing aggression. For what happens to the inhibited aggression?

> Something very remarkable, which we should never have guessed and which is nevertheless quite obvious. His aggressiveness is introjected, internalized; it is in point of fact, sent back to where it came from − that is, directed toward his own ego. There it is taken over by a portion of the ego which sets itself over against the rest of the ego as superego, and which now in the form of conscience, is ready to put into action against the ego the same harsh aggressiveness that the ego would have liked to satisfy upon other extraneous individuals.[6]

But how does civilization do this? After all, civilization is not itself an actor, a participant in history. Freud needs a naturalistic account of how this 'achievement' of civilization comes to be. Only then will Freud distinguish himself from Nietzsche. In *On the genealogy of morality*, Nietzsche argues that guilt and bad conscience result from human aggression turned in on the self.[7] But he gives no account of how this transformation occurs. Freud, by contrast, tries to work out a dynamic psychological account of how this inversion of aggression comes about.[8] His account is derived from his clinical work with patients, and it has two aspects.

The first aspect concerns socialization within the family. As we saw in our discussion of the Oedipus complex in the last chapter, the process of a child entering the family necessarily involves some turning inward of aggression. Here Freud describes it at the right level of generality:

> A considerable amount of aggressiveness must be developed in the child against the authority which prevents him from having his first, but none the less most important, satisfactions ... but he is obliged to renounce the satisfaction of this revengeful aggressiveness. He finds his way out of this economically difficult situation with the help of familiar mechanisms. By means of identification he takes the unattackable authority into

himself. The authority now turns into his superego and enters into possession of all the aggressiveness which a child would have liked to exercise against it.[9]

This is a strategic outcome no one planned. As we have seen, these are basic mental tropisms that are not themselves the outcome of choice. Once lodged inside, the superego figure becomes a vehicle through which the child's own aggression is now turned on herself. This configuration is selected because it is socially advantageous.

The second aspect is the social institution of morality. Morality provides a cultural vehicle by which the psychic transformation of the child is reinforced and given a particular cultural form. Morality functions as a 'cultural superego': it provides an explicit and shared set of practices, customs and rules that bind the members of society together both socially and psychically. These are rules that can be internalized; and as such they come to form part of the adult's superego. The individual members of society are bound together in part because each person's superego has been shaped according to a common cultural template. This is the psychic precipitate of morality. According to Freud, morality is basically a set of cultural practices and precepts that takes hold of the natural vicissitudes of the Oedipus complex and turns them to society's advantage.

This account of how morality comes to take hold has a number of significant consequences – none of them pleasant for the individual:

- Morality makes us unhappy.

The idea that morality promotes human happiness or fulfillment is, Freud thinks, exposed as wishful fantasy. For the psychic structure that morality fosters is a structure of individual human suffering: a punishing superego is set over against an inhibited ego. Outwardly and consciously, the person may be an upstanding member of society. Inwardly, and perhaps unconsciously, he is inhibited from pursuing his desires; and thus lives in frustration. Virtue is not its own reward.[10] Indeed, the moral life, according to Freud, is necessarily and constitutionally a life of suffering. 'The two processes of individual and cultural development must stand in hostile opposition to each other, and mutually dispute the ground.'[11]

- The relation between individual and society is necessarily unharmonious.

Freud understood that this insight was unsettling because it provided a blow to 'the naive self-love of men' – the sense of their deserved place in the world.[12] Society is not there to serve human purposes, humans are there to serve society – often at significant psychic cost to themselves. A person may carve out a life for herself in society; but the essence of morality, Freud thinks, is constraint and prohibition. Morality is the institution that distorts individual human well-being for the sake of civilization.

- Morality facilitates a special kind of viciousness.

The prohibitions of morality are not just demands of society; they are internalized and become prohibitions of a person's own superego. Since the superego is sensitive to a person's thoughts as well as deeds, there is no place to hide.[13] A person's wishful and aggressive thoughts will inevitably contradict the prohibitions of society. And thus people will inevitably incur the wrath of their own superegos. Guilt is thus an inevitable condition of living in civilization. And given the way in which the superego enables people to turn their aggression onto themselves, a truly terrifying economy is established:

> here at last comes an idea which belongs entirely to psycho-analysis and which is foreign to people's ordinary way of thinking. This idea is of a sort which enables us to understand why the subject-matter was bound to seem so confused and obscure to us. For it tells us that conscience (or more correctly the anxiety that becomes conscience) is indeed the cause of instinctual renunciation to begin with, but that later the relationship is reversed. Every renunciation of instinct now becomes a dynamic source of conscience and every fresh renunciation increases the latter's severity and intolerance.[14]

This is a kind of sorcerer's apprentice of moral asceticism: the more 'moral' one becomes, the more aggression is inhibited from discharge in the social world, and thus it is turned inward on oneself.

There arises the furiously moral person – the 'saint' – who takes himself to be such a sinner. Freud thinks that such a person has a basically correct assessment of his internal situation. So too arises the phenomenon Freud called moral masochism: the person perversely dedicated to castigating himself for being so awful.

2 The morality system

Freud has, I think, given a psychodynamic account of what the philosopher Bernard Williams called 'the morality system.'[15] This is 'a *special* system, a *particular variety* of ethical thought.' Williams thinks that in coming to understand it we will at the same time see 'why we would be better off without it.'[16] Note that the critique is not about moral life *per se*, but about an unhealthy yet ultimately optional distortion. The morality system, Williams argues, takes our ordinary notion of obligation, which on its own has important uses, and turns it into a special, highly charged notion of *moral* obligation – to which it attaches too much significance.

> Moral obligation is inescapable. ... Once I am under the obligation there is no escaping it, and the fact that a given agent would prefer not to be in this system or bound by its rules will not excuse him; nor will blaming him be based on a misunderstanding. Blame is the characteristic reaction of the morality system. The remorse or self-reproach or guilt ... is the characteristic first-personal reaction within the system, and if an agent never felt such sentiments, he would not belong to the morality system or be a full moral agent in its terms.[17]

The morality system, Williams tells us, tries to turn everything into an obligation and it 'encourages the idea, *only an obligation can beat an obligation.*'[18]

In morality so conceived, we have a closed system of blame and guilt with no upper bound on stringency and no escape from obligation. Freud gives the psychological account of how this system can take hold of us. But he also raises a problem for Williams about the difficulty of a way out. Williams says: 'In order to see around the intimidating structure that morality has made out of the idea of obligation, we need an account of what obligations are when they are rightly seen as merely one kind of ethical consideration among others. This account will help to lead us away from morality's special notion of moral obligation, and eventually out of the morality system altogether.'[19] From a Freudian perspective, Williams is being too optimistic about the power of a thoughtfully reasoned 'account' to lead us out of the morality system. If Freud is right about the psychodynamics by which the morality system takes hold of us, then a reasoned account on its own will not do the trick. We need a psychodynamic account about how, over time, the morality system might loosen its grip. What would be required for the superego to give up its punishing stance of guilt and obligation? What cultural developments might facilitate this process in terms of large-scale cultural shifts? And is there a particular form of political critique that would be appropriate – one that used psychoanalytic insight to offer alternatives to political societies that make undue use of the morality system to organize and subdue its citizens? These are the kind of questions an informed psychoanalysis might help us answer. Freud had a marvelous ability to turn a problem – for instance, transfer-ence – into a solution. If the problem of the morality system is a punishing superego, why isn't the solution the conditions of healthy relations between ego and superego? This would be a natural place for psychoanalysis to make a lasting contribution to moral psychology. In effect, this is what would be involved in taking up the inheritance of an Aristotelian approach. For Aristotle, as for Plato before him, happiness required psychic harmony between the rational and non-rational parts of the soul – and such harmony was a condition of an ethically virtuous life. If Freud had been able to make the same kind of move as he made with transference, he would have gone from intrapsychic relations as a problem for moral life, to intrapsychic relations as the conditions for a satisfying moral life.

3 Pleasure versus happiness

I suspect there is a contingent reason he did not go down this route: in his theoretical research he focused on pleasure, rather than on happiness. His concern with pleasure goes back to the beginning of his career, long before he had a structural theory of the mind – and thus before he could formulate an Aristotelian approach to moral psychology. What attracted him to the phenomenon of pleasure is that he thought he could give a quasi-mechanistic account of it. It fit his conception of a naturalistic project by which one could plausibly show how complex workings of the mind could be built up from elementary operations of a 'psychic mechanism.' The aim of the psychic mechanism, as he conceived it, was to discharge pent-up psychic energy, and this discharge was experienced as pleasure.[20] This schematic picture has heuristic value: humans do live under psychic pressure, and Freud was a master at charting the myriad ways they seek release. But this picture also blinkered Freud's thinking. For if built-up tension is in itself unpleasurable, it becomes easy to assume that such tension is itself a condition of unhappiness. If one holds onto this theory of pleasure-as-discharge, the subsequent discovery of psychological structure will not seem like an occasion to rethink the possibilities of human happiness. The ego and superego are variously in the business of inhibiting, reshaping, redirecting the wishes of the id. But if the gratification of these wishes would provide the most immediate and direct discharge, it should provide the most pleasure. According to this mechanistic theory, then, psychological structure itself inhibits pleasure and is thus an occasion for unpleasure. Again it becomes easy to assume that psychic structure inevitably causes unhappiness. This would seem to be confirmed by Freud's clinical realization that a punishing superego was the key to the individual's discontent in civilization. Since the human condition would then appear to be inevitably bound up with unhappiness, the only real questions would be how to minimize it and fend off pathological distortions. There would not be room for the question of a psychologically harmonious, happy ethical life to arise. None of this reasoning is ultimately justified, but one can see how it hangs together. There were disruptions in Freud's thought that could have been the basis for a thorough reconceptualization of his theory of pleasure. By the time he wrote 'The economic problem of masochism' (1924), Freud realized that increases in tension can be pleasurable.[21] This recognition could have been an occasion to consider how certain forms of tension-filled dynamic psychological structure could in themselves be pleasurable. For whatever reason, Freud did not take up this opportunity, and thus he was not in a position to use the discovery of psychological structure to think afresh about the possibilities for human happiness.

4 Critique of religious belief

Freud argued that religious belief is illusion. He meant this in a precise sense: a belief is an *illusion* if it is derived from human wishes.[22] Illusions are by their very nature misleading. For people take their beliefs to be responsive to the way things are. So if a belief is held in place by wishes, people are misled about their orientation to the world. Beliefs can be true or false; the same holds for illusions. It is not out of the question for an illusion to be true. The essential problem for an illusion, then, is that we are mistaken about the basis of our commitment to it. We take it to be a belief based on responsiveness to the world; in fact, it is held in place by primordial wishes of which we are unconscious.

Freud's argument is oblique. He does not address religion directly; and ostensibly he makes no claims about whether religious beliefs are true or false.[23] His claim is rather that religious beliefs are illusions. That is, whatever the truth of religious claims, the fact that we believe them is not based on that truth, but rather on infantile wishes. His expectation seems to be that once we recognize these beliefs as illusions, and come to see the kind of wishes they gratify, the temptation towards religious belief will fall away. At the very least, we will see that we *ought* to give up religious belief.

His argument is flawed. But before looking for the flaw, it is worth noting that Freud's aim is more than the dissolution of religious belief. He is also attacking what he takes to be the foundation of morality. Morality, he thinks, depends on its claim to be carrying out the teachings of the Hebrew and Christian Bibles. The ultimate authority for morality is the Word of God. Thus morality, on Freud's understanding, provides a genealogical defense of its authority that is absolute and supernatural. In response, we can now see, Freud offers a counter-genealogy that is meant to be de-legitimating and naturalistic. We have already seen the first stage of Freud's argument by which he offers an alternative, deflationary account of how the moral capacity arises in people. We are now at the second stage in which Freud seeks to undermine morality's appeal to a religious foundation. Religious belief, Freud argues, arises from an infantile prototype: our earliest experiences of helplessness.[24] Religion emerges as a cultural elaboration of childhood fantasies whose function is to protect us against a sense of utter vulnerability. In response, Freud says, we wishfully imagine that the world is ordered according to a higher purpose and we each have a proper role within it.

> Over each one of us there watches a benevolent Providence which is only seemingly stern and which will not suffer us to become a plaything of the over-mighty and pitiless force of nature. Death itself is not extinction, is not a return to inorganic lifelessness, but the beginning of a new kind of existence which lies on the path of development to something higher.[25]

Freud diagnoses this as a manifestation in adult life of an infantile longing for the father – a wish for a powerful, protective figure.[26] This is why Freud thinks religion is an illusion: it is held in place by 'the oldest, strongest and most urgent wishes of mankind. The secret of their strength lies in the strength of those wishes.'[27] And he is scathing in his judgment: 'The whole thing is so patently infantile, so foreign to reality, that to anyone with a friendly attitude to humanity it is painful to think that the great majority of mortals will never be able to rise above this view of life.'[28] Even more pathetic, Freud thinks, are those educated people who ought to know better, but still try to defend religion 'in a series of pitiful rearguard actions.' I suspect that would be Freud's charge against the author of this chapter.

That said, there is a problem in Freud's argument. In a nutshell, it contains its own kernel of wishfulness. And this wishfulness compromises his argument. It is helpful to ask how Freud's argument is meant to persuade. That is, what is its rhetorical strategy? If we take the idea of illusion seriously, there is a question of how we could come to recognize any of our beliefs as illusions. An illusion does not seem to be an illusion to those who are in its grip. And if illusions are held in place by primordial wishes, one would expect them to be tenacious. In particular, one should not expect people to recognize their illusions simply by being told by another that their purported beliefs are illusory. So, if we are suffering from illusion, how will it help us for Freud simply to tell us that we are?

Obviously, if Freud's intended readers are only other non-believers, then there is no need to persuade them. It is easy enough for author and readers to agree that *other people* suffer from illusion. Illusion tends to be the kind of thing other people suffer from.

This would be the atheist version of preaching to the choir. The more interesting case is to think that Freud is also writing for religious believers, as well as for agnostics and those who are suspended in a limbo between belief and non-belief. How, one might ask, is Freud's diagnosis meant to reach such readers? Even if one accepts Freud's diagnosis that religious belief has a wishful component, this need not on its own give a person reason to abandon religious commitment. It is a longstanding belief among religious thinkers that, precisely because we come into the world as children, religion needs a childish – that is, age-appropriate – component. From such a religious perspective, this is the point of many myths and stories. It is thus not a criticism, from this perspective, to point out that there is an infantile dimension to religious belief. The crucial question would be: what, religiously speaking, are the possibilities for growing up? Perhaps the wishful illusions of childhood were no more than steps on a spiritual ladder that was meant to be kicked away at a later stage. To elim-inate this possibility, Freud would need to show that there is nothing to religious belief *other* than illusion. He does not try to do this. For whom then might Freud's critique function *as* a critique? The argument seems designed to appeal to three broad groups: agnostics, atheists and people who are merely going through the motions of religious rituals. Perhaps they are lazy; perhaps they are sitting on the fence. For agnostics and atheists, Freud's argument would likely seem to confirm their doubts; for the person who has been going through the motions, it might tip her into viewing her own behavior as childish. It might be a step along a path of dis-enchantment. We have examined a case where Freud's argument fails to persuade, and cases where it would. What we can see is this: whether the argument does or does not persuade does not depend on accepting Freud's premise that religious belief has a wishful component. All sides we have considered accept that. For

Freud's argument to have the rhetorical force he intended, one needs to consider the context in which he took himself to be writing. Freud took himself to be writing within an historical epoch of secularization within Europe, and he intended his critique to further that process. His argument is directed at those who have *already* lost their religious belief or those who are *already* wavering in agnosticism or those who are *already* participating in the social rituals of religion in a weak way. For such a reader, the argument may facilitate their journey towards a non-religious life. In this way, Freud takes his argument to be helping history along. But what is Freud's view of history?

5 The illusion of a future

Freud thinks we have reached an historic epoch in which we can simply see that his analysis is true. If we look to individual development, Freud says, we see that a person develops through psychological stages. In particular, the inevitable Oedipal crisis of childhood is eventually outgrown, and falls away. 'In just the same way,' he says, 'one might assume, humanity as a whole, in its development through the ages, fell into states analogous to the neuroses, and for the same reasons.'

> Religion would thus be the universal obsessional neurosis of humanity; like the obsessional neurosis of children, it arose out of the Oedipus complex, out of the relation to the father. If this view is right, it is to be supposed that a turning-away from religion is bound to occur with the fatal inevitability of a process of growth and that we find ourselves at this very juncture in the middle of that phase of development.[29]

On Freud's account, then, his interpretation will be persuasive because we are historically ready to face the truth. But just how wishful is such an image of historical progress? Freud gives us no reason to believe the history of civilization proceeds 'in just the same way' as the development of an individual out of childhood. And, of course, there are reasons to reject this picture as a progressivist fantasy. But Freud was unwilling to countenance any other explanatory hypotheses for this movement other than an inevitably emerging truth of which he is an avatar.[30] But if we look to the argument, a comparison with the Danish philosopher Søren Kierkegaard is illuminating. Kierkegaard thought that Christendom was a 'dreadful illusion.'[31] He did not, like Freud, have an explicit and technical definition of illusion. We can nevertheless see an important area of agreement with Freud.

Christendom, for Kierkegaard, referred to the totality of social practices, customs and rituals of his day that were accepted as an expression of Christian faith. To say that Christendom was an illusion was, for Kierkegaard, to say that these social practices trapped one in a misleading fantasy of religious commitment. But, for Kierkegaard, this recognition was meant to be preparatory to a more genuine religious engagement. To do this, however, one would have to buck the trends of age. The illusion of Christendom was itself part of a general decadence of the historical epoch. The modern age had produced changes in mass communication – in particular, the capacity to publish newspapers and pamphlets – and increased production in consumer goods – and this led to what Kierkegaard called the leveling of the age.[32] Newspapers tell one what one should believe – although they are doing little more than passing along unsubstantiated gossip – and advertisements tell one what one should want. This, Kierkegaard thought, led to the collapse of the individual (in particular, an individual's sense of responsibility) and in its place a 'crowd' formed, governed by rumor and fashion. In a crowd, genuine religious engagement becomes impossible. This is obviously a thumbnail sketch, but it is enough to see that while Freud and Kierkegaard start from the same phenomenon – the decline of religious conviction in contemporary Europe – and they both believe that common religious practice is illusion, they draw opposite conclusions.

Once one sees that Freud's argument need not push one in only one direction, it is easier to see the conclusion Freud does draw as wishfully heroic. He imagines a conversation with a religious interlocutor:

> We desire the same things, but you are more impatient, more exacting, and – why should I not say it? – more self-seeking

than I and those on my side. You would have the state of bliss begin directly after death; you expect the impossible from it and you will not surrender the claims of the individual. Our God, Λογος [Logos], will fulfill whichever of these wishes nature outside us allows, but he will do it very gradually, only in the unforeseeable future, and for a new generation of men. He promises no compensation for us, who suffer grievously from life. On the way to this distant goal your religious doctrines will have to be discarded, no matter whether the first attempts fail, or whether the first substitutes prove to be untenable. You know why: in the long run nothing can withstand reason and experience, and the contradiction which religion offers to both is all too palpable. Even purified religious ideas cannot escape this fate, so long as they try to preserve anything of the consolation of religion.[33]

Why should Freud of all people believe this? Has he not taught us that we are always subject to wishful and aggressive fantasies of which we are largely unaware? If so, should one not expect that whatever genuine achievements of reason and experience occur, they will tend to be fragile and subject to reversal? Whatever one thinks about religion and religious belief, one should by now see that this is less the future of an illusion, than the illusion of a future. History is assumed to be progressive, inevitable and truth-revealing. This is a triumphal story of human progress in which one can play a decisive role if only one is brave enough to face the emerging truth. Obviously, there is no reason to go along with this Enlightenment fantasy about the significance of human history.[34] So, in the name of analyzing the fantasy underlying religious belief, Freud participated in his own fantasy of inevitable historical progress, which included secularization as a hallmark of that progress. There is reason to think that this closed down Freud's curiosity: he was disposed to see religious commitment as historically retrogressive. If he could find a kernel of wishfulness in that commitment that was sufficient; it was as though there was nothing more to look for. As a result, Freud blinded himself to the possible complexity of religious belief. We are still living in Freud's shadow. Instead of assuming ahead of time that religious commitment must be illusion, we need to know more than we now do about the place of religious belief in analysands' lives. This is a place where psychoanalysis could make a contribution: helping us to understand in robust detail the myriad places of religious commitment in individuals' lives. We get in the way of that project by assuming ahead of time that there is only one such place, and we already know what it is.

6 Primal crime

Freud also had an illusion of the past. He claimed that history as we know it was inaugurated by a murder of the 'primal father' by the brothers and sons.[35] In prehistory, humans were organized in hordes. Each horde was ruled by a primal father who subjugated the other men, and had sexual access to all the women. Eventually the men banded together and killed the primal father; and society was organized around an agreement that no one else would take his place. Instead, the incest taboo was established, which facilitated the sharing of women among the men, and social relations between them. But this primal crime also laid down an archaic heritage of guilt. For the father who was hated was also the father who was loved. The murder was so traumatic that permanent memory trace was laid down in the human race – a phylogenetic inheritance as Freud called it. (Genes had not yet been discovered, but I suspect Freud would have been happy with the idea that the murder made a genetic difference; and this genetic alteration continues to be passed down through the generations.) At the end of his career, Freud makes a further astonishing claim: that the Jewish people murdered Moses as a repetition and recreation of that primal crime.[36] According to Freud, Moses was an Egyptian who tried to impose monotheism on the recalcitrant Hebrews. It is, says Freud, the murder of Moses that provokes the wishful fantasy of the return of the Messiah. And it is the cover-up of this murder that results in official Judaism taking on the form of an obsessional neurosis: structured by endless rituals of cleanliness and purification.[37] Moreover, Christ's coming and his killing was another repetition and re-creation of the primal crime:

If Moses was the first Messiah, Christ became his substitute and successor, and Paul could exclaim to the peoples with some historical justification: 'Look the Messiah has really come: he has been murdered before your eyes!' Then too there is a real piece of historical truth in Christ's resurrection, for he was the resurrected Moses and behind him the returned primal father of the primitive horde, transfigured and, as the son, put in the place of the father.

The poor Jewish people, who with their habitual stubbornness continued to disavow the father's murder, atoned heavily for it in the course of time. They were constantly met with the reproach 'You killed our God!' And this reproach is true, if it is correctly translated. If it is brought into relation with the history of religions it runs: 'you will not admit that you murdered God (the primal picture of God, the primal father, and his later reincarnations).' There should be an addition declaring: 'We did the same thing, to be sure, but we have admitted it and since then we have been absolved.'[38]

These are extraordinary claims – and they are based on almost no evidence. Freud admits that, when it comes to a memory-trace of an ancient crime, he has nothing more to go on than the tenacity of Oedipal fantasies in the psychoanalytic situation.[39] He does not think that the power of guilt, ambivalence and aggression that he sees in his neurotic patients can be explained on the basis of their imaginative and emotional life alone, nor on the basis of their experiences with others. Similarly, he did not think it possible for religion to be transmitted from generation to generation using only cultural and psychological means. To explain the tenacity with which the Jews held onto their religion it was not enough, Freud thought, to cite Jewish rituals, festivals and teachings. Nor was it enough to include an account of how wishful infantile fantasies get entwined in religious myths. In Freud's opinion, these facts alone could not explain the stubborn persistence of Judaism. There had to be an actual crime whose trace was laid down in human memory, a primal murder that was repeated by the Jews, but never acknowledged.[40] Freud is making a bold assertion, but there is really no basis for it. And if we consider the place of this speculation in the larger framework of his thought, Freud is in effect attacking his own life's work. He has spent his career showing the power of unconscious fantasy to shape a life, but when it comes to our religious lives, he claims this cannot be explained by the power of human imagination, culture and rituals alone. He is talking particularly about Judaism and Christianity: religions in which God intervenes in history and interacts with specific human individuals. Freud agrees with the religions to this extent: for these religions to be possible there must have been a significant *actual* historical event. These religions cannot, he thinks, be understood simply as a product of the human imagination. But he takes that actual event to be secular: the murder of the primal father, followed by subsequent re-enactments with Moses and then with Jesus.[41] If Freud's argument had been sound, he would have given a thoroughly naturalist account of religious experience. Obviously, it is in principle possible to give a naturalist account only invoking human imagination and culture. But by invoking an actual event, Freud thought he had uncovered the hidden meaning of these fantasies. He thought he had given a secular and naturalist counterpart to original sin (the primal crime) and to the transmission of hereditary sin (phylogenetic inheritance). Without the actual crime, there would always be a question of why human imagination and culture took this form rather than some other – and there would be no place to look other than further delving into imagination and culture. Freud wants the primal crime to serve as an Archimedean point. But this isn't an Archimedean point; it's a fantasy of having achieved one. In effect, Freud constructs his own myth of origins. He hides this from himself by cloaking his myth in the garb of a naturalistic account of human development. Freudian psychoanalysis aims to be a naturalistic account of human mental life – an account that includes culture, rituals and social institutions. It is within this important project that Freud embeds his own illusion: that science will answer the fundamental question of how to live. So, he thinks that any rational person who accepts the findings of science *ought* to give up religious belief. This is a wishful illusion of rationality and scientific progress. It captured Freud's imagination, but there is no reason for us to be in its thrall.

Further reading

Readings from Freud

Civilization and its discontents, SE XXI: 57–145. Presents Freud's argument that humans are necessarily uncomfortable, not at home, in civilization. This is his critique of morality as a social institution.

The future of an illusion, SE XXI: 1–56. His critique of religious belief as illusion.

Moses and monotheism, SE XXIII: 1–137. His argument that Moses was in fact an Egyptian, killed by the Jews in a repetition of the primal crime. That monotheism arises out of guilt for that crime.

Other readings

R. B. Blass, 'Beyond illusion: psychoanalysis and the question of religious truth,' *International journal of psychoanalysis*, 85 (2004), pp. 615–34.

J. Cottingham, *Philosophy and the good life* (Cambridge: Cambridge University Press, 1998). How psychoanalytic ideas can be used in an ethics that emphasizes human flourishing.

S. Kierkegaard, *The present age*, trans. W. Kaufmann (New York: Harper and Row, 1962). Gives a similar critique of the moral and religious *social* institutions of nineteenth-century Europe but, unlike Freud, uses that as an occasion for renewed moral and religious commitment.

J. Lacan, *The ethics of psychoanalysis, 1959–1960; The seminar of Jacques Lacan Book VII* (London and New York: Routledge, 1992). Makes stunning use of Freud's insight into the dynamics of aggression and guilt. Difficult and obscure, but worth the effort.

W.W. Meissner, *Psychoanalysis and religious experience* (New Haven: Yale University Press, 1984).

F. Nietzsche, *On the genealogy of morality*, trans. C. Diethe (Cambridge: Cambridge University Press, 1994). A similar tale to Freud's, told with breathtaking panache.

R. Paul, *Moses and civilization: the meaning behind Freud's myth* (New Haven: Yale University Press, 1996). If one has to pick one's all-time favorite in the secondary literature on Freud, this is my choice. It reads like a detective novel, and makes stunning use of Freud's account of the Moses myth.

Notes

1 See H. Loewald, 'Psychoanalysis and modern views on human existence and religious experience', *Journal of pastoral care* 7, no. 1 (1953), pp. 1–15.

2 See Raymond Geuss' helpful article, 'Nietzsche and genealogy', *European Journal of Philosophy* 2, no. 3 (December, 1994), pp. 274–92.

3 *Oxford English Dictionary Online* (Oxford University Press, 2004).

4 When Freud does talk about virtue, he is referring to the Judeo-Christian conception. See J. Church, 'Morality and the internalized other,' in J. Neu (ed.), *The Cambridge companion to Freud* (Cambridge: Cambridge University Press, 1991), pp. 209–23.

5 See, for example, the case that Thrasymachus makes in *Republic* I and Glaucon makes in *Republic* II. And see T. Hobbes, *Leviathan* (Harmondsworth and New York: Penguin, 1985).

6 Freud, *Civilization and its discontents*, SE XXI: 123–24.

7 F. Nietzsche, 'Second essay: "guilt," "bad conscience" and related matters,' in *On the genealogy of morality*, trans. C. Diethe (Cambridge: Cambridge University Press, 1994), pp. 38–71.

8 I discuss this in Lear, 'The idea of a moral psychology: the impact of psychoanalysis on philosophy in Britain,' *International journal of psychoanalysis* 84 (2003), pp. 1351–61.

9 Freud, *Civilization and its discontents*, SE XXI: 129–30.

10 Ibid, SE XXI: 125–26.

11 Ibid, SE XXI: 141.

12 See, for example, *Introductory lectures on psychoanalysis*, SE XVI: 284–85; 'A difficulty in psychoanalysis,' SE XVII: 140; 'Resistances to psychoanalysis,' SE XIX: 221.

13 Freud, *Civilization and its discontents*, SE XXI: 125; cf. 127–28.

14 Ibid, SE XXI: 129. Cf. Lacan, *The ethics of psychoanalysis, 1959–1960; The seminar of Jacques Lacan Book VII* (London and New York: Routledge, 1992), pp. 191–204.

15 Bernard Williams, *Ethics and the limits of philosophy* (Cambridge MA: Harvard University Press, 1985), pp. 174–96.

16 Ibid, p. 174, my emphasis.

17 Ibid, p. 177.

18 Ibid, p. 180.

19 Ibid, p. 182.

20 Freud, *Project for a scientific psychology*, SE I: 295–397; *The interpretation of dreams*, SE V: 533–625.

21 Freud, 'The economic problem of masochism,' SE XIX: 159–70.

22 Freud, *The future of an illusion*, SE XXI: 31.

23 Ibid, SE XXI: 33.

24 Ibid, SE XXI: 15–19.

25 Ibid, SE XXI: 18–19.

26 Ibid, SE XXI: 24.

27 Ibid, SE XXI: 30; cf. 33.

28 Freud, *Civilization and its discontents*, SE XXI: 74.

29 Freud, *The future of an illusion*, SE XXI: 43, my emphasis.

30 Note that in Freud's family, the break in the transmission of Jewish teaching seems to come with Freud's father Jacob failing to educate his son in Hebrew and Jewish rituals. And later in life Freud both regretted his lack of Jewish education and blamed his father. (See P. Gay, *Freud: a life for our time*, pp. 599–600.) Thus there is reason to think that Freud's relation to being a Jew was bound up (somehow) with his relationship with his father.

31 See S. Kierkegaard, 'The point of view for my work as an author: a direct communication, report to history,' in H. Hong and E. Hong (eds.), *The point of view* (Princeton: Princeton University Press, 1998), pp. 21–97; see especially pp. 41–44, 48–49; S. Kierkegaard, *Attack upon 'Christendom,'* trans. W. Lowrie (Princeton: Princeton University Press, 1991).

32 S. Kierkegaard, *The present age*, W. Kaufmann (New York: Harper and Row, 1962), pp. 33–86.

33 Freud, *The future of an illusion*, SE XXI: 54.

34 See R. Rorty, *Contingency, irony and solidarity* (Cambridge: Cambridge University Press, 1989).

35 Freud, *Totem and taboo*, SE XIII: 143; *Civilization and its discontents*, SE XXI: 131; *Moses and monotheism*, SE XXIII: 98–102.

36 Freud, *Moses and monotheism*, SE XXIII: 90.

37 Cp. Freud, *Civilization and its discontents*, SE XXI: 127.

38 Freud, *Moses and monotheism*, SE XXIII: 89–90.

39 Ibid, SE XXIII: 98ff: 'Granted that at the time we have no stronger evidence for the presence of memory-traces in the archaic heritage than the residual phenomena of the work of analysis which call for a phylogenetic derivation, yet this evidence seems to us strong enough to postulate that such is the fact.'

40 Ibid, SE XXIII: 101: 'A tradition that was based on communication could not lead to the compulsive character that attaches to religious phenomena.'

41 It is striking how similar the form of this explanation is to Freud's original seduction hypothesis. In each case he feels the need to trace the 'symptom' back to a real life event. The assumption seems to be that discovering the real life event one has reached a kind of explanatory bedrock. There is another irony: although the quality of Freud's argument here is poor, it has generated some of the most fascinating secondary literature in the entire corpus of Freudian criticism. See, for example, R. Paul, *Moses and civilization: the meaning behind Freud's myth* (New Haven: Yale University Press, 1996); Y. Yerushalmi, *Freud's Moses: Judaism terminable and interminable* (New Haven: Yale University Press, 1991); J. Assman, *Moses the Egyptian: the memory of Egypt in Western monotheism* (Cambridge, MA: Harvard University Press, 1997).

Conclusion
Freud's legacy

Freud was a controversial figure in his lifetime, and he remains a controversial figure after his death. The controversies swirl around two important issues: whether another form of therapy is better at treating this or that ailment; and whether Freud overstated some of his claims – for instance, his insistence on the hidden importance of sexuality in human suffering. These are questions that need to be argued through.

But the controversies should not blind us to the elegance and importance of Freud's method. In Freudian psychoanalysis, the analysand is asked to try to speak *whatever* comes to his or her mind. The psychoanalytic situation is designed to provide the private and safe space in which it is ever more comfortable for the analysand to do just that. From a Freudian perspective, the analyst's task is to work with the analysand to facilitate this process. In this way, psychoanalytic practice gives us one concrete determination of what we might mean by *encouraging the free flow of self-conscious activity in an individual*. This ought not to be a controversial claim: one can see its truth simply by looking at the structure of the psychoanalytic situation.

Freudian psychoanalysis is not a cure-all. Even within psychoanalysis, much research after Freud has centered on revisions of technique in order to reach patients who could not be helped by Freud's classic method.[1] But to grasp Freud's legacy, it is helpful to concentrate on those who *can* be helped by psychoanalysis according to the fundamental rule. Their sufferings do flow from inhibitions and blockages in the free flow of self-conscious activity. Here we do see the travails of self-consciousness trying to unfold according to its own inner principle.

Philosophy has long considered human life to be distinctive (and valuable) in virtue of its capacity for self-conscious awareness. The Freudian question to philosophy is: why settle for only a partial exercise of this capacity? But the issue raised goes deeper. From its inception, philosophy has invoked a special capacity of the human psyche, *reason*. But we cannot properly understand what this capacity is if we have only a schematic understanding of what its proper exercise consists in. From the time of Plato and Aristotle — that is, from the inception of philosophy's reflection on reason — one of reason's central tasks has been taken to be the thoughtful, self-conscious integration of the human psyche. The point is not merely that psychoanalysis provides insight into how such integration might be achieved — far beyond anything Plato or Aristotle imagined — it is that psychoanalytic activity itself is the very exercise of self-conscious, thoughtful integration of the psyche. That is, psychoanalysis when carried out according to Freud's principle would seem to be a quintessential activity of reason.

Although much more work needs to be done, we seem to be on the verge of answering a longstanding philosophical question: how can reason itself be efficacious in structuring the human psyche? Freud did not explicitly formulate this himself, but it is the meaning of the ideal he set at the center of his therapeutic technique. Psychoanalysis gives us unparalleled access to the microcosm of reason's working at the interface of (what Aristotle called) the rational and non-rational parts of the soul. In the psychoanalytic situation, the interface is so intimate between self-conscious awareness and the irruptions and movements of the unconscious that it becomes possible for the analysand to become aware *immediately and directly* of the efficacy of her own self-conscious thought. One is not restricted to inferring the unconscious from manifest behavior, nor need one rely simply on theoretical insight into how one's mind works. Rather, one can experience one's mind working immediately in self-conscious awareness, and can *thereby* directly appropriate unconscious mental activity — via the activity of self-conscious understanding. This is, I think, a practical-poetical exercise of reason. It is practical in that the efficacy runs directly through the self-conscious understanding of what the mind is doing. It is poetical in the sense that this activity can genuinely reshape the mind. This is not simply a matter of *changing one's mind* in the sense of changing one's beliefs or altering one's emotional state. Psychoanalysis is a conversation that, when done well, can structure the psyche.[2] So, to take a notable example, through a successful psychoanalytic conversation, a punishing super-ego can diminish and fade away. What emerges is a harmoniously functioning ego, living with ideals in ways that harmoniously promote human flourishing. And, at least in principle, there should be no mystery about how this happens.

Psychoanalysis also provides unusual insight into the macrocosm of unconscious desire. It is an empirical discovery of some magnitude – although one can find intimations of it throughout literature and poetry – that the unconscious is not a teeming cauldron of atomic wishes but an astonishingly organized and unifying imaginative activity, often focused on fundamental problems of human existence. What would it be to have a father? What would it be to be a mother? Is intimacy possible? What is it to be gendered? What would it be to accept my vulnerability in the world? What is it to trust? What am I to do with my anger? How destructive am I? Can I tolerate the creativity of others? Can I risk my own creativity in the face of the envy of others? The list can be extended, I suspect indefinitely – but the unconscious imagination of humans does seem to be preoccupied with basic questions of human finiteness and vulnerability. I said in the Introduction that the unconscious seemed to think like a philosopher who happened to lack the capacity for rational thought. But now, by the end of the book, we can see that the unconscious is not properly thought of as *lacking* a capacity, but as possessed of poetic, creative capacities of its own. The unconscious has its own form of mental activity. We are, I think, at an early stage of understanding what a thoughtful engagement of reason with the non-rational part of the soul could be. Psychoanalysis gives us the best insight we yet have into what it would be for thoughtful self-consciousness to take the non-rational part of the soul into account. This is the irony of Freud's legacy. Freud is often taken to be the person who showed us how irrational the human soul is. But if we think of his legacy in terms of the enduring significance of his method, Freud has bequeathed us a hitherto unavailable possibility for coming to understand what the

activity of reason consists in. This is crucial for any ethics that hopes
to ground itself in a conception of human flourishing. We are only
beginning to understand what it is to live well with an alternative
(largely unconscious) activity of mind.

Our humanity – so a thought running through the Western
tradition goes – is not a biological given, but an ethical task.
We become distinctively human via our self-conscious struggles to
face up to challenges and be who we want to be.[3] Such humanistic
self-constitution is a contingent achievement. We can imagine the
human species losing interest in its struggles, perhaps inducing
a genetic alteration that eliminated anxiety and discontent once and
for all. The human mind as we know it would fade away, while
the biological species continued. This may at the moment look like
science fiction, but there are currents alive in the culture that so
valorize comfortable lives that the image of a *trouble-free* life can come
to seem an ideal.

What would it mean to maintain solidarity with the opposite
ideal, with humanity as achievement and response to challenge and
suffering? It seems to me that we need to find ways to accept – to
honor – the fact that in our unconscious imaginations we are always
already at work on some such project. Our unconscious minds are
going over our past sufferings (and perhaps imaginatively elaborat-
ing them); anxiously fearing dangers; imagining angry responses;
and wishfully hoping our desires will be fulfilled. Psychoanalysis is a
creative repetition of these mindful activities at the level of self-
conscious awareness. Psychoanalysis is as much the capacity to *mourn*
our sufferings – and thereby transform them – as it is to *celebrate* our
imaginative grapplings with life. Thus it is a constituent moment of
human mindedness, as we have come to value it.

One last word in conclusion. We have throughout this book been
exploring the lasting significance of Freud's thought. But the beauty
of Freud's method – analysis in accordance with the fundamental
rule – is that we do not have to rely on his authority for the answer
to any question of psychological or philosophical importance. His
case histories and theoretical essays are no more than guideposts.
Whatever is true about psychoanalysis should emerge again and
again in individual psychoanalyses, as people are encouraged to
speak their minds.

Notes

1 For a brief sample, see: Heinz Kohut, 'The two analyses of Mr. Z,' *International journal of psychoanalysis* 60 (1979), pp. 3–27; W.R. Bion, 'Attacks on linking,' in E.B. Spillius (ed.), *Melanie Klein today: developments in theory and practice*, Vol. 1, *Mainly theory* (London: Routledge, 1988), pp. 87–101; C. Botella and S. Botella, *The work of psychic figurability: mental states without representation* (London: Routledge, 2005); Andre Green, *The fabric of affect in psychoanalytic discourse* (London: Routledge, 1999); Betty Joseph, *Psychic equilibrium and psychic change* (London and New York: Routledge, 1989); H.B. Levine, G.S. Reed, D. Scarfone (eds.), *Unrepresented states and the construction of meaning: clinical and theoretical contributions* (London: Karnac, 2013); Edna O'Shaughnessy, 'W.R. Bion's theory of thinking and new techniques in child analysis', in E.B. Spillius (ed.), *Melanie Klein today*, Vol. 2, *Mainly practice* (London and New York: Routledge, 1988), pp. 177–90; H. Rosenfeld, *Impasse and interpretation: therapeutic and anti-therapeutic factors in the psychoanalytic treatment of psychotic, borderline and neurotic patients* (London and New York: Tavistock, 1987).

2 I discuss how a conversation can structure the soul in Lear, *Therapeutic action.*

3 One excellent exploration of this thought is Soren Kierkegaard, *Concluding unscientific postscript to the philosophical crumbs* (by the pseudonymous author Johannes Climacus), ed. and trans. Alastair Hannay (Cambridge: Cambridge University Press, 2009). I discuss Kierkegaard's approach in J. Lear, *A case for irony* (Cambridge, MA: Harvard University Press, 2011).

The reader who wishes to delve into the meaning of any psycho-analytic term is strongly advised to consult J. Laplanche and J-B. Pontalis, *The language of psychoanalysis* (London: Hogarth Press, 1983). This book provides a definition of each term, an essay on the subject and references to the relevant occurrences of the term in Freud's work. It is a masterful achievement. There is also, B. Moore and B. Fine (eds.), *Psychoanalytic terms and concepts* (New Haven: Yale University Press and American Psychoanalytic Association, 1990). This provides solid and clear entries for all major psychoanalytic terms. The glossary below provides only a minimal orientation.

acting-out A person in the grip of an unconscious fantasy may dramatize that fantasy in a social situation, or in the analytic situation. The dramatization will often be surprising to the person as well as to those around him/her. But since the person has no conscious awareness of the fantasy as such, he or she will be motivated to see themselves as acting for reasons (see Chapter 4, section 6; and Chapter 2, sections 3–5). On occasion, analysts will call acting-out, when it occurs in the analytic situation, acting-in.

catharsis Freud's first form of therapy — the cathartic method — supposedly relied on finding a hidden emotion or memory that, because of its upsetting nature, was split off from conscious awareness. The method was supposed to purge this memory through an emotionally vivid recall in the therapeutic situation. Thus Freud and Breuer harkened this method to ancient Greek practices of purgation and purification, which were called catharsis. Freud discards this method as fundamentally flawed very soon after adopting it.

condensation Along with displacement, a hallmark of unconscious mental functioning: the energy from various (repressed) ideas and wishes can be concentrated on one idea that is innocuous in itself. The innocuous idea becomes intense – as in a dream – and thereby stands for the repressed ideas. Freud's dream of the botanical monograph is a classic example (see Chapter 3, section 3).

death drive In Freud's final theory of the drives, he posits a basic tendency toward decomposition and death. He uses it to explain aggression as the (temporary) deflection outwards of this internal tendency to fall apart (see Chapter 5, sections 4–6).

displacement Along with **condensation**, a hallmark of unconscious mental functioning: psychic energy flows loosely among ideas according to primary process, and thus energy can easily move from a forbidden idea or wish onto another idea that is innocuous in itself. The forbidden idea loses its intensity, the innocuous idea gains in intensity. But the innocuous idea comes thereby to stand for the forbidden one (see Chapter 3, section 3).

dream-work The activities of the mind by which repressed unconscious wishes are transformed into the manifest content of a dream.

drive From the German *Trieb*; an internal and innate pressure, arising in the body and directing the organism towards some kind of act (mental or physical) that will bring about a discharge of tension. For Freud, the paradigm of a drive is the sexual drive in humans (see Chapter 2, sections 4–5).

ego The term comes from the German *Ich* (I), not Latin, and is used by Freud both to mean the self – I as an agent in the world – and a particular agency within the psyche. The ego's task is to mediate between the wishful demands of the **id** and the inhibiting criticisms of the **superego**. It is also to mediate between the conflicting internal demands of the self and the demands of the external social world. It is thus responsible for the public presentation of self.

Eros In Freud's final theory of the drives, a basic force for life, love and development. In opposition to the **death drive**, Eros seeks the formation of greater differentiated unities. He uses it to explain human development, differentiation and integration. And he self-consciously brings psychoanalysis into the Platonic tradition that sees human being as essentially erotic (see Chapter 2, section 6).

fantasy (or phantasy) An imaginary scenario in which a wish is represented as fulfilled. These scenes can be modified in all sorts of ways due to conflicting forces within the mind. A paradigm of a conscious fantasy in puberty and adult life are the daydreams that surround masturbation as well as other sexual activity. Analysis reveals primordial unconscious fantasies, formed in childhood, which continue to structure adult life.

free association An important psychoanalytic method in which the patient is encouraged to say whatever thoughts and feelings come to conscious awareness. Patients are encouraged to let their minds wander where they will; and asked not to inhibit themselves in speaking whatever comes to mind.

id The term comes from the German Es (it), not Latin; and it is used by Freud in his structural theory to designate that part of the psyche which contains repressed wishful and aggressive impulses. The **ego** and **superego** will typically inhibit id impulses. Freud takes the id to be an important source of **psychic energy**. Thus a person's vitality will depend on how well or badly they can incorporate id-impulses into daily life.

identification A fantasy by which a person transforms himself so as to be another person. The fantasy is that by molding oneself in the image of another person – taking on a certain character trait, or aspect as part of oneself – one succeeds not simply in being *like* that person, but in *being* that person (see Chapter 6, sections 4–6).

illusion A belief caused by a wish. We take our beliefs to be responsive to reality; thus when we are in the grip of an illusion we are misled about the source and authority of our belief.

introjection A fantasy by which a person takes emotions, character traits or other qualities of people in the external world and takes them into him- or herself. Freud thought that early introjective fantasies play a crucial role in the development of psychological structure, a sense of self, and character (see Chapter 6, sections 4–7).

latent content The initially hidden meaning of a dream (or act) that emerges in the course of analysis.

manifest content The remembered content of a dream, before it has been subject to analytic inquiry.

pleasure principle Along with the **reality principle**, the pleasure principle serves as one of the two principles of mental functioning. It aims at immediate discharge of accumulating tension that typically results in hallucinatory gratification. The pleasure principle can exercise a kind of gravitational pull on the reality-testing functions of the mind, leading people to distort their perceptions of others and of their situation in wishful ways.

preconscious An arena of the mind or of mental activity that, while not conscious, is distinct from what Freud called the unconscious. These may be thoughts that are simply unconscious in the sense that we are not consciously aware of them or they may be actively kept out of conscious awareness. Still, even these repressed or disavowed thoughts tend to have an articulated propositional structure. They thus tend to cluster in articulated structures of propositional thought. In this way they differ from the wishes and fantasies of the unconscious (see Chapter 1, sections 2–5).

primary process A distinct type of mental functioning, characteristic of the unconscious and distinct from the **secondary process** of conscious thought. In this process psychical energy flows loosely and easily across ideas, seeking discharge in a hallucinatory gratification (see Chapter 3, sections 6–7).

projection A fantasy of removing something from inside the psyche and placing it onto or into a person or object in the external world. So, for instance, a person who projects her anger will typically experience another person as angry at her. Freud thought that projection had its origin in early infantile fantasies (see Chapter 6, sections 4–5).

psychic energy Freud saw that people live under pressure, that there is a certain intensity to life, and that that intensity is variable and transferable: from mind to body, from idea to idea, from body part to body part. He posited psychic energy as a psychological force, along the lines of physical energy, to describe the routes of transfer of that intensity. In *The ego and the* *id* (1923) he posits two kinds of psychic energy, libido (the energy of the sexual drive) and aggressive energy.

reality principle Along with the **pleasure principle**, the reality principle serves as one of the two principles of mental functioning. It seeks realistic gratifications of wishful impulses and desires. This regularly requires tolerating delays, making compromises, following a series of practical steps towards a goal. And this puts it in conflict with the pleasure principle, which seeks immediate gratification in hallucinatory discharges of tension. Freud often writes as though he is talking of a simple perceptual capacity, but his use of the reality principle has an essential ethical dimension (see Chapter 6, sections 1–3).

repetition compulsion Freud thought that the compulsive repetitiveness he saw in the lives of neurotics was due to a force whose aim was repetition. This repetition compulsion, he thought, operated independently of the **pleasure principle** and **reality principle** (see Chapter 6, sections 4–5).

repression A mental activity (or set of mental activities) by which an idea, wish, thought or fantasy is actively kept out of conscious awareness. Repression expresses an elemental motivation of the mind to keep certain ideas unconscious (see Chapter 1, sections 4–5; Chapter 2, section 2; Chapter 4, section 4).

secondary process A process of thought typical of conscious reasoning, where one idea connects to another according to its meaning and logical connections. This type of thinking is in the service of the **reality principle**, and requires that the flow of **psychic energy** be restricted to connections between ideas that are logically related (see Chapter 5, sections 1–2).

sublimation A process by which the energy of the sexual drive is redirected onto non-sexual aims. For Freud, all forms of human creativity – artistic, scientific, philosophical – were the outcome of sublimation. He did not really explain how sublimation works – and thus the nature of sublimation remains an outstanding problem for psychoanalysis.

superego In Freud's structural theory of the psyche, the superego functions as a voice of conscience, an image of ideals, and as a punishing judge and censor. It typically represses the wishes of the **id** and inhibits the desires of the **ego**. The superego is formed in childhood in response to the childhood fears of their own aggression and thus, in the first instance, it is an infantile solution to an infant's problem.

transference Freud used transference to describe two related processes. First, in the dream-process, a forbidden wish will transfer its intensity onto a relatively innocent idea. That idea will then represent the forbidden wish, and show up in the **manifest content** of a dream. This is transference as a process occurring inside the mind (see Chapter 3, sections 6–7). Second, transference is a process by which unconscious wishes and impulses show up in a social situation, most notably the analytic situation. Wishful emotions, repressed thoughts, hidden conflicts are transferred from some past time, or even simply from the hidden recesses of the mind, onto the analyst and the analytic situation (see Chapter 4 for an account of how best to understand this phenomenon).

unconscious The term is used variously to mean: a) contents of the mind that are simply not present to conscious awareness; b) contents of the mind that are not present to consciousness because they are repressed and are thus unavailable; c) a part of the mind that is the home of these repressed unconscious ideas. The latter is referred to as the unconscious. Freud argues that, due to typical vicissitudes of human development, the unconscious is the home of repressed infantile wishes and aggressive impulses.

wish Basic desiring force in the **unconscious**, of a different type than conscious desire, in that it operates in the mind according to primary process mental functioning, and thus tends towards hallucinatory gratification. Wishes exert an influence upon the conscious and preconscious mind, but operate largely independently of the belief–desire system of rationality (see Chapter 3, sections 6–7; Chapter 5, sections 1–3).

wish-fulfillment The experience of gratification of a **wish** in dreams, symptoms and acted-out fantasies. In a dream, a wish is not merely represented as fulfilled, it is experienced as fulfilled. However, the experience of gratification is typically disguised from conscious awareness (see Chapter 3, sections 6–7).

working-through The process by which a person transforms a relatively theoretical insight into their unconscious motivations into a practical understanding of how they permeate myriad aspects of their lives. It is above all the acquisition of a practical skill by which a person comes to recognize the fractal nature of unconscious conflicts, and acquires the ability to intervene in these processes as they are unfolding. It lies at the heart of the psychoanalytic process (see Chapter 1, section 7; Chapter 2, section 6; Chapter 4, section 6).

Bibliography

A note on Freud texts: All references to Freud's writings in this book are to: Sigmund Freud, *The standard edition of the complete psychological works of Sigmund Freud* (London: Hogarth Press; New York: Norton, 1981). The German text I have relied on is S. Freud, *Gesammelte Werke*, ed. A. Freud, E. Bibring, W. Hoffer, E. Kris, O. Isakower (Frankfurt am Main: S. Fischer Verlag, 1960–87).

The main Freud texts are easily available in paperback. In the USA: *Introductory lectures on psychoanalysis, The ego and the id, Beyond the pleasure principle, Group psychology and the analysis of the ego, Totem and taboo, Civilization and its discontents, The future of an illusion, Inhibitions, symptoms and anxiety, An outline of psychoanalysis, Five lectures on psychoanalysis* are all available in the Norton Paperback Library. *Three essays on the theory of sexuality* and *Studies on hysteria* are published by Basic Books. *Three case histories* (which includes the Rat Man, Wolf Man and Dr. Schreber), and the Dora case history, *Analysis of a case of hysteria* are published by Collier Books, Macmillan Publishing Company. Collier-Macmillan also publishes two excellent collections of articles under the titles, *General psychological theory* and *Therapy and technique. The interpretation of dreams* is published by Avon. In the United Kingdom there is *The Penguin Freud library*, eds. A. Richards and A. Dickson, which has all the major works.

Appignanesi, L. and J. Forrester, *Freud's women* (New York: Basic Books, 1992).
Aristotle, *History of animals* (many texts and editions).
——*Nicomachean ethics* (many texts and editions).
——*On the soul* (many texts and editions).
——*Parts of animals* (many texts and editions).
——*Posterior analytics* (many texts and editions).

——Rhetoric (many texts and editions).

Assman, J. *Moses the Egyptian: the memory of Egypt in Western monotheism* (Cambridge, MA: Harvard University Press, 1997).

Bartsch, S. and T. Bartscherer (eds.) *Erotikon: essays on Eros ancient and modern* (Chicago: University of Chicago Press, 2005).

Bernheimer, C. and C. Kahane (eds.) *In Dora's case: Freud, hysteria, feminism* (New York: Columbia University Press, 1985).

Bion, W. *Learning from experience* (London: Karnac, 1984).

——'Attacks on linking,' in E.B. Spillius (ed.), *Melanie Klein today: developments in theory and practice*, Vol. 1, *Mainly theory* (London: Routledge, 1988), pp. 87–101.

——'Differentiation of the psychotic from the non-psychotic personalities,' in E.B. Spillius (ed.), *Melanie Klein today*, Vol. 1, *Mainly theory* (London and New York: Routledge, 1988), pp. 61–78.

——'A theory of thinking,' in E.B. Spillius (ed.), *Melanie Klein today: developments in theory and practice*, Vol. 1, *Mainly theory* (London and New York: Routledge, 1988), pp. 178–86.

Bird, B. 'Notes on transference: universal phenomenon and hardest part of analysis,' in A.E. Esman (ed.), *Essential papers on transference* (New York: New York University Press, 1990), pp. 331–61.

Blass, R. B. 'Beyond illusion: psychoanalysis and the question of religious truth,' *International journal of psychoanalysis* 85 (2004), pp. 615–34.

Bollas, C. *Hysteria* (London and New York: Routledge, 2000).

Boris, H. *Envy* (Northvale, NJ: Aronson, 1994).

Botella, C. and S. Botella, *The work of psychic figurability: mental states without representation* (London: Routledge, 2005).

Boyle, M. 'Essentially rational animals,' in G. Abel and J. Conant (eds.), *Rethinking epistemology*, Vol. 2 (Berlin: Walter de Gruyter, 2012), pp. 395–427.

——'Additive theories of rationality: a critique,' forthcoming in *European Journal of Philosophy*, online: http://dash.harvard.edu/handle/1/8641840.

Bromwich, D. *A choice of inheritance: self and community from Edmund Burke to Robert Frost* (Cambridge, MA: Harvard University Press, 1989).

Bruch, H. *Eating disorders: obesity, anorexia nervosa and the person within* (New York: Basic Books, 1973).

——*The golden cage: the enigma of anorexia nervosa* (Cambridge, MA: Harvard University Press, 1978).

——*Conversations with anorexics* (New York: Basic Books, 1988).

Burge, T. 'Individualism and the mental,' in D. Rosenthal (ed.), *The nature of mind* (Oxford and New York: Oxford University Press, 1991), pp. 536–65.

Canguilhem, G. *The normal and the pathological* (New York: Zone Books, 1989).

Cavell, M. *The psychoanalytic mind: from Freud to philosophy* (Cambridge, MA: Harvard University Press, 1993).

Chodorow, N. 'Freud on women,' in J. Neu (ed.), *The Cambridge companion to Freud* (Cambridge: Cambridge University Press, 1991), pp. 224–48.

Church, J. 'Morality and the internalized other,' in J. Neu (ed.), *The Cambridge companion to Freud* (Cambridge: Cambridge University Press, 1991), pp. 209–23.

Cottingham, J. *Philosophy and the good life* (Cambridge: Cambridge University Press, 1998).

Crews, F. *The memory wars: Freud's legacy in dispute* (New York: New York Review of Books, 1995).

Davidson, D. *Essays on actions and events* (Oxford: Clarendon Press, 1980).

——'Hume's cognitive theory of pride,' in *Essays on actions and events* (Oxford: Clarendon Press, 1980).

——'Paradoxes of irrationality,' in R. Wollheim and J. Hopkins (eds.), *Philosophical essays on Freud* (Cambridge: Cambridge University Press, 1982).

——*Inquiries into truth and interpretation* (Oxford: Clarendon Press, 1984).

——*Subjective, intersubjective, objective* (Oxford: Clarendon Press, 2001).

Decker, H. *Freud, Dora and Vienna 1900* (New York: Free Press, 1991).

de Sousa, R. *The rationality of emotion* (Cambridge, MA: MIT Press, 1987).

Dostoyevsky, F. *The brothers Karamazov*, trans. R. Pevear and L. Volokhonsky (New York: Farrar, Straus and Giroux, 1990).

Ellenberger, H.F. *The discovery of the unconscious: the history and evolution of dynamic psychiatry* (New York: Basic Books, 1970).

Esman, A.E. (ed.) *Essential papers on transference* (New York: New York University Press, 1990).

Etchegoyen, R.H. *The fundamentals of psychoanalytic technique* (London: Karnac, 1991).

Finkelstein, D. *Expression and the inner* (Cambridge, MA: Harvard University Press, 2003).

Fonagy, P. *Attachment theory and psychoanalysis* (New York: Other Press, 2001).

Fonagy, P., G. Gergely, E. Jurist and M. Target, *Affect regulation, mentalization and the development of the self* (New York: Other Press, 2002).

Fonagy, P., H. Steele, G. Moran, M. Steele and A. Higgitt, 'The capacity for understanding mental states: the reflective self in parent and child and its significance for security of attachment,' *Infant mental health journal* 13 (1991), pp. 200–17.

Freud, S. *The complete letters of Sigmund Freud to Wilhelm Fliess, 1887–1904* (Cambridge, MA: Harvard University Press, 1985).

——*The interpretation of dreams*, trans. J. Crick (Oxford and New York: Oxford University Press, 1999).

Friedman, L. *The anatomy of psychotherapy* (New Jersey: The Analytic Press, 1988).

Gabbard, G. 'Challenges in the analysis of adult patients with histories of childhood sexual abuse,' *Canadian journal of psychoanalysis* 5 (1997), pp. 1–25.

Gabbard, G. and D. Westen, 'Rethinking the concept of therapeutic action,' *International journal of psychoanalysis* 84 (2003), pp. 823–41.

Gardner, S. 'The unconscious,' in J. Neu (ed.), *The Cambridge companion to Freud* (Cambridge: Cambridge University Press, 1991), pp. 136–60.

——*Irrationality and the philosophy of psychoanalysis* (Cambridge: Cambridge University Press, 1993).

Gay, P. *Freud: a life for our time* (New York: W.W. Norton, 1988).

Geuss, R. 'Nietzsche and genealogy,' *European journal of philosophy* 2, no. 3 (December 1994), pp. 274–92.

Goldberg, A. *A fresh look at psychoanalysis: the view from self psychology* (Hillsdale, NJ: Analytic Press, 1988).

——*The problem of perversion: the view from self-psychology* (New Haven and London: Yale University Press, 1995).

Gordon, R.M. *The structure of the emotions* (Cambridge: Cambridge University Press, 1987).

Gray, P. '"Developmental lag" in the evolution of technique,' in *The ego and analysis of defense* (Northvale, NJ: Aronson, 1994), pp. 29–61.

——*The ego and analysis of defense* (Northvale, NJ: Aronson, 1994).

Green, A. *The fabric of affect in psychoanalytic discourse* (London: Routledge, 1999).

Greenson, R.R. *The technique and practice of psychoanalysis* (New York: International Universities Press, 1967).

Grünbaum, A. *The foundations of psychoanalysis: a philosophical critique* (Berkeley: University of California Press, 1984).

Hamburg, P. 'Bulimia, the construction of a symptom,' in J.R. Bemporad and D.B. Herzog (eds.), *Psychoanalysis and eating disorders* (New York: Guildford Press, 1989), pp. 131–40.

Hinshelwood, R.D. *Clinical Klein* (New York: Basic Books, 1994).

——'The death instinct and envy,' in *Clinical Klein* (New York: Basic Books, 1994), pp. 135–43.

Hobbes, T. *Leviathan* (Harmondsworth and New York: Penguin, 1985).

Hopkins, J. 'The interpretation of dreams,' in J. Neu (ed.), *The Cambridge companion to Freud* (Cambridge: Cambridge University Press, 1991), pp. 86–135.

Johnston, M. 'Self-deception and the nature of mind,' in C. and G. Macdonald (eds.), *Philosophy of psychology: debates on psychological explanation* (Oxford: Blackwell, 1995).

Jones, E. *The life and work of Sigmund Freud*, ed. L. Trilling and S. Marcus (New York: Basic Books, 1961).

Joseph, B. 'Addiction to near death,' in *Psychic equilibrium and psychic change* (London and New York: Routledge, 1989), pp. 127–38.

——'Envy in everyday life,' in *Psychic equilibrium and psychic change* (London and New York: Routledge, 1989), pp. 181–91.

——*Psychic equilibrium and psychic change* (London and New York: Routledge, 1989).

——'Transference: the total situation,' in *Psychic equilibrium and psychic change* (London and New York: Routledge, 1989), pp. 156–67.

Kandel, E.R. 'A new intellectual framework for psychiatry,' *American journal of psychiatry* 155 (1998), pp. 457–69.

——'Biology and the future of psychoanalysis: A new intellectual framework for psychiatry revisited,' *American journal of psychiatry* 156 (1999), pp. 505–24.

——'Nobel Banquet Speech', 2000, http://nobelprize.org/medicine/laureates/2000/kandel-speech.html.

Kant, I. 'Religion within the boundaries of mere reason,' in *Religion and rational theology*, trans. A. Wood and G. Di Giovanni (Cambridge: Cambridge University Press, 2001), pp. 39–213.

Kernberg, O. *Severe personality disorders: psychotherapeutic strategies* (New Haven and London: Yale University Press, 1984).

——*Object relations theory and clinical psychoanalysis* (Northvale, NJ: Aronson, 1986).

Kierkegaard, S. *The present age*, trans. W. Kaufmann (New York: Harper and Row, 1962).

——[Johannes de Silentio, pseud.] *Fear and trembling*, ed. and trans. H.V. Hong and E.H. Hong (Princeton: Princeton University Press, 1983).

——[Anti-Climacus, pseud.] *Sickness unto death: a Christian psychological exposition for edification and awakening*, trans. A. Hannay (New York: Penguin, 1989).

——*Attack upon 'Christendom,'* trans. W. Lowrie (Princeton: Princeton University Press, 1991).

——'The point of view for my work as an author: a direct communication, report to history,' in H. Hong and E. Hong (eds.), *The point of view* (Princeton: Princeton University Press, 1998), pp. 21–97.

——[Johannes Climacus, pseud.] *Concluding unscientific postscript to the philosophical crumbs*, ed. and trans. Alastair Hannay (Cambridge: Cambridge University Press, 2009).

Klein, M. *The psychoanalysis of children* (London: Hogarth Press, 1980).

——'Envy and gratitude,' in *Envy and gratitude* (London: Hogarth Press, 1984), pp. 176–235.

——*Narrative of a child analysis* (London: Hogarth Press, 1984).

Kohut, H. 'The two analyses of Mr. Z.' *International journal of psychoanalysis* 60 (1979), pp. 3–27.

——*The restoration of the self* (Madison, CT: International Universities Press, 1986).

——*The analysis of the self: a systematic approach to the psychoanalytic treatment of narcissistic personality disorders* (Madison, CT: International Universities Press, 1987).

Korsgaard, C. *The sources of normativity* (Cambridge: Cambridge University Press, 1996).

——*Self-constitution: agency, identity and integrity* (Oxford: Oxford University Press, 2009).

Krohn, A. *Hysteria: the elusive neurosis* (New York: International Universities Press, 1978).

Lacan, J. 'Intervention on transference,' in C. Bernheimer and C. Kahane (eds.), *In Dora's case: Freud, hysteria, feminism* (New York: Columbia University Press, 1985), pp. 92–104.

——*The ethics of psychoanalysis, 1959–1960; The seminar of Jacques Lacan Book VII* (London and New York: Routledge, 1992).

——*The four fundamental concepts of psychoanalysis* (New York: Norton, 1998).

——*Le séminaire, Livre VIII, Le transfert* (Paris: Seuil, 2001).

——*Ecrits*, trans. B. Fink (New York: Norton, 2002).

——'The mirror stage as formative of the I function, as revealed in psychoanalytic experience,' in *Ecrits*, trans. B. Fink (New York: Norton, 2002), pp. 3–9.

——'The subversion of the subject and the dialectic of desire in the Freudian unconscious,' in *Ecrits*, trans. B. Fink (New York: Norton, 2002), pp. 281–312.

Laplanche, J. *Life and death in psychoanalysis* (Baltimore: Johns Hopkins University Press, 1970).

——*New Foundations for Psychoanalysis* (Oxford and Cambridge, MA: Basil Blackwell, 1989).

——*Entre séduction et inspiration: l'homme* (Paris: Presses Universitaires de France, 1999).

——*Essays on otherness* (London and New York: Routledge, 1999).

——'The unfinished Copernican revolution,' in *Essays on otherness* (London and New York: Routledge, 1999), pp. 52–83.

Laplanche, J. and J.-B. Pontalis, *The language of psychoanalysis* (London: Hogarth Press, 1983).

Lear, J. *Love and its place in nature: a philosophical interpretation of Freudian psychoanalysis* (New Haven: Yale University Press, 1990).

——'Inside and outside *The Republic*,' in *Open minded: working out the logic of the soul* (Cambridge, MA: Harvard University Press, 1998), pp. 219–46.

——'An interpretation of transference,' in *Open minded: working out the logic of the soul* (Cambridge, MA: Harvard University Press, 1998), pp. 56–79.

——'On killing Freud (again),' in *Open minded: working out the logic of the soul* (Cambridge, MA: Harvard University Press, 1998), pp. 16–32.

——*Open minded: working out the logic of the soul* (Cambridge, MA: Harvard University Press, 1998).

——'Restlessness, phantasy and the concept of mind,' in *Open minded: working out the logic of the soul* (Cambridge, MA: Harvard University Press, 1998), pp. 80–122.

——*Happiness, death and the remainder of life* (Cambridge, MA: Harvard University Press, 2000).

——'Jumping from the couch,' *International journal of psychoanalysis* 83 (2002), pp. 583–93.

——'The idea of a moral psychology: the impact of psychoanalysis on philosophy in Britain,' *International journal of psychoanalysis* 84 (2003), pp. 1351–61.

——*Therapeutic action: an earnest plea for irony* (New York: Other Press, 2003).

——'Allegory and myth in Plato's *Republic*,' in G. Santas (ed.), *The Blackwell companion to Plato's Republic* (Oxford: Blackwell, 2005).

——'Give Dora a break!,' in S. Bartsch and T. Bartscherer (eds.), *Erotikon: essays on eros ancient and modern* (Chicago: University of Chicago Press, 2005).

——*A case for irony* (Cambridge, MA: Harvard University Press, 2011).

——'Integrating the non-rational soul,' *Proceedings of the Aristotelian Society* 114 (April 2014), pp. 75–101.

——'Wisdom won from illness: the psychoanalytic grasp of human being,' *International journal of psychoanalysis*. Published electronically 12 April 2014. doi: 10.1111/1745–8315.12209.

Le Doux, J. *The emotional brain: the mysterious underpinnings of emotional life* (New York: Simon and Schuster, 1996).

Levenson, L. 'Superego defense analysis in the termination phase,' *Journal of the American Psychoanalytic Association* 46 (1998), pp. 847–66.

Lévi-Strauss, C. *The elementary structures of kinship* (Boston: Beacon Press, 1969).

Levine, H.B., G.S. Reed and D. Scarfone (eds.) *Unrepresented states and the construction of meaning: clinical and theoretical contributions* (London: Karnac, 2013).

Likierman, M. '"So unattainable": two accounts of envy,' in *Melanie Klein: her work in context* (London and New York: Continuum, 2001), pp. 172–91.

Loewald, H. 'Psychoanalysis and modern views on human existence and religious experience.' *Journal of pastoral care* 7, no. 1 (1953), pp. 1–15.

——'The transference neurosis: comments on the concept and the phenomenon,' in A.E. Esman (ed.), *Essential papers on transference* (New York: New York University Press, 1990), pp. 423–33.

——'Ego and reality,' in *The essential Loewald* (Hagerstown, MD: University Publishing Group, 2000), pp. 3–20.

——*The essential Loewald* (Hagerstown, MD: University Publishing Group, 2000).

——'Instinct theory, object relations and psychic structure formation,' in *The essential Loewald* (Hagerstown, MD: University Publishing Group, 2000), pp. 207–18.

——'On the therapeutic action of psychoanalysis,' in *The essential Loewald* (Hagerstown, MD: University Publishing Group, 2000), pp. 221–56.

——'Sublimation: inquiries into theoretical psychoanalysis,' in *The essential Loewald* (Hagerstown, MD: University Publishing Group, 2000), pp. 439–525.

——'The waning of the Oedipus complex,' in *The essential Loewald* (Hagerstown, MD: University Publishing Group, 2000), pp. 384–404.

Mahler, M., F. Pine and A. Bergman, *The psychological birth of the human infant* (London: Karnac, 1975).

Mahony, P. *Freud's Dora: a psychoanalytic, historical and textual study* (New Haven: Yale University Press, 1996).

Main, M., N. Kaplan and J. Cassidy, 'Security in infancy, childhood and adulthood: a move to the level of representation,' in I. Bretherton and E. Waters (eds.), *Growing points of attachment theory and research: monographs of the Society for Research in Child Development* (Chicago: University of Chicago Press, 1985), pp. 66–104.

Malcolm, R. 'The mirror: a perverse sexual phantasy in a woman seen as a defense against a psychotic breakdown,' in E.B. Spillius (ed.), *Melanie Klein today*, Vol. 2, *Mainly practice* (London and New York: Routledge, 1988), pp. 115–37.

Mann, Thomas *Freud, Goethe, Wagner* (New York: Knopf, 1937).

Marcus, S. 'Freud and Dora: story, history, case history,' in C. Bernheimer and C. Kahane (eds.), *In Dora's case* (New York: Columbia University Press, 1985), pp. 56–91.

Mayes, L.C. and D.J. Cohen, 'The development of a capacity for imagination in early childhood,' *Psychoanalytic study of the child* 47 (1991), pp. 23–48.

McGrath, W. *Freud's discovery of psychoanalysis, the politics of hysteria* (Ithaca, NY: Cornell University Press, 1986).

Meissner, W.W. *Psychoanalysis and religious experience* (New Haven: Yale University Press, 1984).

Moore, B. and B. Fine (eds.) *Psychoanalytic terms and concepts* (New Haven: Yale University Press and American Psychoanalytic Association, 1990).

Moran, R. *Authority and estrangement: an essay on self-knowledge* (Princeton: Princeton University Press, 2001).

Nagel, T. 'Universality and the reflective self,' in C. Korsgaard (ed.), *The sources of normativity* (Cambridge: Cambridge University Press, 1996), pp. 200–209.

Nasio, J.-D. *Hysteria from Freud to Lacan* (New York: Other Press, 1998).

Neu, J. Emotion, thought and therapy: a study of Hume and Spinoza and the relationship of philo-sophical theories of the emotions to psychological theories of therapy (Berkeley and Los Angeles: University of California Press, 1977).

——(ed.) The Cambridge companion to Freud (Cambridge: Cambridge University Press, 1991).

——'Freud and perversion,' in J. Neu (ed.), The Cambridge companion to Freud (Cambridge: Cambridge University Press, 1991), pp. 175–208.

Nietzsche, F. On the genealogy of morality, trans. C. Diethe (Cambridge: Cambridge University Press, 1994).

——'Second essay: "guilt," "bad conscience" and related matters,' in On the genealogy of morality, trans. C. Diethe (Cambridge: Cambridge University Press, 1994), pp. 38–71.

Nussbaum, M. The therapy of desire: theory and practice in Hellenistic ethics (Princeton: Princeton University Press, 1994).

——Hiding from humanity: disgust, shame and the law (Princeton: Princeton University Press, 2004).

O'Shaughnessy, E. 'W.R. Bion's theory of thinking and the new techniques in child analysis,' in E.B. Spillius (ed.), Melanie Klein Today, Vol. 2, Mainly practice (London and New York: Routledge, 1988), pp. 177–90.

Pape, R.A. 'The strategic logic of suicide terrorism,' American political science review 97 (2003), pp. 21–42.

Paul, R. Moses and civilization: the meaning behind Freud's myth (New Haven: Yale University Press, 1996).

Plato, Laches (many texts and editions).

——Phaedrus (many texts and editions).

——Republic (many texts and editions).

——Symposium (many texts and editions).

Proust, M. In search of lost time, trans. and ed. C.K. Scott Moncrieff, D.J. Enright and T. Kilmartin (New York: Modern Library, 2003).

Reeve, C.D.C. Philosopher-kings: the argument of Plato's Republic (Princeton: Princeton University Press, 1988).

Reiser, L. 'Love, work and bulimia' in H.J. Schwartz (ed.), Bulimia: psychoanalytic treat-ment and theory (Madison, CT: International Universities Press, 1988), pp. 373–97.

Reiser, M. Mind, brain, body: towards a convergence of psychoanalysis and neurobiology (New York: Basic Books, 1984).

——'The dream in contemporary psychiatry,' American journal of psychiatry 158 (2001), pp. 351–59.

Rieff, P. Freud; the mind of the moralist (Chicago: University of Chicago Press, 1979).

Ritvo, S. 'The image and uses of the body in psychic conflict – with special refer-ence to eating disorders in adolescence,' Psychoanalytic study of the child 39 (1984), pp. 449–69.

——'Mothers, daughters and eating disorders,' in H.P. Blum, Y. Kramer, A.K. Richards and A.D. Richards (eds.), Fantasy, myth and reality: essays in honor of Jacob A. Arlow, M.D. (Madison, CT: International Universities Press, 1988), pp. 423–34.

Roberts, R.C. 'What an emotion is: a sketch,' Philosophical review 47 (1988), pp. 183–209.

Rödl, S. *Self-consciousness* (Cambridge, MA: Harvard University Press, 2007).

Rorty, R. *Contingency, irony and solidarity* (Cambridge: Cambridge University Press, 1989).

Rosenfeld, H. 'On the psychopathology of narcissism: a clinical approach,' in *Psychotic states: a psychoanalytical approach* (London: Hogarth Press, 1965), pp. 169–79.

——*Psychotic states: a psychoanalytical approach* (London: Hogarth Press, 1965).

——*Impasse and interpretation: therapeutic and anti-therapeutic factors in the psychoanalytic treatment of psychotic, borderline and neurotic patients* (London and New York: Tavistock, 1987).

——'A clinical approach to the psychoanalytical theory of the life and death instincts: an investigation into the aggressive aspects of narcissism,' in E.B. Spillius (ed.), *Melanie Klein today: developments in theory and practice*, Vol. 1, *Mainly theory* (London and New York: Routledge, 1988), pp. 239–55.

Sachs, D. 'In fairness to Freud: a critical notice of *The foundations of psychoanalysis* by Adolf Grünbaum,' in J. Neu (ed.), *The Cambridge companion to Freud* (Cambridge: Cambridge University Press, 1991), pp. 309–38.

Sartre, J.P. *Being and nothingness: a phenomenological essay on ontology*, trans. H. Barnes (New York: Washington Square Press, 1993).

Scheffler, S. *Human morality* (Oxford and New York: Oxford University Press, 1992).

Schwartz, D. *In dreams begin responsibilities* (Norfolk, CT: New Directions, 1938).

Segal, H. 'Depression in the schizophrenic,' in E.B. Spillius (ed.), *Melanie Klein today, developments in theory and practice*, Vol. 1, *Mainly theory* (London and New York: Routledge, 1988), pp. 52–60.

——'Notes on symbol formation,' in E.B. Spillius (ed.), *Melanie Klein today*, Vol. 1, *Developments in theory and practice* (London and New York: Routledge, 1988), pp. 160–77.

——'Some aspects of the analysis of a schizophrenic,' in E.B. Spillius (ed.), *Melanie Klein today*, Vol. 2, *Mainly practice* (London and New York: Routledge, 1988), pp. 96–114.

Slade, A. 'Quality of attachment and early symbolic play,' *Developmental psychology* 17 (1987), pp. 326–35.

Slade, A., J. Belsky, L. Aber and J.L. Phelps, 'Mothers' representations of their relationships with their toddlers: links to adult attachment and observed mothering,' *Developmental psychology* 35 (1999), pp. 611–19.

Solms, M. 'New findings on the neurological organization of dreaming: implications for psychoanalysis,' *Psychoanalytic quarterly* 64 (1995), pp. 43–67.

——'Freudian dream theory today,' *The psychologist* 13 (2001), pp. 618–19.

——'The interpretation of dreams and the neurosciences,' *Psychoanalysis and history* 3 (2001), pp. 79–91.

Solms, M. and O. Turnbull, *The brain and the inner world: an introduction to the neuroscience of subjective experience* (New York: Other Press, 2002).

Spillius, E.B. 'Varieties of envious experience,' *International journal of psychoanalysis* 74 (1993), pp. 1199–1212.

Strachey, J. 'The nature of the therapeutic action of psychoanalysis,' in A.E. Esman (ed.), *Essential papers on transference* (New York: New York University Press, 1990), pp. 49–79.

Velleman, J.D. 'The voice of conscience,' *Proceedings of the Aristotelian Society* 99 (1998), pp. 57–76.

——'Love as a moral emotion,' *Ethics* 109 (1999), pp. 338–74.

——'A rational superego,' *Philosophical review* 108 (1999), pp. 529–58.

Westen, D. 'Toward an empirically and clinically sound theory of motivation,' *International journal of psychoanalysis* 78 (1997), pp. 521–48.

——'The scientific status of unconscious processes: is Freud really dead?,' *Journal of the American Psychoanalytic Association* 47 (1999), pp. 1061–1106.

Westen, D. and G. Gabbard, 'Developments in cognitive neuroscience 1: conflict, compromise and connectionism,' *Journal of the American Psychoanalytic Association* 50 (2002), pp. 54–98.

——'Developments in cognitive neuroscience 2: implications for the concept of transference,' *Journal of the American Psychoanalytic Association* 50 (2002), pp. 99–113.

Williams, B. *Ethics and the limits of philosophy* (Cambridge, MA: Harvard University Press, 1985).

——*Shame and necessity* (Berkeley: University of California Press, 1993).

——'Naturalism and morality,' in J.E.J. Altham and R. Harrison (eds.), *World, mind and ethics: essays on the ethical philosophy of Bernard Williams* (Cambridge: Cambridge University Press, 1995), pp. 202–5.

——'Nietzsche's minimalist moral psychology,' in *Making sense of humanity and other philosophical papers* (Cambridge: Cambridge University Press, 1995), pp. 65–76.

——*Truth and truthfulness: an essay in genealogy* (Princeton: Princeton University Press, 2002).

Winnicott, D.W. 'Anxiety associated with insecurity,' in *Through paediatrics to psychoanalysis* (London: Hogarth Press, 1982), p. 99.

——'Appetite and emotional disorder,' in *Through paediatrics to psychoanalysis* (London: Hogarth Press, 1982), pp. 33–51.

——'The depressive position in normal emotional development,' in *Through paediatrics to psychoanalysis* (London: Hogarth Press, 1982), pp. 262–77.

——'Ego distortion in terms of true and false self,' in *The maturational process and the facilitating environment* (London: Hogarth Press, 1982), pp. 140–52.

——*The maturational process and the facilitating environment* (London: Hogarth Press, 1982).

——'On the contribution of direct child observation to psychoanalysis,' in *The maturational process and the facilitating environment* (London: Hogarth Press, 1982), pp. 109–14.

——'String: a technique of communication,' in *The maturational process and the facilitating environment* (London: Hogarth Press, 1982), pp. 153–57.

——*Through paediatrics to psychoanalysis* (London: Hogarth Press, 1982).

——*The piggle: an account of the psychoanalytic treatment of a little girl* (Harmondsworth and New York: Penguin, 1983).

——*The child, the family and the outside world* (Harmondsworth and New York: Penguin, 1984).

——'Mirror-role of mother and family in child development,' in *Playing and reality* (London and New York: Routledge, 1996), pp. 111–18.

——Playing and reality (London and New York: Routledge, 1996).

——'Transitional objects and transitional phenomena,' in Playing and reality (London and New York: Routledge, 1996), pp. 1–25.

Wollheim, R. Sigmund Freud (Cambridge: Cambridge University Press, 1971).

——'Wish-fulfilment,' in R. Harrison (ed.), Rational action: studies in philosophy and social science (Cambridge: Cambridge University Press, 1979), pp. 47–60.

——The thread of life (Cambridge: Cambridge University Press, 1984).

——The mind and its depths (Cambridge, MA: Harvard University Press, 1993).

——On the emotions (New Haven: Yale University Press, 1999).

Wolstein, B. (ed.) Essential papers on countertransference (New York: New York University Press, 1988).

Wood, A. Kant's moral religion (Ithaca, NY: Cornell University Press, 1970).

——Kant's rational theology (Ithaca, NY: Cornell University Press, 1978).

Yeats, W.B. Responsibilities and other poems (New York: Macmillan, 1916).

Yerushalmi, Y. Freud's Moses: Judaism terminable and interminable (New Haven: Yale University Press, 1991).